Politics, Language
and Time

J. G. A. POCOCK

Politics, Language and Time

Essays on Political Thought and History

NEW YORK Atheneum 1971

The second of these essays originally appeared in *Political Science* (Victoria University of Wellington, New Zealand), volume 16, no. 1 (March 1964); the third in *Il Pensiero Politico* (Casa Editrice L. S. Olschki, Florence, Italy) *anno* 1, no. 2 (1968); the fourth in *The William and Mary Quarterly* (Institute of Early American History, Williamsburg, Virginia), 3rd series, volume XXII, no. 4 (October 1965); the fifth in *The Diversity of History: Essays in Honour of Sir Herbert Butterfield*, edited by J. H. Elliott and H. G. Koenigsberger (London: Routledge and Kegan Paul; Ithaca: Cornell University Press, 1970); the sixth in *The Historical Journal* (Cambridge University Press), volume III, no. 2 (1960); and the seventh in *Politics and Experience: Essays Presented to Michael Oakeshott*, edited by Preston King and B. C. Parekh (Cambridge University Press, 1968). I express my indebtedness to all these journals, to Routledge and Kegan Paul Ltd. and the Cornell University Press, and to the Syndics of the Cambridge University Press. The first and eighth essays were written especially for this volume.

To Quentin Skinner and John Wallace;
and to the University of Canterbury in New Zealand,
where half of these papers were written

Contents

Politics, Language
and Time

[1]

Languages and Their Implications:
The Transformation of the Study
of Political Thought

THE TERM "revolution" may soon cease to be current, emptied of all meaning by constant overuse; so that, for both revolutionary and conservative reasons, it should be employed sparingly. Let it rather be said, then, that during the last ten years scholars interested in the study of systems of political thought have had the experience of living through radical changes, which may amount to a transformation, in their discipline. These changes have had historians and philosophers at their center, and have consisted essentially in a revaluation of the ways in which history and philosophy meet in this particular study; but other disciplines—political science, literature and possibly sociology—have been involved and have contributed. The present author, who seems to himself to have been concerned in this transformation from an early stage, here brings forward a number of essays designed to illustrate its character. The first and last excepted, they have been published previously, and all were written while he variously bore the official denominations of historian and political scientist; and the first

3

part of their dedication, to a Cambridge student of history and philosophy and a Chicago student of English literature, emphasizes the interdisciplinary nature of what is going on.

To trace the history of a revolution is, almost of necessity, to start with a straw man. The rhetoric of the exercise compels the construction of an account of the way things stood before change began which neglects the extent to which change had begun already and the activities of men under the old regime resembled the activities which were to receive emphasis as a result of the process of transformation. In describing certain intellectual confusions which it has been necessary to attack and seek to dispel, I do not wish to ascribe them to my seniors and predecessors indiscriminately; but neither do I wish to minimize the extent to which they live on, and are inflicted upon novices to the present day. It seems to follow, then, that I am not tracing the history of a revolution but rather of that very different thing known, in current jargon, as a confrontation. (Like most academic debates, it is scarcely a dialogue.) The "transformation" of my title is a change of emphasis, a heightening of awareness, which has made this "confrontation" possible. If it is now clear that what I am describing is a matter of degree rather than kind, it should be easier to recognize that my straw man is a methodological or narrative device (if at the same time a cap that will fit many if they will wear it), and that I do not intend to ascribe all intellectual confusions to some group of rivals, or all intellectual clarity to the group to which I myself belong.

In illo tempore, then, the study of political thought was confused to the point where one did not know whether "political thought," "theory," or "philosophy" was the appropriate designation for the field one had chosen. A canon of major works had been isolated by academic tradition, running from Plato to Aristotle to Augustine to Aquinas to Marsilius to Machiavelli to Hobbes to Locke to Hume to Rousseau to Burke to Hegel to

4

Marx. Here, if no earlier, confusion set in; there was vague talk of a "collapse of the classical tradition," and in the Cambridge Historical Tripos, for example, a paper on "The History of Political Thought" (Plato to Rousseau, or is it Marx?) gives place, even at this day, to one on "Theories of the Modern State"—a title which seems unmistakably to reveal its authors' uncertainty as to whether what they are studying is any longer history at all, and if not, what. The political thought of the nineteenth and twentieth centuries has remained uncanonized by the organizers of this tradition and—where its study has not been actually discouraged—is all the better for it. But the figures in the classical canon held their places there because most of them could with fair plausibility be described as philosophers. It was true that many of them had at the same time practiced disciplines as diverse as theology, jurisprudence, history, economics or aesthetics, and that here and there the startled face of a Florentine diplomat or a Cromwellian soldier peered out of the *galère*, as if wondering why others as remote from formal philosophy as himself had not obtained admission; but such divergencies of thought were dealt with by treating them as if they had been political philosophy, and consequently as commentaries upon or moments within its uninterrupted course. Alone among the major branches of historical study in the middle twentieth century, the history of political thought was treated as the study of a traditional canon, and the conversion of tradition into history was in this case conducted by the methods of philosophic commentary on the intellectual contents of the tradition, arbitrarily defined as philosophy.

Neither the philosophers nor the historians—nor, when they became involved from their own angle of approach, the political theorists—were more to blame than the others; each group was as anxious to escape from the confusion as its neighbors; but the root of the trouble lay in a maladjusted relationship between history and philosophy. As has been amply documented and accurately criticized by a number of writers in recent years,[1] the coherence of a work or body of political writing, as political philosophy or as political theory, was mistakenly identified with its character as a historical phenomenon. The historical interpretation, explication or explanation of the text was consequently identified with the discovery of its coherence in one or other of the above forms, and this identification persisted alongside the otherwise historically correct principle that the interpreter's aim should be to present the text as it bore meaning in the mind of the author or his contemporary reader. Acceptance of this principle did not always save the scholar from focusing his efforts on the rediscovery of coherence, or even on the suggestion of means whereby the text might be endowed with a coherence which the author had failed to give it. This latter objective, even when pursued by means which were those of historical insight and reconstruction, was plainly unhistorical, since it is as possible in principle that a thinker fails to achieve coherence as that he succeeds in achieving it; and when this becomes a historical question, it is obviously no part of the historian's business to furnish his author with a degree of coherence he did not in fact achieve. The most the historian may attempt is to show that, once we realize as historians that a man's ideas are to be interpreted in a certain way, we may understand in the light of that knowledge what his problem in achieving coherence was, and why he believed that he had solved it by proceeding as he did. Even this hypothesis presupposes that the author aimed at achieving a certain degree of formal coherence, which further historical research may show that he did not.

But if even the interpretation of a man's thought by histori-

---

[1] Quentin Skinner, "Hobbes's *Leviathan*," *The Historical Journal*, VII, 2 (1964); "The Limits of Historical Explanations," *Philosophy*, XLI (1966); "Meaning and Understanding in the History of Ideas," *History and Theory*, VIII, 1 (1969). John Dunn, "The Identity of the History of Ideas," *Philosophy*, XLIII (1968); *The Political Thought of John Locke* (Cambridge University Press, 1969).

cal means may be deployed in ways that are historically illegitimate, it follows even more clearly that interpretation by the
philosopher, the political theorist, or—when he too enters the
arena—the critic of literature should not be identified, or rather
confounded, with interpretation by the historian. The statements made by any one of these practitioners are not historical
statements; they are designed to produce, or elicit, formal relationships or empirically testable propositions, not with what
eigentlich happened or—the special form which this takes in
the history of thought—what *eigentlich* was meant. The non-
historical practitioner is not concerned with what the author of
a statement made in a remote past meant by it so much as with
what he in his present can make it mean: what he can do with
it for purposes of his own, which may or may not—and therefore do not have to—coincide with those of the author. Either
the formal nature of the enterprise in which author and interpreter share, or considerations of historical continuity, may
bring it about that to some degree they do so coincide, and that
to this degree effective communication between the dead and
the living is possible; it may well be that unless there is some
degree of communication of this kind, the interpreter will be
unable to use the author's words even to his own purpose. But
only the historian, or more precisely the man engaged for the
moment in historical inquiry, is interested in the question of
how far the author's use of his words coincided with his modern
interpreter's use of them. From his standpoint, he must observe
that communication between author and interpreter is of the
kind which Petrarch imagined between himself and Cicero or
Livy—"from you, in your age of the world, to me in mine"—
and necessarily entails an element of translation, and consequently of *traduttore traditore*. But since he is prepared to allow autonomy to disciplines other than his own, he will also
observe that if this kind of treason prosper, it is no longer
treason. "Hobbes did not mean that by those words," he will
murmur to the philosopher or political theorist, "at least not

7

exactly; but you may if you find it useful. Do not, however, preface your thought by the words 'Hobbes said,' still less by the dishonest pseudo-present 'Hobbes says.' Something like 'if we repeat these words of Hobbes under given conditions, there ensue the following results' is more your meaning."

The philosopher, theorist or critic *in illo tempore* might with reason resent his apparent obligation to study what he knew to be history, and still more his apparent obligation to write it. There is a legitimate activity—it would be proper to term it a humanist one—of restating the thought of ancients and predecessors in the language of one's own day, in order to see what they have to say, when so stated, as to its concerns; the humanist in this sense is one who would rather learn about politics from Aristotle than from behavioral science. But twentieth-century men are averse from regarding themselves as dwarfs on the shoulders of giants, and many of them would rather not take their conceptual apparatus from tradition, preferring to construct their own. The division of labor between humanists and operationalists is a wholly legitimate one. The trouble arose *in illo tempore* less because students were drafted into humanism against their will than because, when philosophers became involved in humanist activities, they found themselves expected to do work of historical interpretation for which they were not equipped; and whether they resented the task or eagerly embraced it, the results were often equally unfortunate. A classic instance of the substitution of philosophical for historical explanation that sometimes ensued is to be found in the work of R. I. Aaron. Becoming interested in Locke's apparent indifference to any historical explanation of politics, he accounted for it by saying that the age Locke lived in was rationalist and was uninterested in any other kind of explanation.[2] Historical inquiry, however, revealed that Locke was unique among the theorists of his age, including his closest associates, in his indif-

[2] R. I. Aaron, *John Locke* (2nd ed.; Oxford: at the Clarendon Press, 1955), p. 271.

8

ference to historical explanation and that it is very difficult to
account for this characteristic;[3] from which it further appears
that Aaron's allegedly historical explanation was drawn from
his philosophical analysis of Locke's text, that it is wholly circu-
lar and that it masqueraded in his own mind as a piece of history. Faulty division of labor—the chief cause of methodological debate—was clearly to blame for this sad confusion.

But the historian was no less to blame, and no less confused,
when he allowed the philosopher's modes of thought to be
foisted upon his own. Since the philosopher's business is to
formalize the relations between ideas, he very properly drew out
the bodies of political thought presented to him into systems
of philosophy at least as formalized as their authors had sought
to make them, and at times more so. When the authors had
themselves aimed at a philosophical degree of formalization,
this was not an illegitimate activity and had much to teach the
historian; but this was not always the case. Even when it was,
however, the philosophical explanation of how the ideas in a
system are related to one another is generically different from,
and only contingently coincident with, the historical explanation of what the author meant to say, let alone of why he
wanted to say it or chose to say it in that way; the two are
arrived at by different procedures and answer different questions. The result for the historian *in illo tempore* was that he
found himself confronted by a chronologically ordered sequence of major intellectual systems, allegedly (and sometimes
verifiably) constituting historical phenomena. The intellectual
similarities between these systems were supposed to constitute
the continuities, the dissimilarities between them the processes
of change, of a historical order; but the order had not been built
up by the methods of the historian.

[3] J. G. A. Pocock, *The Ancient Constitution and the Feudal Law*
(Cambridge University Press, 1957), chs. 8 and 9; Peter Laslett, ed.,
Two Treatises of Government by John Locke (Cambridge University
Press, 1960), introduction; and Dunn, op. cit.

He was therefore required to deal with a para-history or meta-history, consisting of philosophical systems and existing alongside the other historical sequences or orders with which he dealt, and to which he was expected in some way to relate it. The task was plainly impossible if, as this analysis has suggested, the "history of political thought" presented to him did not belong to his universe of discourse at all; but he did not escape from his difficulties merely by denying that it so belonged. He might, that is to say, respond as Marxists did, by stigmatizing the whole erection as "idealism," and indeed it is such contemporary idealists as W. H. Greenleaf who profess themselves happiest with a "history of political philosophy" so constructed [4] (though some would wish to ask why the idealist universe of discourse in which Greenleaf operates is to be called "history" at all). But the counterpart of idealism is materialism; and the historian often reacted to his predicament by seeking to reduce the order of ideas to identity with some other order which he was better equipped to handle. If a Marxist (at least of the Old Left), he declared that "ideas" were a mere reflection of social reality; if a Namierite, that they were rationalizations of political interests independently perceived and arrived at. But this did not do either. Reductionism failed to rescue the historian from the circumstance that the intellectual constructs he was trying to control were not historical phenomena at all, to the extent to which they had been built up by non-historical modes of inquiry; to the extent that at best they were historical phenomena only by the luck of some intelligent non-historian's discovery. The reductionist technique was simply an attempt to explain how the apple got into the dumpling, the ghost into the machine.

The above strictures should not be read as meaning that

[4] W. H. Greenleaf, *Oakeshott's Philosophical Politics* (London: Hutchinson, 1966) and "Hobbes: The Problem of Interpretation" in Reinhart Koselleck and Roman Schnur, eds., *Hobbes-Forschungen* (Berlin: Duncker and Humblot, 1969).

much excellent history of political thought was not written by scholars operating under these limitations; the mind overcomes limitations of this kind before it sets about dismantling them. But good work done in a context of methodological confusion is in a sense done by chance, or by some coincidence of *virtù* and *fortuna*; it is done despite the available methods, and lacks the critical autonomy which comes only when the method is operating positively to produce the work. The transformation we can claim to be living through is nothing more or less than the emergence of a truly autonomous method, one which offers a means of treating the phenomena of political thought strictly as historical phenomena and—since history is about things happening—even as historical events: as things happening in a context which defines the kind of events they were. Ghosts still stalk the battlefield; it can still be seriously asked whether the history of political thought consists of the study of classical texts or of perennial problems, whether the choice lies between an idealist or a materialist scheme of interpretation. But we are beginning to see historical daylight; and since it has been emphasized that much of the previous confusion originated in a confounding of the functions of the historian and the philosopher, it is gratifying to record that philosophic analysis was the agency which began to liberate the historian for the pursuit of his own method.

The positivist and linguistic philosophies ascendant some fifteen years ago [5]—difficult as it is to recall that time in the present moment of romantic agony—raised the question whether such a thing as political philosophy could exist at all; whether the business of the philosopher were not simply to explore and clarify the statements which other men made about

[5] I have in mind the appearance in 1956 of the first series of *Philosophy, Politics and Society*, edited by Peter Laslett, and its editor's claim that "for the present, anyhow, political philosophy is dead." For the revenant's subsequent adventures see, e.g., the second series issued under the same title, edited by Laslett and W. G. Runciman (Oxford: Basil Blackwell, 1962).

subjects that might include the political. If to clarify might be considered a normative activity, to explore might be either analytical or historical. The distinction between first-order and second-order statements, between statements and statements about statements, evoked the image of a world in which some men employed language—or languages, or language structures, or language-"games" possessing "rules" by which they might be "played"—to make statements, including political statements and statements about politics, while other men employed language (the concept could be similarly refined at this level) to explore the statements which had been made and the vocabularies, structures or rules by which they had been made. It needed only the step—which a historian should take instinctively—of viewing "language" as a product of history and as possessing history of its own, to reach the point where it could be seen, first, that the exploration of language might yield historical results, might produce second-order statements about languages used which would be historical statements; second, that this activity could be considered a historical agent, helping to produce changes in linguistic consciousness and so in the history of language-use itself. What seemed to many, about 1956, the subversion of political philosophy by linguistic analysis helped to liberate the history of political thought by converting it from a history of systematization ("philosophy" in an old sense) into one of linguistic use and sophistication ("philosophy" in a new).

But to analyze the logical structure of a statement—as we already know, and as has been the recurrent theme of this critique—is not to bring out its concrete character as a historical phenomenon. Neither can this be done—though it can be approached a great deal more nearly—by the techniques which critics and students of literary expression employ to uncover the full wealth of association, implication and resonance, the many levels of meaning, which a living language contains when used by those who are masters of its powers of expression. The rigor with which some schools of "new criticism" insist that theirs is and must be an altogether a-historical discipline demonstrates, even if one does not accept this doctrine, that the critic is not self-defined as a historian dedicated to the recovery of an actual past. Still less will this be the aim of the sort of analysis conducted by pure linguistics, especially if one accepts that the mental structures constituting language lie at a level of the personality too deep to be readily associated with history in any of its usual senses. At this stage in the reconstruction which we are conducting, the methodological autonomy of the history of political language remains to be established.

Perhaps the most valuable single contribution to its establishment has been made indirectly, by a historian of science. Thomas S. Kuhn's *The Structure of Scientific Revolutions* has accustomed readers to think of the history of science as essentially a history of discourse and of language. In what he calls periods of "normal science," paradigms—controlling concepts and theories—so satisfactorily discharge the intellectual functions expected of them that they authoritatively indicate not merely the solutions to problems, but the kinds of problems which are to be conceptualized as requiring solution; and so, dictating the direction, the pattern, the distribution and organization of intellectual endeavor, indicate further the ascription and definition of authority among the individuals and groups composing the "scientific community." Scientific revolutions occur when the paradigms cease to function satisfactorily, and it is discovered not merely that problems are remaining unsolved, but that the problems which the paradigms indicate are incapable of solution because they are now seen as misconceived; that something has happened which necessitates a redefinition of the problems to be solved, a reordering and redefinition of the discipline itself, a new paradigmatic structure, a new language and a new distribution of authority within the scientific community. A "take-off" or "permanent revolution" might be envisaged in the case of a community so flexibly or-

13

ganised that the process of paradigmatic reconstruction, or "scientific revolution," was constant and continuous; but on the assumption that a successful paradigmatic change is one which discovers (or constitutes) a whole new class of problems awaiting definition and solution, it is likely to generate a period of "normal science" in which it will become a conservative force, or Hegelian thesis, necessitating antithesis, revolution and synthesis at a later moment.

The exciting thing about Kuhn's methodology, from the point of view of one concerned with the problems of this essay, is that it treats a branch of the history of thought as a process both linguistic and political. To treat a highly formalized activity of thinking as an activity of communicating and distributing authority by linguistic means may very well be unwelcome to many readers at present, if they view Kuhn's treatment (wrongly but inevitably) as normative or recommendative; but its value to the historian is that, by defining the "paradigm" both in terms of the intellectual (heuristic) function it performs and in terms of the authority, both intellectual and political, which it distributes as between human actors in a social system, we acquire two sets of criteria by which to define the language in general and the paradigm in particular,[6] in which we are interested, in their social context and their historical con-

---

[6] In thus defining the "paradigm" in strictly linguistic terms, I have already begun to diverge somewhat from Kuhn's employment of a term so much his own. He has recently (*Comparative Studies in Society and History*, vol. XI, no. 4, p. 412) emphasized that "paradigms are not to be entirely equated with theories. Most fundamentally, they are accepted concrete examples of scientific achievement, actual problem-solutions which scientists study with care and upon which they model their own work." In what follows, I have consistently treated them as *verba* rather than *exempla*; but I believe this can be justified on the grounds that politics (as distinct from political science) is not a problem-solving activity and involves an even more intricate structure of communication; and the verbal paradigm as I seek to present it—a historical event or phenomenon to which there can be many responses—retains much of the character of Kuhn's concrete *exemplum*. It will, I fear, be Professor Kuhn's fate to see his concepts taken from him and used for purposes not his own; but this is proof of the essential value of his theory.

creteness. Men think by communicating language systems; these systems help constitute both their conceptual worlds and the authority-structures, or social worlds, related to these; the conceptual and social worlds may each be seen as a context to the other, so that the picture gains in concreteness. The individual's thinking may now be viewed as a social event, an act of communication and of response within a paradigm-system, and as a historical event, a moment in a process of transformation of that system and of the interacting worlds which both system and act help to constitute and are constituted by. We have gained what we lacked before: the complexity of context which the historian needs.

It is hard to exaggerate the attractiveness, to the historian of political thought, of the suggestion that Kuhn has provided an anatomy applicable to his or to any field of intellectual history. Not only does this scheme offer him a means of furnishing the history of political thought with methodological autonomy; the implication that any formalized language is a political phenomenon in the sense that it serves to constitute an authority structure is agreeable to his sense that, in studying the history of political thought, he must at the same time be studying the history of political society. What has hitherto been rather vaguely termed "political thought" is now redefined as the exploration and sophistication of political language, and the connections between language system and political system begin to seem possible to draw. However, if we proceed to say that political language consists of the paradigms of the political community in a way analogous to that in which scientific language consists of the paradigms of the scientific community, complications arise which have to be recognized. The political community is not like the scientific community, and its language differs accordingly. The reason is that the scientific community may without distortion be thought of as organized for a single purpose, that of intellectual inquiry of a certain kind. It is true that the extent to which this is so may be questioned.

We have defined intellectual inquiry as itself displaying a political aspect, in so far as it consists of the construction and reconstruction of authority-structures; and we may bow the knee to the Double Helix by admitting both that considerations other than purely intellectual enter into the motivation and behavior of scientists, and that the decisions by which scientific paradigms are modified or abandoned are processes of consensus in which the exact moment of decision cannot be isolated and intellectualized, and into which the politics of group behavior may conspicuously enter.[7] Nevertheless, there is a difference. The scientific community is formally constituted by the paradigms of intellectual inquiry of a specific sort, and by the concept of that inquiry itself acting as a paradigm. A man is a member of the scientific community only because he has assumed the *persona* of one engaged in that form of inquiry and acknowledging the authority of its paradigms; and this will not cease to be true should his community pass through the restructuring process of a scientific revolution. Consequently, the extent to which the language and thought of the scientific community will be disciplined by the paradigms of a single mode of intellectual inquiry, as that is from time to time redefined, may be predicted as high. The same may be said of other communities of intellectual specialists, though with varying degrees of specificity; the paradigms of the community of historians, for example, will prove maddeningly elusive. But the history of political thought is not the history of the thought, language or paradigms of the community of political scientists; only very recently has that community developed to the point where its language and its history may attain to the dignity of a subsystem. The political thinker is assumed to be thinking as a member, and in the context, of the political community itself, and therefore to be speaking a specialized variation of its public language. Where a subcommunity of political scientists

[7] J. M. Ziman, *Public Knowledge: An Essay Concerning the Social Dimension of Science* (Cambridge University Press, 1968); James D. Watson, *The Double Helix* (New York: Atheneum, 1968).

has developed to the point of professional or methodological autonomy, we shall ask whether its language is continuous or discontinuous with that of the political community at large. The more the two languages are continuous, or the less the specialized subcommunity is seen to be autonomous, the more will the "political thinker" be supposed to be making second-order statements, to be exploring, modifying and using at a higher level of abstraction, some area of the language of politics itself. He will be communicating with his fellow citizens—as Socrates was judged by them—in terms of what he has done with their publicly approved paradigms of value and authority.

The language of politics is obviously not the language of a single disciplined mode of intellectual inquiry. It is rhetoric, the language in which men speak for all the purposes and in all the ways in which men may be found articulating and communicating as part of the activity and the culture of politics. Political speech can easily be shown to include statements, propositions and incantations of virtually every kind distinguished by logicians, grammarians, rhetoricians and other students of language, utterance and meaning; even disciplined modes of inquiry will be found there, but coexisting with utterances of very different kinds. It is of the nature of rhetoric and above all of political rhetoric—which is designed to reconcile men pursuing different activities and a diversity of goals and values—that the same utterance will simultaneously perform a diversity of linguistic functions. What is a statement of fact to some will symbolically evoke certain values to others; what evokes a certain cluster of factual assertions, and value judgments concerning them, to one set of hearers will simultaneously evoke another cluster and recommend another resolution of conduct in the ears of another set. Because factual and evaluative statements are inextricably combined in political speech, and because it is intended to reconcile and coordinate different groups pursuing different values, its inherent ambiguity and its cryptic content are invariably high.

The consequence is that if we are to define political speech as controlled by paradigms—and these, in the forms of highly authoritative linguistic formulations, are very evidently present —we must revise our theoretical definition of a paradigm and its function. A Kuhnian paradigm prescribed the isolation of certain problems and their solution in certain ways, and in so doing prescribed certain definitions of authority within the scientific community. Since speech is a political operant, it visibly performs the latter kind of function within the political community; but since it is not confined to the activity of problem-solving, it arrives at these functions by a different route. It invokes values, it summarizes information, it suppresses the inconvenient; it makes many kinds of statement and does so by means of formulations which can often convey several kinds of statement at once, while simultaneously diverting attention from others. Its paradigms, therefore, even those institutionalized to the point where to utter them is itself an invocation of authority, must be thought of as operating in several simultaneous contexts, performing several simultaneous functions, and as doing so in ways which deliberately fail to distinguish these contexts and functions from one another. When we define the paradigm as prescribing an authority-structure in the act of performing an intellectual (or linguistic) function, it must follow that a multivalent paradigm, simultaneously performing diverse functions in diverse contexts, must simultaneously designate and prescribe diverse definitions and distributions of authority; nor is this surprising once we remember that a political society contains a great variety of authority-structures, variously indicated and prescribed, and that the purpose of political activity —including political speech—is to appeal to numbers of these simultaneously, by means which can neither politically nor linguistically be identical.

It follows for the post-Kuhnian student of political speech that the paradigms whose careers he is tracing must be thought of as existing in many contexts and on many levels simultaneously. He may analyze the rhetorical (which are also political) structures in which they were employed to say many things to many men at once; but as he traces their history, in terms of men's responses to their use and their subsequent re-employment, he must recognize the theoretical probability that each of them may have had as many histories as there were levels on which its use was recognized and provoked response, and that given the semantic diversity of these levels, these histories may have diverged widely from one another. Even if they did not, the levels remain as semantically distinguishable as ever, so that rhetorically complex speech has a semantically complex history; and all this is part of the linguistic and therefore political texture of the human societies and lives whose history the student is ultimately tracing. It does not follow that a paradigmatic revolution—the equivalent in political speech of one of Kuhn's "scientific revolutions"—will entail the occurrence of a political revolution; a power-structure may survive by successfully transforming its idiom; but these are phenomena between which relations can be found.

At this stage we are considering the possibility of a politics of language: a series of devices for envisaging the varieties of the political functions which language can perform and of the types of political utterance that can be made, and the ways in which these utterances may transform one another as they interact under the stress of political conversation and dialectic. Some theoretical, as well as historical, exercises in such a politics may be found in the seventh essay in this book, where political statements concerning the past of society are envisaged in transit from symbolic legitimation *via* pragmatic criticism to historical reconstruction. It will be observed that while the earlier conventions of utterance are not superseded, but survive alongside the later modes superimposed upon them, the process of debate itself does operate to clarify the distinctions between the different types of statement being confusedly intimated, as men respond to the different aspects of the communication which stimulate and provoke them. Confusion and clarification exist together. The prototype of the second-order statement thus appears quite spontaneously, without the necessity of intervention by specialized intellectuals, as men argue over, as well as for and against, the exact meanings of the message intimated to them; but it is along the same line of development that the specialized intellectual makes his appearance, either as one whose function it is to make second-order statements concerning the level of meaning on which the intimated statement is to be interpreted, or as one practicing the special skill of interpreting and refining the statement and others like it on some one of these levels, where a distinct and autonomous intellectual activity is now being carried on. It is very important, above all when we are engaged in revising the relation between political philosophy and the history of political thought, to recollect that philosophy, whether in its classical or in its modern sense, is only one of the specialized intellectual activities which can be generated by discussion and exploration of the language in which the articulation of politics is carried on. Historiography is another; and others again may be identified, to varying degrees emerged from the merely ancillary (as historiography, it may be argued, has emerged altogether).

Whether the intellectual has specialized in the clarification of speech itself, or in one or other of the abstract crafts to which clarification gives rise, his increasingly rarefied diction continues to perform political functions; since the paradigms of his discourse, even if they are not merely the paradigms of ordinary political language raised to a higher level of abstraction, still inescapably recommend (even if only by emphasizing) this or that deployment of speech, and so this or that definition and ascription of authority. He does not emerge from the multiple structures of political language and the political community. But at this point we are rendered conscious once again of the diversity of "languages" in which "political thought" may be carried on, the diversity of contexts in which its paradigms may function linguistically and exert political effects. A theoretical politics of language has carried us so far, by demonstrating that political speech consists of a dense texture of undifferentiated intimations, that these may be differentiated into a variety of specialized linguistic (and political) activities, but that nothing can prevent these from continuing to affect and redound upon one another. It is part of the plural character of political society that its communication networks can never be entirely closed, that language appropriate to one level of abstraction can always be heard and responded to upon another, that paradigms migrate from contexts in which they have been specialized to discharge certain functions to others in which they are expected to perform differently. If the philosopher is concerned to keep statements of different orders distinct from one another, the historian is concerned with whether or not they were kept distinct, and with what happened as a result of either.

To render the texture denser still, a politics of language, though it may succeed in predicting the functions of political paradigms and even the theoretical processes of change in those functions, cannot be expected to predict the specific contents and referents of political speech; this has to be left to empirical investigation. Political speech does not refer alone to the structure of political activities, institutions and values conceptualized as the subject matter of political theory, and conceivable as theoretically constant in a wide range of political societies. It refers also to all those activities, together with their institutions and values, which it is the business of politics to order and coordinate and which may, in the specific society whose language and thought we choose to study, have been seen for so long as relevant to politics that their vocabularies and values have entered the political language and become part of it. Governors must learn and speak the language of the governed; individuals enter the governing elite by way of specialized subelites whose characteristic vocabularies they bring with them; for these and other reasons, political speech becomes impreg-

21

nated with the more or less institutionalized idioms of the
social activities for which politics has developed a special concern. And it is the history of the political culture which has determined which these are—Burke's perception [8] that Englishmen conducted debate largely in the language of common law
and real property is a perception of the history of English political thought—so that there does not appear to be a politics
which can predict which they shall be. The language of one
society is impregnated with terms of theology, of a second with
law, of a third with economics, and so on; we may trace how
this has happened, we may observe it in process of happening,
but in either case we are studying history, not constructing
models of hypothetical processes. Furthermore, it must be recognized that as the languages of the subpolitical activities migrate into the political speech, they bring with them paradigms
of their own, which not only exercise a political function in the
sense that they perform authoritatively within their subcom-
munities, but encourage definitions and distributions of authority within the political community at large which continue
the value-assumptions and thought-forms of the subpolitical
communities in which they originated. A complex plural society will speak a complex plural language; or rather, a plurality
of specialized languages, each carrying its own biases as to the
definition and distribution of authority, will be seen converging
to form a highly complex language, in which many paradigmatic structures exist simultaneously, debate goes on as between
them, individual terms and concepts migrate from one structure
to another, altering some of their implications and retaining
others, and the processes of change within language considered
as a social instrument can be imagined as beginning. Add to
all this the presence of a variety of specialized intellectuals,
making second-order statements of many different kinds in explanation of the language or languages they find to be in use,

[8] See below, pp. 206–12.

and we shall have some image of the richness of texture to be discovered in what we term the history of political thought.

That history might be defined as a history of change in the employment of paradigms, the exploration of paradigms and the employment of paradigms for the exploration of paradigms. But in considering the character of the political paradigm, we have established that diversity of function and diversity of origin both operate to ensure that its employment remains multivalent and ambiguous. Political statements are such that they may convey more than one meaning and be of more than one order; they are made up of terms of many origins, bearing many possible implications. We have now to consider the significance of this for the historian. In the first place it seems to guarantee, in a specifically political way and for specifically political reasons, the truth for his purposes of the general rule that a historical document can always be made to yield more information than it overtly conveys, more even than its maker intended to convey: as when a charter reveals more about medieval society than the scribe intended to communicate or knew that he was communicating. The author of a political statement may intend to be ambiguous; he is employing a language by its nature inherently ambiguous; but because the language and the range of its ambiguities are given him by society and exist in a context of use and meaning whose multivalency he cannot expect to control, his statement may convey meanings to others (especially after the processes of linguistic change have had time to proceed some way) outside any range of ambiguity he may have intended. It is true that he could not have meant to convey any message which the resources of language in his lifetime did not render it possible for him to have meant; it may be that he could not have meant anything which no contemporary hearer or reader could have understood him as meaning; but within these limits there is room for it to have happened to him (as happens to all of us) to mean more than he said or to say more than he meant. It could be argued that

23

among its political functions language operates to ensure something like the exchanges of hostages which interest the conflict theorists: it always implicitly conveys more than we intend, and we commit ourselves, by the mere act of using the language, to these implications as soon as some hearer becomes aware of them and uses them to control or modify the meaning of our communications and acts. To speak at all is to give some other power over us, and some assert their own power by refusing to speak at all, to speak intelligibly or (so far as this is possible) within any frame of reference they cannot unilaterally prescribe. An author who burns his manuscripts on his deathbed is refusing posterity the power which comes of interpreting him. Alice's Humpty Dumpty existed in the linguistic equivalent of a Hobbesian state of nature.[9]

But if the author of a political utterance cannot wholly control the levels on which his utterance may be taken to have meaning, or—once the making of second-order statements has entered the context of discourse—the levels of abstraction on which it may be discussed, it follows, first, that (unlike Humpty Dumpty) he is not fully in command of the "meaning" of his own utterance; secondly, that it will have a multiple history, proceeding on as many levels as those on which it is taken to have meaning; thirdly, that this history will consist of moments, events and processes more widely distributed than those constituting the articulation—the formation and utterance—of the author's own meaning, which now represents a limited

---

[9] " 'When I use a word,' Humpty Dumpty said in rather a scornful tone, 'it means just what I choose it to mean—neither more nor less.'
" 'The question is,' said Alice, 'whether you can make words mean different things.'
" 'The question is,' said Humpty Dumpty, 'who is to be master—that's all.' " The reader will find that as the dialogue progresses Humpty Dumpty is unable to maintain this posture of ascendancy and is forced to resort to obfuscation. "Impenetrability! That's what I say!" He falls off his wall as Alice leaves him. At a later point the Red Queen remarks: "When you've once said a thing, that fixes it, and you must take the consequences."

area of the history of the statement. Once history is seen in linguistic depth such as this, the paradigms with which the author operates take precedence over questions of his "intention" or the "illocutionary force" of his utterance,[10] for only after we have understood what means he had of saying anything can we understand what he meant to say, what he succeeded in saying, what he was taken to have said, or what effects his utterance had in modifying or transforming the existing paradigm structures. Authors—individuals thinking and articulating—remain the actors in any story we may have to tell, but the units of the processes we trace are the paradigms of political speech. As these function, they prescribe the levels on which the author's communications may be transmitted and (by no means the same thing) received; as they change, so the pattern of these levels of meaning changes also. If an author was what we call "creative," "seminal" or "revolutionary," we can ascribe to him a definite effect (and perhaps intention also) of changing the paradigm structure by some force which his utterances exerted.

The historian's first problem, then, is to identify the "language" or "vocabulary" with and within which the author operated, and to show how it functioned paradigmatically to prescribe what he might say and how he might say it. This task can more easily be imagined if we suppose (as was generally the case in the "early-modern" or "late-Renaissance" period with which most of the following essays deal) that his society possessed a number of distinguishable idioms, diverse in both their cultural origins and their linguistic functions, with which to discuss questions of politics—theological, legal, humanist, and so on. It then becomes easier to identify which of these the author employed or criticized—the thought of Burke, as

[10] I take the use of these terms from Skinner's article in *History and Theory*, VIII, 1, cited above, n. 1. It seems to me that if the intention and the utterance itself can be thought of as occurring or existing at different moments, "intention" and "illocution" can never be quite identical; the possibility that one's intention is modified in the act of uttering a statement which then exerts illocutionary force can never be eliminated.

discussed later on, is largely an examination of what languages have been, and what appropriately may be, employed in English political debate—and to show what functions, political and intellectual, they discharged or prescribed, what assumptions and implications they contained, and what were normally the consequences of employing them along the lines they themselves suggested, after which we can consider the consequences of the author's employing them as he did. If at this stage we are asked how we know the languages adumbrated really existed, or how we recognize them when we see them, we should be able to reply empirically: that the languages in question are simply there, that they form individually recognizable patterns and styles, and that we get to know them by learning to speak them, to think in their patterns and styles until we know that we are speaking them and can predict in what directions speaking them is carrying us. From this point we may proceed to study them in depth, detecting both their cultural and social origins and the modes, linguistic and political, of assumption, implication, and ambiguity which they contained and helped to convey.

It is difficult to say which has been the more striking experience: the excitement of discovering the languages in which political discourse and discussion were actually carried on, or the astonishment of realizing the extent to which their presence—easily visible and not at all esoteric—has been neglected or ignored. We have been enriched by learning that French thought of the sixteenth century, English thought of the seventeenth century, was conducted largely in terms of rival visions, some of them highly sophisticated, of the legal and institutional past; [11] that Machiavelli's political vocabulary is strik-

[11] W. F. Church, *Constitutional Thought in Sixteenth-Century France* (Cambridge, Mass.; Harvard University Press, 1941); Myron P. Gilmore, *Argument from Roman Law in Political Thought, 1200 to 1600* (Cambridge, Mass.; Harvard University Press, 1941); Julian H. Franklin, *Jean Bodin and the Sixteenth-century Revolution in the Methodology of Law and History* (New York: Columbia University Press, 1963); V. De

ingly continuous with the language of debate in the Florentine *pratiche*; [12] that Puritan thinking was organized around eschatological and apocalyptic concepts largely discountenanced by Calvin, and that the apocalyptic mode was as often employed by ruling structures as by rebellions; [13] that Hobbes's *Leviathan* can be located as a contribution to the Engagement debate of 1649–51; [14] that the significance of Locke in eighteenth-century political discussion requires a complete reassessment; [15] that the conservative style of the mid-eighteenth century was anti-historical rather than Burkean; [16] that the American revolutionaries and founding fathers were obsessed by the fear of Machiavellian corruption.[17] On the other hand, we have had to acknowledge that the third and fourth books of *Leviathan*, though equal in length to the first and second, have been seriously neglected by scholars because the subject matter is exegesis and eschatology, not philosophy, with the result that it was assumed that they could not matter and Hobbes could not have meant them seriously; that the first and longer of Locke's *Two Treatises of*

Caprariis, *Propaganda e Pensiero Politico in Francia durante le Guerre di Religione, 1559–1572* (Naples: E.S.I., 1959); Herbert Butterfield, *The Englishman and his History* (Cambridge University Press, 1944); Pocock, *The Ancient Constitution and the Feudal Law.*

[12] Felix Gilbert, *Machiavelli and Guicciardini: Politics and History in Sixteenth-century Florence* (Princeton University Press, 1965).

[13] W. Haller, *Foxe's Book of Martyrs and the Elect Nation* (London: Jonathan Cape, 1963); William M. Lamont, *Marginal Prynne* (London; Routledge and Kegan Paul, 1963) and *Godly Rule: Politics and Religion, 1603–1660* (London: Macmillan, 1969).

[14] Quentin Skinner, "History and Ideology in the English Revolution," *The Historical Journal,* VIII, 2 (1965) and "The Ideological Context of Hobbes's Political Thought," *ibid.,* IX, 3 (1966). John M. Wallace, *Destiny His Choice: The Loyalism of Andrew Marvell* (Cambridge University Press, 1968).

[15] Dunn, *op. cit.,* and "The Politics of Locke in England and America in the Eighteenth Century," in John W. Yolton, ed., *John Locke: Problems and Perspectives* (Cambridge University Press, 1969).

[16] See below, pp. 142–44, 265–6, 267–8.

[17] Bernard Bailyn, *The Ideological Origins of the American Revolution* (Cambridge, Mass.: Belknap Press, 1967); Gordon S. Wood, *The Creation of the American Republic* (Chapel Hill: University of North Carolina Press, 1969).

Government suffered similar neglect because it too failed to fit into a philosophically-constructed canon; [18] that R. L. Schuyler, editing the works of Josiah Tucker, omitted one whole book on the grounds that, being historical argument and so neither political nor economic theory, it could be of no interest to anyone; [19] and much more of the same kind. The essays in this volume are offered as evidence that there are still striking discoveries to be made by scholars prepared to look empirically at the language, rather than immediately at the theory, of philosophy; even of thinkers whose works have been the subject of centuries of discussion.

To know a language is to know the things which may be done with it, so that to study a thinker is to see what he attempted to do with it; and the first of these goals may be reached through the theoretically (if not practically) uncomplicated procedures of learning to speak it. But this is not always possible by the empirical method alone. If a society speaks in a diversity of language-styles, they need not all be so explicitly distinct and recognizable that they can be identified and learnt through a process of familiarization; we shall have to demonstrate that they are in fact there and functioning as we aver that they function. We have furthermore acknowledged that the paradigmatic functions to be found in political speech are multiple, simultaneously present and so imperfectly distinguished that it is by nature multivalent. It follows that the loads of implication and intimation which such a speech bears are extremely heavy and that, even on levels where speech is being used and explored with considerable sophistication, the political and linguistic functions it may discharge, the universes of discourse into which it may be pursued by intensified discussion and critical analysis, are indefinitely numerous. It is in a sense this which constitutes the "history" of political

[18] Laslett, *op. cit.*
[19] R. L. Schuyler, ed., *Josiah Tucker: A Selection from His Economic and Political Writings* (New York: Columbia University Press, 1931), preface.

28

"thought." A man makes a political utterance, which we have resolved to treat as an event or moment in a history of paradigm change. But the utterance is intelligible as more than one kind of political act, as possessing more than one logical status, as belonging to more than one level of abstraction, more than one context of references, more than one universe of discourse. The author may not have intended his statement to be interpreted in all of these contexts, but he cannot prevent his readers from interpreting it in any or all contexts in which their minds can place it; and as time goes on and men's conceptual universes undergo change, the statement will certainly be interpreted in contexts which the author did not intend or envisage. At any given moment, therefore, the "meanings" (one cannot avoid the plural) of a given utterance must be found by locating it in a paradigmatic texture, a multiplicity of contexts, which the verbal force of the utterance itself cannot completely determine; and if we wish to trace some aspect of its history by making statements of our own, we must, by our own deployments of language, isolate the context or universe in which we say this piece of history took place. Speech is not self-locating; the thought of Machiavelli will not state for us the history of the thought of Machiavelli. Whether *Il Principe* is being written in 1513, or responded to by counter-utterance in (say) 1613, we have to locate in the contemporary texture the level of meaning on which it is most illuminating to conduct our interpretation; and this necessitates our proceeding both by rendering explicit what may have been implicit before, and by selecting the area or level of implication to be explicated.

Selection is necessary because an utterance may, at any moment in its career, have more than one meaning and participate in more than one history; we are merely responding to the obligation to choose, and declare our choice of, that history which we feel competent to tell. It is not subjective or solipsistic because, as historians, we are committed to offering accounts of events which, in some sense or other, actually happened. Machiavelli, we say, did operate at such a level of meaning in 1513;

he was interpreted at such a level of meaning in 1613; if he was interpreted in 1613 as meaning something he had or could have meant in 1513, this is to say that the paradigm-structure had remained sufficiently stable over the intervening centuries for this to be possible. On the one hand, then, we assert that paradigm-structures are historical realities, whose presence and character can be detected by the methods that historians use. On the other, the fact that they are multivalent structures of speech, composed to a great extent of the implicit and the covert, compels us to employ techniques of detection and discovery which are of a sophisticated kind.

We have to get from the merely possible to the theoretically testable, to frame hypotheses about a realm of meaning which *may* have been present and operative, such that they will enable us to say whether, as a matter of historical fact, it *was* or not. The latter part of this operation—the verification—must obviously be conducted by methods which are rigorously historical; the former part may be, but need not. That is to say, our hypothesis that such and such a realm of meaning (or paradigm-function) was possible may be intimated to us by our historical sensitivity to the language being spoken and the society which spoke it; but we may equally well construct a hypothesis on the basis of some affirmation about language and its possibilities which is not a historian's affirmation. We may borrow from a philosopher or some other specialist in meaning or communication a thesis to the effect that an utterance of a certain order is conducive to utterances of other orders, and test to see whether this colligation existed in the historical situation we are examining. This is one way in which philosophy of a highly analytical kind can be useful to the historical investigation of political philosophy, and it is held by some that the possibilities of this sort of collaboration have not yet been sufficiently explored.[20] The point of immediate importance,

[20] Skinner, *History and Theory, loc. cit.,* pp. 49–50. Dunn, *Philosophy, loc. cit.,* pp. 86 *et seq.*

however, is that a heuristic construction does not become a historical hypothesis until it is reworded in such a form that it can be tested by the rules of historical evidence.

The point is illustrated by the second essay in this volume. I know no Chinese, and little enough about the history of China in the era of the Hundred Schools and the Warring States; but some years ago, I chanced to read a number of translations from ancient Chinese philosophers by different hands, which struck me as containing a definite political meaning and as coalescing to form a definite pattern of ideas about political values, political authority and the changes contingent on their transmission by linguistic or non-linguistic means. This pattern—which I have found employable in teaching introduction to political theory—is set out in the essay as here printed. But in writing it, I was (I hope) sufficiently careful to avoid putting it forward as a statement about the way in which ancient Chinese actually thought about politics, and to exclude as many historical referents as possible. Since my lack of knowledge of the historical period precludes me from making or testing statements about what actually happened or obtained then, it was clearly my duty to offer my reconstruction purely as an account of a notional situation. From time to time I show this piece to friends who are acquainted with ancient China as a historical reality, and inquire of them whether it might be an account of the actual thinking of men of that time. They have usually replied that it is probable that men did think in some such way as I hypothecate; i.e., my reconstruction is testable as a historical hypothesis; but a situation of far greater methodological interest would arise if they were to reply that on the basis of independent evidence it is historically impossible that the ancient Chinese thought in the way I have described. What, in that event, would be the status of the pattern of ideas I have put forward? I have abstained from advancing it as a historical hypothesis, though it is a usable one, so that to say that it was a falsified historical hypothesis would not exhaust all that could be said about it. It should be reusable in another context and as a hypothesis offered for a different sort of testing—as a piece of theory about the relations between authority and language, perhaps, or about the sociology of political concepts. As matters stand at the moment of including the essay in this volume, it appears to be an open-context hypothesis: a hypothetical structure capable of being turned to the purposes of more than one specialized mode of inquiry, not unlike the multivalent paradigms to be found in political speech itself, and therefore perhaps worth reading for the hypotheses it might suggest. The way of discourse by which we trace a path between the different modes of studying political thought is one to be trod delicately.

But the hypotheses constructed by the historian in this field aver that a certain level of meaning, a certain paradigmatic situation, existed in the mental activity of the past in such a way that men's thinking may be said actually to have gone on along the lines indicated by it. We know that a number of such levels may be simultaneously present and operative; but the greater the number that we distinguish, the more probable it becomes that we are going outside the author's "intention" and interpreting his statements as bearing meanings he did not consciously attach to them. Reasons have already been indicated why this is not an impossible situation, but it is a dangerous one insofar as it tempts the historian to take liberties and indulge in undisciplined interpretations. We deal with it by drawing distinctions between the implicit and the explicit. It is part of normal experience to find our thought conditioned by assumptions and paradigms so deep-seated that we did not know they were there until something brought them to the surface; we suspect, if we are historians, that there are others present and operative of which we shall never be aware because they will only be visible from the vantage-points provided by historical moments in the future. As historians, then, we are justified in seeking to make the implicit explicit and to find levels of meaning in a man's thought which he did not directly express and of which he was not consciously aware. We have, however, to be particularly careful—more careful than has sometimes been the case—to indicate the historical moment at which the implicit is seen as becoming explicit. We may mean that there was a level of meaning, a set of assumptions and paradigms, situated just below the normal level of critical consciousness in men of the author's era, so that they could in principle have been aware of it but as a rule took it for granted. In such a case the tests to be applied for historical verification of our hypothesis are relatively simple: there must be reasons of a contemporary nature that render it plausible that their thought should have been so conditioned; men's utterances and intellectual behavior should in general be consistent with their having acted on these assumptions; and there should if possible be one or two occasions on which the implicit surfaced into explicitness and authors spelled out in so many words that these were indeed the assumptions on which they acted. To satisfy these requirements is almost identical with demonstrating that there existed a language or paradigm-structure whose presence has not hitherto been realized; the study of "Burke and the Ancient Constitution," in the present volume, is an exercise of the kind. But the situation becomes more complex if we wish to say that the pattern of implication revealed was one which became visible only in a historical era later than that of which we are writing. If we mean that it became visible at some period intermediate between the author's lifetime and our own, we must say of those who did perceive it—as, for example, of Burke's analysis of the thought of the seventeenth century—either that the original paradigm-structure persisted into their time, but in such a way that what had been implicit now became explicit; or that the paradigm-structure had changed, so that they became conscious of characteristics of their predecessors' thought which they had not noticed before; or that they were performing exercises in historical reconstruction of the same kind that we perform ourselves. These three statements are not exclusive of one another, and each of them might with some plausibility be made of Burke in the case examined in this book.

Suppose next that we wish to declare that the implications uncovered in the thought of the past were never rendered explicit before we ourselves did so. We are claiming, that is, to know something about an author's paradigm-situation and his response to it of which he was not himself conscious, at least in the (paradigmatically determined) terms that we use to present it, and which has not been noticed or described before; how long the paradigm-situation we describe is said to have lasted is a secondary consideration. We may mean simply that we have performed a historical reconstruction of the sort described above; that we have uncovered a new paradigm structure and revealed its existence in the past. We may mean that we have erected a paradigm structure which suggests a new interpretation of the author's thought, but that—as in the Chinese case—we are uncertain whether the paradigms can be said to have existed historically, or whether the interpretation can be advanced as a historical hypothesis; we may even be certain that such is not the case and that we are not figuring *qua* historian at all. Or we may mean that we have erected some general rule or "law" concerning the paradigms of political thought and their functioning, which we now offer both as the sort of hypothesis which isolates and predicts a regular occurrence and as a source of historical hypotheses concerning authors and their paradigm-situations at moments in the past. The historian— being, as someone has put it, a consumer of general laws rather than a producer [21]—will be chiefly interested in the latter of the two functions which a general law may serve; but he will regard all these operations as legitimate.

[21] The phrase is that of Carey B. Joynt and Nicholas Rescher, "The Problem of Uniqueness in History," *History and Theory*, I, 2 (1961), p. 158.

"Laws" or general hypotheses of this kind will be statements concerning the paradigms of political speech as a category: the ways in which they originate, function or change under specified conditions. In putting forward such statements we shall be moving back towards the idea of a "politics of language" discussed earlier, and we shall be relating paradigms to some set of specified but generalized conditions in which they are seen as existing. It is therefore virtually inevitable, given the prevalent paradigms of historiography and the other social sciences, that we shall find ourselves talking about the paradigms of political speech as existing under "social" conditions and as intelligible in relation to the "social" positions of those using them or likely to be using them habitually; and that we shall find ourselves faced with colleagues who declare that the paradigms, concepts, ideas and utterances must be understood as rigorously controlled by our knowledge of social structure as something extraneous to them, and that not to understand them in this way is to be guilty of "idealism," "false consciousness," "abstractness," "unreality" and a variety of other terms for intellectual sin. Here it should be plain that we are back at the idealist-materialist dichotomy, and the problem of reduction discussed earlier; and some very careful definitions of our task have become necessary. The techniques discussed in this essay are techniques for identifying and exploring the paradigmatic languages in which political discourse has been carried on; stress has been laid on identification of the rhetorical, political and intellectual functions which they perform and of the implications and intimations which they contain and which may become operative and explicit as the political conversation continues. Now languages plainly denote, both consciously and unconsciously, elements of experience, feeling, and conditioning outside the structure of intellectuality; a social language exists to do just that, and it has been emphasized here that political language is saturated with references to elements outside the narrowly political field, of innumerable and unpredictable

35

variety. To explore political language is to explore the changing character of these references. We shall be constantly inquiring, therefore, to what elements of social experience the language under study can be shown to refer? at what levels of implication? at what levels of abstraction? The charge that we do not relate thought to social structure should be utterly untenable. The technique, however, does necessarily involve starting with the language and working outwards, to show what meanings it can be said to have borne; it does not involve starting with the assumption that language "reflects" social reality, selecting in obedience to conventional wisdom some aspect of social structure as predictably "reflected," and endeavoring to demonstrate parallels, correlations or connexions between the two. It should be thought of as an inquiry into the process of "reflection," rather than as based on a simple mirror-object assumption concerning its nature; we are interested in what elements of social experience are articulated in political speech, in how the process of articulation goes on, in how the articulations come to be organized in paradigmatic languages and elaborated in theoretical, philosophical, historical and other intellectually autonomous structures, and in the history of the entire process thus rendered visible. If it be said that political thought consists of "abstraction" from social reality, the word may simply be inserted in the foregoing sentence in place of "reflection."

But there is a procedure—somewhat dismissively summarized just above—which the approach through paradigms and conventional language does not undertake: that of seeking to establish correlations between the saying of certain things by certain men and the occupation by those men of certain places in a social structure and of certain moments in its history, and of seeking to demonstrate connections between the phenomena correlated which in no way need to have been denoted or implied by the previously-existing structure of the language they employed. This is an entirely legitimate (even if it remains a problematic) procedure when conducted with sufficient experimental rigor, as it has been, for example, by C. B. Mac-pherson.[22] He lays down the hypothesis that seventeenth-century England was a society in which a "market economy" was becoming important to the point where it should have had impact upon abstract political theory; he then enumerates the characteristics of such an economy which he expects to find discussed or implied in its works of theory, and tests in a variety of seventeenth-century English theorists to see if the expected allusions, implications or assumptions are really there. There may be two opinions as to whether Macpherson has found what he is looking for, but there can be no question that his procedure, as described, is wholly legitimate. If nothing like it is attempted in a book such as the present one, there is no more profound reason for this than the time has come for a change. One may entertain a measure of skepticism as to whether procedures which isolate certain social phenomena, and then seek to show that these were "reflected" in thought, may not impute to contemporary minds processes of conceptualization which it is difficult to show taking place; but there can be no possible objection to procedures which undogmatically explore problems of this kind. The point is rather that, under pressure from the idealist-materialist dichotomy, we have been giving all our attention to thought as conditioned by social facts outside itself and not enough of our attention to thought as denoting, referring, assuming, alluding, implying, and as performing a variety of functions of which the simplest is that of containing and conveying information. For this reason it is not necessary—though it may be useful—to make metaphysical statements about the relation of ideas to reality, epistemological statements about the relation of concepts to phenomena or sociological statements about the conditioning of thought by social structure, in order to discover that there is a great deal of valuable and neglected information, both theoretical and em-

[22] C. B. Macpherson, *The Political Theory of Possessive Individualism* (Oxford: the Clarendon Press, 1962).

pirical, to be got by systematic exploration of such questions as "what was he saying?", "what language was he saying it with?" and "what was he talking about?"—to say nothing of the further problems, concerning implication, level of meaning, and perfect or imperfect communication, which open out from this point.

There is one linguistic muddle, or pseudo-philosophical statement, stemming from the idealist-materialist dichotomy, which the historian of paradigmatic, and especially political, thinking has altogether to repudiate. This is the practice of referring to the extra-intellectual or extra-linguistic as "reality," and to the intellectual or linguistic equipment, at least by implication, as non-reality; a practice so rooted and widespread that this is the only branch of historical inquiry which faces constant reductionist pressure to abolish itself and restate its findings in other men's terms. Something called "reality," we are constantly assured, itself determines the paradigms by which men order it; but the word so used, whether by historians or by social scientists (who should know better), can bear no other meaning than "social and historic reality ordered by paradigms and concepts other than those by which the men who lived in it ordered it," as if only the concepts actually used in a given society were assured of unreality in their relation to it. The absurdity of the implication should remind us that the paradigms which order "reality" are part of the reality they order, that language is part of the social structure and not epiphenomenal to it, and that we are studying an aspect of reality when we study the ways in which it appeared real to the persons to whom it was more real than to anyone else. Certainly an aspect only; it is equally, but not more, legitimate to order their reality by paradigms other than theirs and to use the insights so gained to study their use of their paradigms; but in the last analysis, when we study the history of thought we are studying the conscious and subjective aspects of history. We can afford to ignore those who will at this point automatically accuse us of idealism, as we can afford to ignore the metaphysicians who will accuse us of setting up a counter-metaphysics; and if anyone accuses us of "abstraction," we can afford to reply that what we are studying is, precisely, the history of abstraction, that is to say the history of systematic thinking. For as long as the present confusions last, we shall be accused, in one way or another, of claiming as everything what our accusers claim to be nothing; but the simplest strategy may be to take no notice. When the confusions end, it may be observed that looking at language from the inside is complementary to looking at it from the outside and that all we have been doing is remedying the neglect which has, for various reasons, been visited upon the former.

In the essays that follow, one law or general hypothesis—concerned not with the conditions under which paradigm systems operate, so much as with the characteristics they regularly display—is constantly present and operative. Each essay is concerned with time: with the conceptualizations of time that may be elicited from systematic bodies of political thought; and the implicit generalization is simply that any such body of thought, and every paradigmatic language, contains a structure of implications concerning time, which can further be shown to embody a mode or modes of conceptualizing political society itself as existing in time. These structures appear to originate and develop in two ways, themselves interlocking. In the first place, they originate from the institutional forms which in any society are thought of as both defining and legitimizing its continuity; in the second place, they arise from the languages available for stating how an emergent event may be cognized and acted upon as it occurs in an extra-political continuum of time which, because it consists of such emergent events, is conceived of as a dimension of contingency. These two paradigmatic functions, which a politics of time may predict will be performed in the majority of societies, give rise to a variety of languages whose cultural diversity is so great that they can only be studied empirically and historically. Historically, then, the idea of time as the dimension of contingency is sufficiently close to the idea of time to be found in Aristotelian philosophy to make it possible to conceive that a species of historicism may be uncovered in late medieval and Renaissance political thought, originating when the attempt was made to integrate contingent time into the framework of Christian eschatology and gaining in importance as political structures claimed so much autonomy as to make it crucial to be able to show how they maintained themselves in time and dealt with its emergencies. Languages arose in which the political system could be shown existing in both contingent and eschatological time, overcoming and absorbing the contingent event or failing to do so; these were organized around the concepts of custom, providence, apocalyptic, fortune, virtue and corruption. A history can be written of how these languages were employed and modified, from the fifteenth through the eighteenth centuries, as various societies strove to explain what was happening to them and in the process moved some way from the idea of contingency to that of history. The third and fourth essays in this book, parts of a larger work in progress, depict aspects of this story in its movement from a Florentine to an English and American context.

But since time-structures of this kind are found implicit in language-structures, it follows from all that has been said that they can be studied theoretically as well as historically. The treatment of Chinese material set out in the second essay, as has already been shown, cannot be advanced except very tentatively as a historical hypothesis; its themes do, however, offer a pattern of general statements concerning the concepts of time, authority and action which arise when norms are thought of as transmitted verbally or non-verbally, by ritual, language or coercion; and some of these are taken up again in the seventh essay, which is an ambitious yet still tentative attempt at a politics of time considered as a subdepartment of a politics of language. It supposes a single mode of legitimizing the institutions of society through a conceptualization of their continuity, called "traditionalism"; and it attempts to pursue this mode through a number of mutations which occur as the pressures of political debate compel changes of both strategy and context. One of these is seen to be the emergence of critical historiography, which is here considered as an output both of political speech and of the politics of language. In conclusion, since all the historical material employed and the very concept of paradigm change itself presuppose an inherited or transmitted mental and linguistic structure and a consequent—one might say a dependent—willingness to criticize and explain that structure (or tradition), an eighth essay has been added, written after all the pieces that precede it, which raises and considers the charge that the method itself induces bias, towards early-modern themes in history and towards an unacknowledged classicism and conservatism in politics. In both contexts, therefore, I intend charging myself with a neglect of romanticism, in order to see what comes of *orationes accusatoria et defensoria* on this count. In all these essays, however—be this as it may—there will be seen going on a constant endeavor to disengage the structures of implication and paradigmatic function latent in political discourse. That five essays strictly historical are enclosed within three somewhat more theoretical indicates with fair accuracy the distribution of the author's interests and the methodological balance of the whole enterprise.

Ritual, Language, Power: An Essay on the Apparent Political Meanings of Ancient Chinese Philosophy

T HIS ESSAY records the attempts of a historian and political theorist who is no Oriental scholar, and knows no Chinese, to discover a pattern of meanings in the ideas about government and society expressed in the heroic age of Chinese thought—the Warring States period, *circa* 500–200 B.C.—and to present them in such a way as to aid his understanding both of political society and of the character and problems of thought about it.

The writer became interested in the matter of Chinese political theory on learning that an ancient philosopher standing apart from the Confucian canon, Mo Ti or Mo Tzu (? 479– 381 B.C.), had written that in the beginning no one word had had the same meaning for two men, so that disorder had existed until the Emperor or "Son of Heaven" had unified language and thus stabilised human society under his authority. It seemed that there was something here worth investigating; and accordingly, a selection was made of passages relevant to politics which appeared either in standard works on Chinese philosophy, or in such modern translations of important texts as were readily available.[1] All thinkers studied are pre-Han in point of time, and nearly all antedate the Ch'in conquest and unification of the Chinese states about 233 B.C. No claims are made on behalf of the comprehensiveness or representativeness of the selection thus made, and its reliability must rest on the success with which the various translators have performed their bewildering task. Subject to these limitations, however, the passages selected appeared to fall of themselves into an intelligible pattern of ideas, of considerable interest both to the historian of thought and to the analyst of political society, though a complex methodological situation results, reference to which has already been made in the introductory chapter. In what follows, this pattern of ideas is presented in all its procedural ambiguity, for the sake of the different uses which the student of political thought may be able to make of it.

Confucian political theory seems to make the following presuppositions. Society is governed by a comprehensive code of rituals (*li*). Men in a given situation, by following the ritual prescribed as appropriate to it, manifest both actually and symbolically the ways in which men in that situation ought to behave, the relations between men in that situation which ought to exist. In theory, there is a ritual for every conceivable situation and a complete code of ritual behaviour for persons in every grade of society to whom the rituals apply. Only the privileged and noble, however, are governed by *li*; those beneath them are subject to a system of decrees backed by punishments,

---

[1] The following works have been found mainly useful for this purpose: Fung Yu-lan, *A History of Chinese Philosophy*, translated by D. Bodde, vol. I (Peiping and London, 1937); all quotations from Fung, unless otherwise stated, are from this book, not from the condensed one-volume *Short History of Chinese Philosophy* (Macmillan Paperbacks, New York, 1960). Arthur Waley, *Three Ways of Thought in Ancient China* (London, 1939). J. J. L. Duyvendak, ed. and trans., *The Book of Lord Shang* (London, 1928). H. H. Dubs, *Hsüntze, the Moulder of Ancient Confucianism* (London, 1927), and (ed. and trans.) *The Works of Hsüntze* (London, 1928); A. K. Liao, ed. and trans., *Han Fei Tzu* (two volumes, London, 1939 and 1959).

called *fa*—unsatisfactorily rendered in English as "laws." "The ritual does not extend down to the common people; the punishment of the law does not reach up to the Senior Officer." [2] Subject to this provision, however, the values and norms of noble society are all contained in the *li*, and society can be entirely and efficiently controlled by the performance of ritual; if the *li* are carried out, society's disagreements are resolved, its norms and relationships declared and established, and its necessary enterprises co-operatively executed. The performance of *li* is the maintenance of order.

The value of this theory to the student of politics is the emphasis it lays on the government of society by non-verbal means, and the explicit contrast it draws between *li* and *fa*—between government by ritual and government by verbal command. It is assumed that the performance of ritual is the display of virtue in a form which ensures that it acts upon, and is transmitted to, those before whom it is displayed.

> He who is a ruler of men makes it his object to manifest virtue and suppress what is wrong, that he may shed an enlightening influence on his officials, and is afraid lest he should fail in this. Therefore he seeks to display excellent virtue to show an example to posterity. . . . Now when by virtue he is frugal and observant of the statutes, attentive to the degrees of high and low; his character stamped on his elegant robes and his carriage; sounded forth also [with bells] and brightly displayed [with emblems]—when thus he presents himself for the enlightenment of his officials, they are struck with awe and dare not depart from the rules and laws. [3]

But in contrast with this government by ritual and *mana:*

[2] Quoted in S. Kaizuka, *Confucius* (tr. G. Bownas, London, 1956), p. 35.

[3] Fung, pp. 36–37; from the Tso Chuan, a pre-Confucian chronicle which may have undergone Confucian editing.

44

When the people know what the exact laws are, they do not stand in awe of their superiors. They come to have a contentious spirit and make their appeal to the written words, hoping to be successful in their argument. They can no longer be managed. When the government of the Hsia dynasty fell into disorder, the penal code of Yü was made; under the same circumstances in Shang, the penal code of T'ang; and in Chou, the code of the nine punishments. These three codes all originated in times of decay. And now, in your administration of the state of Cheng, you have constructed dikes and ditches, you have established a government which has been much spoken against, and you have framed a law code like those three codes, casting in metal a record of the punishments it provides. Will it not be difficult to keep the people in order? [4]

Words—this seems to be the essential idea behind this passage—are of limited efficiency as a means of government, perhaps because they are of limited efficiency as a means of communication. There is no proposition whose meaning cannot be called in doubt, contested or denied; none of which the contrary cannot be conceived or enunciated. To tell a man to do something, therefore, is to call into his mind the possibility of not doing it. Command entails disobedience, not because human personalities are recalcitrant, but because the nature of command is verbal and intellectual; instructing the penny to show only one side, we remind it that it has two. And because *fa* are verbal, they entail punishments; if you command a man to do something and, understanding your command, he does the contrary, you have no recourse left but to use force upon him. But since rituals are non-verbal, they have no contraries. They can therefore be used to produce harmony of wills and actions without provoking recalcitrance; if a man finds himself playing his appointed part in *li* and thus already—as it were

[4] Fung, *ibid.*, also from the Tso Chuan.

45

de facto—in harmony with others, it no more occurs to him to play a part other than that appointed to him than it occurs to a dancer to move to a different rhythm than that being played by the orchestra. This image is memorably employed by the great third-century Confucian, Hsun Tzu.

> How do we know the meaning of dancing? The dancer's eyes do not look at himself; his ears do not listen to himself; yet he controls the lowering and raising of his head, the bending and straightening of his body, his advancing and retreating, his slow and rapid movements; everything is discriminated and regulated. He exerts to the utmost all the strength of his body to keep time to the measures of the sounds of the drum and bell, and has no rebellious heart. All his purposes are summed up and earnest.[5]

Where Plato required the aid of an elaborate parallelism between the personality and the social structure in order to vindicate his claim that to change the form of music or poetry was to change the form of the state, here music and dancing *are* the form of the state; they stabilise its structure and communicate its values. But precisely because rituals have no contraries, the values of a ritual-controlled society cannot be questioned or doubted, and the Confucian world, being without moral alternatives, is a closed society. Its norms are exclusive and traditional; they are thought of as inherited from a past so remote and mythical that it can be known only by studying the later, but better-documented, period nearest to it in time, and a substantial part of Confucian thought is thought about the continuity of social usages in the past as a source of authority for continuing the same usages in the present. A group of sayings attributed to Confucius (who described himself as "a transmitter and not a creator") exemplify both the strength of his belief in tradition as a source of authority and the strength of his belief in the continuity of Chinese society.

[5] Dubs, *The Works of Hsüntze*, pp. 234–35.

Yuan Hui inquired how to govern a state. "Use the Hsia calendar. Ride in a Yin carriage. Wear a Chou hat. When there is music, let it be that of Shun. Banish the songs of Cheng and keep away from the eloquent, for the songs of Cheng are depraved and the eloquent are dangerous." [6]

"I can describe the civilisation of the Hsia dynasty, but the descendant state of Ch'i cannot render adequate corroboration. I can describe the civilisation of the Yin dynasty, but the descendant state of Sung cannot render adequate corroboration. And all because of the deficiency of their records and wise men. Were those sufficient then I could corroborate my views." [7]

"Chou had the advantage of surveying the two preceding dynasties. How replete was its culture! I follow Chou." [8]

Asked by Tzu Chang if the shape of the government of China ten generations hence could be known, Confucius replied: "Yes, the Yin dynasty, in the formulation of its system of ritual, borrowed from that of the preceding Hsia dynasty, and one can work out what additions were made, and where any part was rejected. Similarly, Chou borrowed from the ritual system of Yin, and again, it is possible to discover what was added, and what rejected. Hence, whatever the date, be it even a hundred generations hence, one can know by inference the corpus of ritual of the royal line which succeeds to Chou." [9]

When usages are thought of as so far continuous that a knowledge of their state in the present, combined with a documented knowledge of what they were like in relatively recent (Chou) times, is a sufficient basis from which to infer what

[6] J. R. Ware, *The Sayings of Confucius* (Mentor Religious Classics, New York, 1955), p. 100.
[7] Fung, p. 55.   [8] *Ibid.*   [9] Kaizuka, p. 112.

they were like in remotest antiquity and will be like in remotest futurity, the closed character of the Confucian world becomes even more evident. Yet there is nothing dead or mechanical about obedience to the Confucian norms. One of the cardinal virtues is "spontaneity," that quality by which one obeys, with an inner immediacy of consent and assent, a rule which has been fixed for all time and from which one never thinks of dissenting; to lack spontaneity is to be gravely inferior. Much of the ethics and aesthetics of Chinese social thought—for Hsun Tzu the value of obedience to the *li* was fully as much aesthetic as normative—is to be found in this concept of spontaneity; and the quality itself presupposes understanding. To be spontaneously obedient to the *li*, one must understand their meaning, and Confucius was a moral teacher whose life was spent in educating men in the virtues which the *li* contained and expressed. Although the practice and the understanding of the rituals was reserved to the governing class—"the people can be made to follow order, but they cannot be made to understand it"—the relations between governors and people are thought of as relations between moral beings, in which the example of one calls forth a response in the other; and this response in the governed must be spontaneous.

> If the people are kept in order by administration, and are treated as equals in the matter of punishment, they may succeed in doing no wrong, but they will also feel no sense of shame. On the other hand, if they are kept in order by excellence and are treated as equals before the rites, they will reform themselves through a sense of shame.[10]

> If the official is himself upright, the people will play their part without orders. If he is not upright, then even under orders the people will be disobedient.[11]

Here the antipathy to words and punishments—the one entailing the other—as a means of government is once more evi-

[10] Ware, p. 25.   [11] Ware, p. 83.

dent, and the antithesis of *fa* is still *li*: if we were to ask Confucius by what means the character of the ruler is communicated to the people—"when the grass has the wind upon it, it assuredly bends" [12]—he would presumably reply that though the people do not participate in the rituals they feel their effects, either directly as an audience at their performance or indirectly through their effects on the ruler's officials. But to the governing class the rituals bring the knowledge of how to behave, and the intensive study of the rituals is the study of this implied knowledge. In this way the science of ritual becomes the science of government; but here we seem to reach a turning-point, and perhaps uncover a contradiction, in the development of Confucian thought.

> Tzu Lu said: "The prince of Wei is awaiting you, sir, to take control of his administration. What will you undertake first, sir?" The Master replied: "The one thing needed is the rectification of names."

> When Duke Ching of Ch'i inquired the principles of government, the Master answered saying: "Let the ruler be ruler, the minister minister; let the father be father, and the son son." "Excellent!" said the Duke. "For truly, if the ruler be not ruler, the minister not minister; if the father be not father and the son not son; though grain exist shall I be allowed to eat it?" [13]

Everything has its nature, its place in society and its function; unless each is what it ought to be, the work of society cannot go on. But with "the rectification of names" we move from the ritual plane to the intellectual. Instead of everything being at once defined, and made to conform to its definition, by participation in the appropriate ritual, everything is now defined by its name; and names are words. Comprehension of a name is an act of thought; and it must be followed by an act of government, which causes the thing to comply with its name. Con-

[12] Fung, p. 60.   [13] Fung, p. 59.

49

fucius perhaps arrived at this point through his insistence that the meaning of the rituals must be taught. Teaching is an act of verbal communication; much of the work of Confucius and his pupils was documentary scholarship; in this way the understanding of words—"who does not know the value of words can never come to understand his fellow men" [14]—may have come to equal if not surpass in importance the understanding of ritual. But the question must be faced: did not the identification of government with "the rectification of names" logically involve the replacement of *li* by *fa?* The ruler defined things by his intellect; he brought them into conformity by his power. What would happen if his definitions were challenged, and if he were successful in governing in this way, what further need would there be of ritual? The kingdom of the word would also be the kingdom of the sword—of jussive authority.

No doubt Confucius conceived both halves of the rectification process in terms so impregnated with ritual that these questions are largely irrelevant to his thought. But in Mo Tzu, the next great thinker in the order of our pattern, we see the rectification of names in action divorced from ritual, and are led to consider fundamental questions of sovereignty and communication. Mo, a rebel against the whole ritualist tradition and reputedly a man of lower-class origin, attacked the social efficacy of ritual in utilitarian terms. The aim of government, he said, was not the maintenance of a generalised ideal of harmony, but the achievement of certain practical results, and it could not be shown that the performance of ritual contributed in any way to their achievement.

> The people have three worries: that the hungry will not be fed, that the cold will not be clothed, and that the tired will not get rest. These three are the great worries of the people. Now suppose we strike the great bell, beat the sounding drum [and play other ritual instruments], can

[14] Ware, p. 125.

the material for food and clothing thus be procured for the people? For me I do not think this is possible. . . . The levy of heavy taxes on the people to construct the big bell, the sounding drum [etc.], is of no help in endeavouring to procure the benefits of the world and to destroy its calamities. Therefore . . . to have music is wrong.[15]

Because the wide rivers and broad valleys were once not crossable, the Sage-kings ordered boats and oars to be made. Boats are to be used on water and vehicles on land, so that gentlemen can rest their feet and lesser people can rest their shoulders and backs. Thus, why was it that the people produced wealth and contributed it, and did not dare to grumble? It was because these things contributed to the benefit of the people. Thus if musical instruments equally contribute to the benefit of the people, even I shall not dare condemn them. Nor if musical instruments are as useful as the boats and carts of the Sage-kings shall I dare condemn them.[16]

But the appeal to common sense—as Mo Tzu seems to have understood well enough—is necessarily an appeal to consensus, and the problem arises of how that consensus is to be established. How are we to decide what is most beneficial to the people and what is the best means of achieving it? Mo Tzu began by putting forward three tests of every proposal: its conformity with ancient tradition, "the deeds of the ancient Sage-kings"; its conformity with "the senses of hearing and sight of the common people"; and its being of practical benefit as observed in action.[17] But to apply these tests meant discussion, and discussion involved the use of words. The concept of "rectification of names" reached a further, and very important, degree of refinement in the passage mentioned earlier, when Mo Tzu put forward the view that the establishment of standards

---

[15] Fung, pp. 89–90.   [16] Fung, p. 86.   [17] Fung, pp. 85–86.

meant, first and foremost, the establishment of a standard in the use of words; and that the establishment of such a standard was identical with the establishment of society. He employed what we should term a state-of-nature model.

> Of old, when people were first produced, before there were penalties or government, the speech of men had for each a different meaning; for one man it had one meaning, for two men it had two meanings, and for ten men it had ten meanings. As the number of people became great, the meanings which the speech uttered by them had became also great in number. Thus people regarded each his own meaning as right and other people's meanings as wrong, and consequently in their intercourse they criticized each other. Consequently at home fathers and sons, elder and younger brothers, became angry with each other, were estranged from each other and could not live in harmony, and the people in the world harmed each other like water and fire, or poison. . . . The disorder in the world was like that of birds or beasts. An examination of this disorder in the world showed that it came from not having government leaders. Therefore the most capable man in the world was chosen and set up as Son of Heaven. . . . Only the Son of Heaven was able to unify all the meanings in the world, so that the world enjoyed order.[18]

The establishment of language as a means of communication was also the establishment of a means of establishing norms. But as with all state-of-nature models, the difficulty arises of showing how men incapable of social behaviour became capable of it; in this case, how men without the means of agreement were capable of agreeing to set up a governor. It is possible (since Mo's thought is strongly theistic) that Heaven, not men, diagnosed the evil and set up the Son of Heaven to supply the

---

[18] Duyvendak, p. 105; cf. Fung, p. 100, where "word" is rendered "idea."

cure. But the difficulty is not merely one inherent in the model; it may be identified with a more permanent problem in Chinese political thought, that of showing how the ruler brings about acceptance of his norms by those under him. If ritual is rejected (as it is by Mo Tzu), what is left? Does he do it by verbal communication, appealing to the intelligence and agreement of his subjects? They have no intelligence, and are incapable of reason, until after that body of norms which constitutes language has been accepted. Does he do it by means of his authority as a ruler? If authority is unintelligible to those on whom it is imposed, we are left with *fa* and punishment; government will not then be the relationship between moral beings which Mo, no less than Confucius, desired it to be.

Mo Tzu considered this problem, not in connexion with the difficulty of conceiving emergence from a state of nature, but by supposing the case of an established ruler whose ability to impose justice depended in part on the willingness of village communities to denounce those whom his edicts defined as evil-doers. There might be a difference of standards, he pointed out; the village might not consider the proscribed acts evil at all and refuse to denounce their perpetrators. The formula he proposed to end this difficulty—he describes it as "agreement with the superior"—seems designed to avoid two extreme positions: that the ruler should, by means of explanation, seek to persuade the villagers that his standard is the right one, and that he should compel them to accept his standard by force. Under "agreement with the superior" the village elders agree to accept standards dictated to them by the local magistrate, the local magistrates agree to accept standards from the provincial ruler, the provincial rulers agree to accept standards from the emperor, and the emperor models his standards on those of Heaven.[19] Mo Tzu is evidently trying to bridge the gap between agreement and authority; men who cannot agree on

[19] Fung, pp. 101-2.

53

the definition of a standard agree on the need for standards, and so agree to accept standards fixed by authority. Deficiencies and ambiguities in his system exist, but remind us that politics is the art of inducing agreement where there is substantive disagreement. Mo Tzu would not have explored the question to this depth if he had not shifted the emphasis of Chinese political thought from ritual to words, and so to the possibility of disagreement and the need for authority. It is worth noticing, however, that an apparently much earlier text hints at a realisation that all harmony presupposes difference, including difference of opinion.[20]

The next school whom we study greatly enrich our thought, at this point in its development, by denying the value of words altogether. The Taoists—in particular Lao Tzu and Chuang Tzu, in the sayings attributed to them—base their philosophy on a monistic insistence upon the unity, both of all experience and of the one experiencing with the one experienced. Consequently they reject everything suggestive of isolation, separation and definition, and words—regarded as names to define isolated concepts—most of all. It is easy to trace the repercussions of this for their thought about both ethics and politics, both of which they regarded as "rectification of names" in a fully Confucian sense. Lao Tzu rejected both the Confucian search for virtue and the ritual in which Confucius had thought it could be found. Repeatedly in Taoist writings we find that to set before oneself virtue as a conscious goal is to

[20] Fung, pp. 34–35; from the Kuo Yu, another pre-Confucian text:
"Harmony results in the production of things, but identity does not. When the one equalises the other, there comes in what is called harmony, so that then there can be a luxurious growth in which new things are produced. But if identity is added to identity, all that is new is finished.
"Therefore the early kings married queens from different families, sought their riches from those of different regions, selected ministers and received expostulations from officials who could offer them different opinions, and held discussions about all sorts of things. They did so because they wanted harmony. If there is only one sound, it is not worth listening to. A thing entirely the same lacks decorativeness. If there is only one taste, there is no satisfaction. And if things are made of one material, there is no solidity."

confess that one has lost it; to define it by means of a concept or name is to ensure that one will not find it again; while to seek to embody it in an elaborate code of behaviour is merely to confess that one does not know how to behave. Only Tao, the Way, is "the way to behave," and Tao can be neither defined in words nor manifested in ritual; to attempt to do either is to have lost Tao, and the Sage who has Tao practices it by in-action, by attempting neither words, rituals nor acts.

When the great Tao becomes obscured, benevolence and justice appear. When knowledge and wisdom are mani-fested, there is much deception. When . . . relationships are not harmonious, filial piety and tenderness arise. When the states and the clans are disordered, there is loyalty and sincerity.

Therefore, when Tao is lost, virtue comes; when virtue is lost, comes benevolence; when benevolence is lost, there is justice; when justice is lost, there are the rules of conduct (*li*). The rules of conduct are the (? measure) of loyalty and sincerity, and the source of disorder.[21]

Here the Confucian criticism of language and command is turned against virtue and ritual themselves. Not only does the definition of a virtue imply the possibility of its opposite; it ensures that the opposite will appear, for once a virtue is de-fined—i.e., separated from Tao—it loses the only quality (unity with Tao) that makes it a virtue. Words, intentions, values, the whole apparatus of conscious action by which we "seek peace and ensue it," make sure that we shall find not peace but disorder. To define government as "the rectification of names" is to admit hopeless defeat, because to use words at all is to set up a situation which cannot be rectified. But if the Sage, who

[21] C. P. Fitzgerald, *China: A Short Cultural History* (London, 1935), pp. 84–85.

has not lost Tao, does nothing, Tao, through him, does (and is) everything.

> By not exalting merit the people are kept from rivalry. By not valuing what is hard to obtain the people are kept from theft; by not contemplating what is desirable the heart is kept untroubled. Therefore the government of the Sage empties the hearts of the people and fills their stomachs. He weakens their ambitions, but strengthens their bones. Always he keeps the people without knowledge and without desire, so that the crafty do not dare to act. By non-action nothing is ungoverned.[22]

A theory of government which rejected all consciously selected norms naturally led the Taoists to reject the authority of tradition.

> The Former Kings that your Master applauds, what are they but straw dogs which have been used in the sacrifice and had their day? Yet he takes his disciples to lodge and sleep in their presence. . . . If, because a boat has taken well to the water, one tries to travel in it by land, one may push to the end of one's life and get no further than a couple of yards. Our time and that of the Former Kings are as different as land from water; the Empire of Chou over which they ruled and this land of Lu are as different as boat from chariot. Your Master tries to treat the Lu of today as though it were the Chou of long ago. This is like pushing a boat over dry land.[23]

Read in isolation, the foregoing passage appears a piece of serious historical criticism, of a kind unusual in ancient civilisations; but there is another passage, of the same import, which suggests rather that it is based on the characteristic Taoist tenet of the unknowability of the particular.

[22] *Ibid.*   [23] Waley, pp. 37–38.

The six scriptures are the dim footprints of ancient kings. They tell us nothing of the force that guided their steps. All your lectures are concerned with things that are no better than footprints in the dust. Footprints are made by shoes; but they are far from being shoes.[24]

The historian would have retorted—as might the Confucian scholar—that the footprint can give a good idea of the shoe that made it. But the Taoist will have nothing of inference or induction; he will have only direct intuitive apprehension of "the force that guided their steps." That force can only be Tao; and it cannot be studied, or remembered, or communicated, or reconstructed, or argued over. To set up a definition of Tao and construct society in the image it enjoins, or to conceive politics as an arbitration between men with different concepts of Tao, are actions of pure absurdity. Government is neither an imposition of norms, nor a choice or adjustment between norms; it can only be intelligently approached as a getting rid of norms altogether—which would be to get rid of government also. Chuang Tzu wrote:

Suppose I am arguing with you and you get the better of me. Does the fact that I am not a match for you mean that you are really right and I am really wrong? Or if I get the better of you, does the fact that you are not a match for me mean that I am really right and you are really wrong? Must one of us necessarily be right and the other wrong, or may we not both be right or both be wrong? But even if you and I cannot come to an understanding, someone else must surely be as a candle to our darkness? Whom then shall we call in as arbitrator to our dispute? If it is someone who agrees with me, the fact that he agrees with me makes him useless as an arbitrator. If it is someone who agrees with you, the fact that he agrees with you makes him useless as an arbitrator. If it is someone who agrees with neither of us, the fact that he agrees with neither of us makes him useless as an arbitrator. If it is someone who agrees with both of us, the fact that he agrees with us both makes him useless as an arbitrator. So then I and you and he can never reach an understanding. Are we then to go on piling arbitrator on arbitrator in the hope that someone will settle our differences? This would lead to the dilemma of the Reformation and the Sage.[25]

If we are not thus to wait in vain, what can we do but smooth out our differences with the Heavenly Pounder, entrust them to the care of eternity, and live out our days in peace? What is meant by smoothing out our differences with the Heavenly Pounder? It means the smoothing away of "is" and "is not," of "so" and "not so." [26]

This passage may appeal to those reared in the democratic belief that since all men are equal there are no objective means of discriminating between them, and that consequently all disagreements are subjective. But it would have to be pointed out to them that Chuang Tzu's philosophy amounts to a denial of the possibility of verbal or logical communication. Where there are words there will be disagreement; where there are categories there will be opposition. No disagreement can ever be solved, so that the only road to peace is the abolition of words and categories. With perfect consistency, Chuang Tzu wrote:

When there is argument, there is something which the argument does not reach; great argument does not require words; speech that argues falls short of its aim.[27]

But it might have been in direct rebuttal that later disciples of Mo Tzu declared:

[25] "This disordered world can only be reformed by a Sage; but so long as the world is disordered, no Sage can appear"—Waley's note.
[26] Waley, pp. 25–26.   [27] Waley, p. 26.

Dialectic is that in which one person says a thing is so and another says it is not so. The one who is right will win.

To hold that all speech is perverse is not permissible. If the speech of the man who says so is permissible, then all speech is not perverse since there it is permissible. But if his speech is not permissible, then it is wrong to take it as being correct.

There is knowledge when there is discussion about it. When there is no knowledge, there is no means by which to discuss it.[28]

Since it was Mo Tzu's cardinal doctrine that the regulation of society consisted in the fixing of verbal meanings, it is not surprising that his followers defended the logical and linguistic possibility of doing so. The "Later Mohists" are blended in tradition with the Dialecticians or "School of Names," deriving in part from a certain Kung-sun Lung, whose method was to pose philosophical paradoxes challenging the accepted meaning of words: e.g., "A white horse is not a horse." His aim, the contrary of Chuang Tzu's, was "to extend this kind of argument to rectify the relation between names and facts in order to transform the world." [29] Nothing could be more Confucian, and we are left wondering whether Kung-sun Lung and his followers supposed that by the logical solution of paradoxes, every word could be given its one and one only proper meaning, or merely that it could be rendered discussible. In the latter event, the process of government by "rectification of names" would become a process of discussion; and we shall at any rate see that in later Chinese philosophers the question is raised of how far the ruler should explain the meaning of his commands to his people. The student is now becoming aware of the difference between a closed society, with only one set of possible

[28] Fung, p. 277.
[29] Fung, *Short History*, p. 10.

norms, and an open, where the meaning of the norms is discussible and there may or may not be final unanimity.

In one respect, however, as the Taoists clearly perceived, the problem of *fa* remained where the Confucians and Mo Tzu had left it. If norms are to be fixed and names rectified, he who resolves disagreements has power over those whose disagreements are resolved for them. If disagreement was unreal, authority was absurd, as the Taoists liked to illustrate by the tale of Three in the Morning, or the Monkeys of Sung.

> In Sung there was a keeper of monkeys. Bad times came and he was obliged to tell them that he must reduce their ration of nuts. "It will be three in the morning and four in the evening," he said. The monkeys were furious. "Very well then," he said, "you shall have four in the morning and three in the evening." The monkeys accepted with delight.[30]

The keeper's power over the monkeys—so far as the point of this story goes—consisted not in the fact that he kept them in a cage or commanded their food supply, but in the fact that the monkeys supposed there to be some difference between $3 + 4$ and $4 + 3$, and expected him to arbitrate upon this difference for them. All disagreements which we submit to an arbitrator, according to the Taoists—including differences between "is" and "is not," "so" and "not so"—are as unreal as this one; and there would be no such thing as normative authority if we did not suppose these unreal differences to be real. The Sage, knowing that separate things are not real, has no need of authority. But an interesting result follows if we imagine the Sage in the keeper's place; is the keeper a Sage, or are keeperhood and Sagehood incompatible? Because the monkeys believed in unreal distinctions, they subject themselves to the keeper's will; what is the relation between such "monkeys" and the Sage who

[30] Waley, p. 27.

knows the unreality of distinctions? Those who make distinctions place themselves at the mercy of Tao, and Tao does with them as it will. But the Sage's will is one with Tao, and—with the proviso that the Sage, himself inactive, rules by Tao rather than his own will—it would seem that "monkeys" find themselves fully as subject to a "keeper" who is a Sage as to one who is not. There is therefore a form of rule conceivable as exercised by the Sage over the non-Sage, of which Lao Tzu was writing in the passage quoted earlier, when he said that "the government of the Sage . . . keeps the people without knowledge and without desire . . . by non-action nothing is ungoverned."

Now if the Sage achieves this result by non-action, he does not govern the people by the exercise of power in the crude sense, but by his personal influence (precept? example? *mana?*) as a Sage; and it is conceivable that to "keep the people without knowledge and without desire" means to open their eyes to the unreality of separate things, in short to make Sages of them. But it is also conceivable that the people remain unenlightened, and that "non-action" means making use of the power which the unenlightened "monkeys" thrust upon their desireless "keeper." In that case the ruler's power over the people would be as limitless as that of Tao over the fool. There is a passage attributed to Chuang Tzu which hints, with strong Platonic overtones to a Western ear, that the Sages form a class of philosopher kings.

By non-activity he can himself administer the empire and yet have energy to spare; but by activity he is himself used by the empire and is yet insufficient. Therefore the men of old valued the principle of non-activity.

But if superiors have non-activity, and their inferiors also have non-activity, this will mean that inferiors will be equal in virtue to their superiors. When they are equal to their superiors they are no longer their subjects. On the other hand, if, while inferiors practise activity, superiors also practise activity, then superiors will have the same practices as their inferiors. And when they have the same practices, they cease being rulers. The superior must practise non-activity so as to administer the empire; and his inferiors must practise activity so as to be used in the empire. This is an invariable law.[31]

Whatever its intention, this passage makes it clear that the Taoist Sage could be thought of as exercising a form of power; and that power itself could be thought of in Taoist terms is evident from a study of a further school of theorists, most commonly described in English as the Legalists. Waley prefers to call them Realists, but neither term is particularly accurate and their true character is best conveyed by adopting the traditional Chinese name for them—the School of *fa* or Power. The Legalists (to follow the predominant usage) are generally regarded as the ideologists of Ch'in, the centralised military state which conquered and unified China in the third century B.C., though their main surviving works may somewhat antedate this event; and their distinguishing characteristic as a school of political theorists is that they placed the non-moral exercise of power at the centre, divorcing it entirely from the actualisation of ethical norms whether by means of ritual or of words. *The Book of Lord Shang*, a compilation of various passages whose central figure—one Kung-sun Yang, Wei Yang, Shang Yang or the Lord of Shang—may or may not be always the same person, early makes a statement which recalls Mo Tzu's rejection of ritual as useless, or the Taoists' as outmoded, but in fact goes beyond either.

Indeed, ordinary people abide by old practices and students are immersed in the study of what is reported from antiquity. These two kinds of man are all right for filling offices and for maintaining the law, but they are not the kind who can take part in a discussion which goes beyond

[31] Fung, pp. 331–32.

the law. The Three Dynasties attained supremacy by different rites, and the five Lords Protector attained their protectorship by different laws. Therefore a wise man creates laws, but a foolish man is controlled by them; a man of talent reforms rites, but a worthless man is enslaved by them. With a man who is enslaved by rites it is not worthwhile to speak about matters; with a man who is controlled by laws it is not worthwhile to discuss reform.[32]

This is not a rejection of ritual or tradition as one possible means of establishing norms, nor is it identical with (though it is akin to) the Taoist-anarchist doctrine that life is best normalised by rejecting the pursuit of norms. It is rather a preparation for the totalitarian doctrine that norms must not be allowed to become established independent of the ruler's will, since they may then act as obstructions of that will and at best may provide standards around which individuals group themselves regardless of what that will may be. The basic premise of Legalism is that only the ruler's will holds the state together, and that consequently nothing—neither ritual, tradition, morality or the family—must be allowed to exist which is not the direct command and creature of that will. *Non quod rectum est, sed quod jubeo,* is the ruler's motto.

If in a country there are the following ten things: odes and history, rites and music, virtue and the cultivation thereof, benevolence and integrity, sophistry and intelligence, then the ruler has no one whom he can employ for defence and warfare. If a country is governed by means of these ten things, it will be dismembered as soon as an enemy approaches, and even if no enemy approaches it will be poor. But if a country banishes these ten things, enemies will not dare to approach, and even if they should they will be driven back.[33]

[32] Duyvendak, pp. 168–73, for the full debate of this question.
[33] Duyvendak, p. 160.

63

If the people are made strong the army will be doubly diminished; if the people are made weak the army will be doubly strengthened.[34]

Indeed, to attack the strong with a strong people spells ruin; to attack the strong with a weak people means the attainment of supremacy.[35]

If virtuous officials are employed, the people will love their own relatives, but if wicked officials are employed the people will love the statutes. To agree with and to respond to others is what the virtuous do; to differ from and to spy on others is what the wicked do. If the virtuous are placed in positions of authority, transgressions will remain hidden; but if the wicked are employed, crimes will be punished. In the former case the people will be stronger than the law; in the latter the law will be stronger than the people. If the people are stronger than the law, there is lawlessness in the state, but if the law is stronger than the people, the army will be strong. Therefore is it said: "Governing through good people leads to lawlessness and dismemberment; governing through wicked people leads to order and strength." [36]

The modern West is the home of totalitarian government, but there is little or nothing in Western totalitarian theory to equal *The Book of Lord Shang*. Everything (other than the state) which unites the people weakens the state; ethical norms unite the people and are the enemy of power. As for the discussion of norms by logicians and rival philosophers, we might expect to hear that this breeds doubt of norms and consequently should be encouraged by the ruler. But the inclusion of "intelligence and sophistry" among the ten "parasitic virtues" [37]

[34] Duyvendak, p. 198.   [35] Duyvendak, p. 199.
[36] Duyvendak, p. 207.
[37] E.g., Duyvendak, p. 199; the phrase is recurrent.

shows that discussion is reckoned as normative, not divisive, and we read elsewhere that

> sages and intelligent princes are what they are, not because they are able to go to the bottom of all things, but because they understand what is essential in all things. Therefore the secret of their administration of the country lies in nothing else than in their examination of what is essential. But nowadays, those who run the state for the most part overlook what is essential, and the discussions at court on how to govern are confused and speakers try to outdo one another in them; thus the prince is dazed by talk, officials are confused by words, and the people become lazy and do not farm.[38]

It becomes a characteristic Legalist idea that government requires the application of only a limited amount of intelligence. Once the people have been satisfactorily atomised and prevented from displaying any unity or solidarity, it is then possible to govern them; and this is done by commanding them to perform tasks which will strengthen the armies and granaries of the state, and ensuring by a system of rewards and punishments that they do so. *The Book of Lord Shang* argues at great length that the desire-fear motivation in human beings is so strong and simple that men can be easily and effectively manipulated by means of what other Legalists were to call "the two handles of power"; and a great deal is made of the idea that reward and punishment—but particularly punishment—should be inevitable, immediate, automatic and rather mechanical than exactly proportioned to the individual case. The Legalist utopia is one in which punishment, being invariably anticipated, need never be applied and the laws are invariably obeyed. In this case government becomes mechanical and can be as well carried on by a ruler who is a fool as by one who is a Sage. It is no longer,

---

[38] Duyvendak, p. 191.

as it had been to Confucians, Mohists and Taoists alike, the radiation through various media of the ruler's moral influence. *The Book of Lord Shang* points out the advantages of this change.

> Indeed, Li Chu saw a hair at a distance of more than a hundred paces, but he could not transfer his sharp sight to others; Wu Huo was able to lift a weight of a thousand *chün*, but could not transfer his great strength to others; and indeed sages cannot transfer to others the personality and nature that is inherent in them.
>
> But that whereby success may be attained—that is the law.[39]

The idea of power as an automatically self-regulating mechanism is, paradoxically enough, the element in Legalist thought most closely linked to Taoism; or at least, it was this that enabled the Legalists to conceive of power as a species of Tao—the uncontrollable unity and reality of the *Tao Te Ching*. The most Taoist of Legalist writers is Han Fei Tzu, the most arresting and "Machiavellian" of ancient Chinese political theorists. Han Fei [40] was a courtier-intellectual, who traditionally had to commit suicide after losing a battle of statecraft on the eve of the Ch'in conquest; and the greater part of his writings are treatises on how to survive in palace politics. Where *The Book of Lord Shang* supposes the case of the absolute administrator, Han Fei supposes that of the ritual king who takes no initiative himself; his ministers propose and execute all policies, and are his sole source of information as to what is going on; and his only hold over them comes from the fact that all public acts must be brought to him for his authentication and authorisation. Given that the ministers are working for themselves and will not hesitate to betray him to his enemies, the problem

[39] Duyvendak, p. 243.
[40] "Tzu," which forms part of the appellation of every Chinese philosopher, is not a name but an honorific.

becomes that of keeping himself alive in this den of crocodiles. The discernibly Taoist element in Han Fei's advice is his recommendation that the ruler should not exhaust his wits trying to guess what his ministers are about, or in trying to out-think and out-manoeuvre them, but should empty his mind of preconceived ideas and desires, and simply observe what his ministers inadvertently reveal of their aims and intentions by the policies that they propose. This is Han Fei's version of "By non-action nothing is ungoverned"; the ruler's non-action places him in the position of Tao, or at least of the inactive Sage, while the ministers' activity leaves them in the role of the "monkeys" or "inferiors" who are used up and left naked by their pursuit of particular aims and objectives. But the ruler has an aim, the maintenance of his power; and it is his possession of power, not any other quality, which makes him analogous to the Sage. He need not display wisdom, and it is not certain that he need even have it.

Accordingly, the ruler, wise as he is, should not bother but let everything find its proper place; worthy as he is, should not take things on himself but observe closely his minister's motives; and courageous as he is, should not be engaged but let every minister display his prowess. So cast off the ruler's wisdom, then you will find the minister's intelligence; cast off the ruler's worthiness, then you will find the minister's strength. In such cases ministers will attend to their duties . . . and everybody will be employed according to his ability. . . .

Thus, the intelligent ruler does nothing, but his ministers tremble all the more. It is the Tao of the intelligent ruler that he makes the wise men exhaust their mental energy and makes his decisions thereby without being himself at his wit's end; that he makes the able men exert their talents and appoints them to office accordingly, without being himself at the end of his ability; and that in case of merit the ruler gets the praise and in case of demerit the ministers take the blame, so that the ruler is never at the end of his reputation. Therefore the ruler, even though not able, becomes the master of the able, and even though not wise, becomes the corrector of the wise men. . . .

Be empty and reposed and have nothing to do. Then from the dark see defects in the light. See but never be seen. Hear but never be heard. Know but never be known. If you hear any word uttered, do not change it or move it but compare it with the deed and see if word and deed coincide with each other. Place every official with a censor. Do not let them speak to each other. Then everything will be exerted to the utmost. Cover tracks and conceal sources. Then the ministers cannot trace origins. Leave your wisdom and cease your ability. Then your subordinates cannot guess at your limitations.

Keep your decision and identify it with the words and deeds of your subordinates. Cautiously take the handles of power and hold them fast. Uproot others' want of them, smash others' thought of them, and do not let anybody covet them. . . . Be too great to be measured, be too profound to be surveyed, identify norms and names, scrutinise laws and manners and chastise those doing as they please. Then there will be no traitor in the country.[41]

In this great passage—so at least it appears to be in translation—unequalled by anything in Machiavelli, the Taoist hermit has become a dramatically sinister figure, an exponent of "palace" or "Stalinist" politics at their most terrifying. Philosopher kings, it can be suggested, may easily become like this, if their philosophy is absolute. But the real point of Han Fei's thought is perhaps to be found elsewhere. Taoism has become little more than a vocabulary, in which the word "Tao" should really be translated "power." Han Fei's ruler possesses no initiative, but he is so situated that he need take none. It is, so to speak, given in the model that all acts of his ministers must be referred to him, and his power consists simply in this. He has an established and impersonal authority; and Han Fei has perceived that he can best maintain it by displaying no qualities and taking no initiative, but waiting for others to reveal their qualities and intentions to him, since the need to obtain his authorisation will force them to take initiatives sooner or later. Where A has power and B has not, it is a sign of weakness for either to take the initiative; but B must take it and A need not. How power is acquired in the first place, Han Fei does not tell us here; but once acquired, it is maintained not by exertion but by inaction; not by imposing norms, but by being prerequisite to their imposition; not by the display of *virtù*, but by the characterless force of its own necessity. The ruler rules not by solving others' problems, but by having none of his own; others have problems—i.e., they desire the power which he has—and by keeping these unsolved he retains his power over them. He is still the keeper of the monkeys of Sung.

Han Fei's Taoist vocabulary is the clue to his Legalism. He is most Legalist in his radical separation of power from any sort of morality, and also in his belief in the ultimate simplicity of human political behaviour. It is because all the ministers want is power that they cannot help revealing themselves to the intelligent ruler, and in the last analysis the ruler controls them by the simplest of mechanisms. The Confucian doctrine of "rectification of names" and the Legalist formula of "rewards and punishments" are conflated, in the above passages and in others from the *Han Fei Tzu*, into a method for the maintenance of power. The ruler does not impose norms; he lets the ministers do that, by proposing their own policies. He then ascertains whether the minister has performed what he promised, and rewards or punishes him accordingly. He retains power, because the ministers have fixed the norms by which they are themselves judged; and he need not take the

69

initiative in establishing norms with which others may disagree. In other sections of his writings, Han Fei advises the minister never to reveal the whole of his policy to the ruler, because to do so would be to place himself at the ruler's mercy; but here the assumption is made that he is at the ruler's mercy already, because their respective positions ensure that he must reveal the whole of his mind sooner or later.

When a ruler wishes to prevent wickedness, he examines the correspondence between names and actuality, words and work. When a subject makes claims, the ruler gives him work according to what he has claimed, but holds him wholly responsible for accomplishment corresponding to this work. When the accomplishment corresponds to the work, and the work corresponds to what the man has claimed he can do, he is rewarded. If the accomplishment does not correspond to the work, nor the work correspond to what the man has claimed for himself, he is punished. . . . Therefore the Sage holds to uniformity and rests in quiescence. He causes names to be self-applying and commands that things remain fixed in themselves. . . . He employs men according to their ability and then lets them work of themselves. They are given according to what they do and are promoted of themselves.[42]

The ruler could, of course, himself fix the norms by which his subjects are to be judged—as *The Book of Lord Shang* seems to envisage and as Pharaoh practised in the matter of the bricks without straw—but Han Fei insists that it is easier for him to let the subjects do this of themselves. There can thus arise no problem of dialectic, of the possibility that the ruler's commands may be misunderstood by his subjects; [43] "agreement with the superior" will be predetermined, and the desires and

[42] Fung, p. 324.
[43] Fung, p. 323.

activities of men in society will automatically guarantee the ruler's power. The Taoist language of quiescence hides the Legalist conception of society under power as a self-regulating mechanism; and the image of the machine is summed up in the description of reward and punishment as "the handles of power"—terminology which may well have appealed to the technocratic element in Ch'in rule and policy.

But the Ch'in system and its Legalist ideology, though they left an enduring mark, were themselves transitory, and under the Han dynasty Confucian principles became part of the permanent establishment. This is one reason why the arrangement of Chinese thinkers here followed deserts chronological order in treating last of the Confucian Hsun Tzu. Though he lived and taught some time before the Ch'in conquest (tradition gives him Han Fei as one of his pupils), and though later Confucianism thought him less sound and orthodox than Mencius, Hsun Tzu's ideas serve as a summary of the Confucian system he helped transmit to later generations. It will also be seen that the three strands—ritual, language and power— here used as clues to ancient Chinese political theory, are exhibited in his thought in ways which display their relationships with each other.

As a Confucian, Hsun Tzu was above all a ritualist and traditionalist repudiating all Mohist, Taoist and (by anticipation) Legalist attempts to overthrow the value of *li*.

A king's institutions should not depart from those of the three dynasties; his methods should not differ from those of the later kings. . . . There are models for garments; there are rules for buildings; there is an established grading of officials and soldiers. Mourning rites, sacrifices and their utensils all have their appropriate gradations. All music which is not correct should be totally abandoned. All colours which are not of the ancient sort should be entirely dispensed with. All utensils which are not of the ancient sort should be destroyed. This is what is meant by return-ing to antiquity. Such are the institutions of a king.[44]

In advocating a "return to antiquity," Hsun Tzu had to meet the Taoist argument that the practice of ancient times differed from that of the present and could no longer be clearly under-stood. His reply illustrates the important point that in tradition-alist systems of identifying norms, it is often the most recent witness to the practice of highest antiquity whose testimony establishes the canon. In what might be a direct reply to a Tao-ist criticism quoted earlier,[45] he says:

> If you wish to see the footprints of the Sage-kings, then look where they are most clear, that is to say at the later kings. . . . To give up the later kings and follow those of highest antiquity is like giving up one's own prince and serving another's. Hence it is said: if you wish to know a thousand years, then consider today; if you wish to under-stand ten or a hundred thousand, then consider one or two; if you wish to know ancient times, then examine the course of the Chou dynasty. If you wish to know the course of the Chou dynasty, you must learn from the Superior Man who is honoured (apparently Confucius).[46]

Confucius had followed Chou on the principle of "latest witness"; Hsun Tzu would follow Confucius. But the injunc-tion to "consider today" might end by being altogether de-structive of the appeal to historical authority. We have seen that the Taoist claim that past and present differed "as land from water" was really a claim that the inner nature of past events (and of present also) could not be apprehended. Hsun Tzu's retort establishes the intelligibility of the past and its unity with the present, but does so by basing it on principles

---

[44] Fung, p. 282. Dubs's text should be compared throughout.
[45] See note 24.
[46] Fung, pp. 282–84.

which are no longer discoverable by a simple appeal to tradition.

> Therefore the natures of a thousand or ten thousand men are as those of one man. The beginning of Heaven and Earth was as the present day. . . . Abandoned incorrigible people say: Ancient and present times are different in nature; the reasons for their order and disorder differ. Many people are misled by this . . . they can be deceived in what they see, and is this not all the more the case with traditions handed down through a thousand ages? . . . But why cannot the Sage be so deceived? I say it is because the Sage measures things by himself. Hence by himself he measures other men; by his own feelings he measures their feelings . . . by his doctrines he measures their merit; by the Way he can completely comprehend things. Past and present are the same. Things that are the same in kind, though extended over a long period, continue to have the self-same principles.[47]

To explain what these unchanging principles are, Hsun Tzu puts forward a philosophy of *li*, in which the making of norms, to be expressed in rituals, is presented as the main means by which man organises both himself and his environment. In what follows there is hardly any difference between "social distinctions" and "distinctions" in general—between the organisation of society through the differentiation of its parts and the cognition of the environment through the distinction and naming of its elements.

> Water and fire have essences, but no life; herbs and trees have life, but no knowledge; birds and beasts have knowledge but no moral sense. Man has an essence, life, knowledge, and in addition has moral sense; hence he is the highest being on earth. His strength is not equal to that of

[47] *Ibid.*

73

the bull, his running is not equal to that of the horse; yet the bull and the horse are used by him. How is that? Men are able to form social organisations, the former are not able to form social organisations. How is it that men are able to form social organisations? Because of their distinctions. How is it that distinctions can be carried out? Because of moral sense. . . .[48]

How is it that men are able to form social organisations? Because of their social distinctions. How can these distinctions be carried out? Through standards of justice (*i*). Thus when there is justice in distinctions, there is harmony. When people are harmonious they can unite; when united they have greater strength; having greater strength they become powerful; being powerful they can overcome other creatures. . . . Hence they can order their actions accordingly to the four seasons, control all things, and take all that is profitable to them in the whole world. They gain this for no other reason than that they have social distinctions and standards of justice.

Hence if men are to live they cannot do without social organisation. If they form a social organisation but have no social distinctions, they will quarrel; if they quarrel there will be disorder; if there is disorder they will break apart; if they break apart they will become weak; and being weak, they will be unable to dominate other creatures. Hence they will no longer have palaces and houses to live in. All of which means that men cannot abandon the *li* and *i* for an instant.

Wherein is it that man is truly man? Because he makes social distinctions. When he is hungry he desires to eat; when he is cold he desires to be warm; when he is tired he desires to rest; he likes what is beneficial and dislikes what is injurious. Man has these ways of acting from birth; he does not depend on something else to get them. In these

[48] Duyvendak, pp. 106–7; a note to his translation of *Lord Shang*.

things Yü (a Sage-king) and Chieh (a tyrant) were alike. However, man is truly man not simply because he has two feet and lacks hair, but rather in that he makes social distinctions. Now the yellow ape also has two feet and no hair on its face; but the Superior Man sips his soup and carves his meat in slices. Birds and beasts have fathers and offspring, but not the affection between father and son; they are male and female, but do not have the proper separations between male and female.

Hence there is no way of human living which does not have its distinctions; no distinctions greater than the social distinctions; no social distinctions greater than the rules of *li*; no rules of *li* greater than those laid down by the Sage-kings.[49]

Hsun Tzu draws very little distinction betweeen "intelligence" and "moral sense." Since he believes in an ultimately harmonious cosmos, to know a thing is to know it in its proper station and function; there is no difference between knowing what it ought to be and knowing what it is, or, conversely, between a moral decision and a simple act of cognition. Man's "moral sense" enables him to rule the cosmos because it enables him, in knowing what things ought to be, to command the forces which make them what they are. There is a long passage [50] on the function of the ruler in a society based on hydraulic agriculture, which makes it clear that there is no distinction between controlling men's acts, controlling the natural environment and commanding those regularities in nature that do not seem immediately dependent on human action. If it was through ritual that men were co-ordinated in performing the tasks of irrigation and harvest, to carry out sacrifices to heaven was just as important a part of the ruler's function as commanding the activities of men. The harmonies of nature and society were identical, and it was man's ability to distin-

[49] Fung, pp. 296–97.
[50] Fung, pp. 300–1.

75

guish them which gave him power. Ritual was a means of differentiating and combining human activities; it was also an expression of the intelligent observation and control of the social and natural environment by man. But the remark that "the Superior Man sips his soup and carves his meat in slices" suggests that the ability to make distinctions is important *per se*, irrespective of the actual content of the distinctions made. Possibly Hsun Tzu considered that table manners were a ritual manifestation of man's knowledge that soup ought to be sipped and meat carved; or he may have held that they displayed man's power to impose pattern and order on himself and the universe, and were rather aesthetic than moral or cognitive in character. There are passages in which he seems to be saying that the beauty of ritual is that it gives daily life the quality of a work of art.

Hsun Tzu's philosophy most probably was that man perceived the eternal harmonies, yet that those harmonies would not be complete without man. Perceived, they are embodied and actualised in ritual; yet whether they exist before, or as a result of, being perceived, the process of actualisation could not be carried on without the use of words. He was a Confucian in his preference for ritual, which did not divide the possibilities of action, over words, which did; but he accepted the central place of language, and followed out in detail the problems of ambiguity, dialectic and authority to which the use of words gave rise. Taoist and Legalist overtones are evident in his thought here. As a conservative moralist, he believed in a single moral order and consequently in a single right meaning for each word. Yet the meaning of words could be doubted, discussed and even denied. What should the ruler do then? Should he use dialectic to explain his commands, or punishment to impose them? Mo Tzu's problem was revived.

Names were made in order to denote actualities, on the one hand so as to make evident the noble and the base, and on the other so as to distinguish similarities and differences. When the distinction between the noble and the base is evident, and similarities and differences are distinguished, a man's mind will not suffer from the misfortune of being misunderstood, and affairs will not suffer from the calamity of being hindered or wasted. This is the reason for having names. . . .

Therefore when the kings had regulated names, when they had fixed terms and so distinguished actualities, and when their principles were carried out and their will everywhere known, they were careful to lead the people towards unity. Therefore making unauthorised distinctions between words, and making new words—thus confusing the correct nomenclature, causing the people to be in doubt and bringing about much litigation—was . . . a crime like that of using false credentials or false measures. . . . Hence the people were guileless. Being guileless, they could be easily ordered. Being easily ordered, they achieved results. . . . Should a true king arise, he must certainly follow the ancient terms and make the new ones.

All heretical doctrines and heinous teachings . . . can be classed among types of fallacy. Hence the wise ruler, knowing to which class they belong, does not dispute about them. Thus the people can be easily united in the Way, although they cannot be given the reasons for all things. Hence the wise ruler deals with the people by authority, and guides them on the Way; he orders things by his decrees, explains things by his proclamations and enforces them by his punishments. Thus his people are turned into the Way as by magic. Why should he use dialectic?

Now the Sage-kings are no more, the world is in disorder, wicked doctrines have arisen, the wise man has no power to compel the people to do right and no punishments to prevent them from doing wrong, and so there is dialectic. When an actuality is not understood its name is brought forward; when its name is not understood it is illustrated; when the illustration is not understood it is explained; when the explanation is not understood dialectic comes into use. Hence names, illustrations, explanation and dialectic are the great refinements of human activity and the beginnings of the achievements of a king.[51]

It seems that Hsun Tzu regarded discussion as the mark of a second-best, though actually existing, society; it is not clear whether he thought it inferior to punishment as a means of dealing with the refractory, or whether he looked for the restoration of society to its state of ideal unanimity.

Thus far the study of Chinese political thought has conducted us in learning the difference between an open and a closed society. But we know that Greek and classical Western political theory are distinguished from the Chinese by the possession of a plurality of political forms, a plurality of social and other values, a moral philosophy which asks pressingly how these pluralities came to exist, a profound divergence between physical and political theory, and a way of life which makes the citizen's role in decision-taking a principal index to his social position and a formative influence upon his personality. The Greek political vocabulary is thus largely our own; whereas if there are Chinese words which can be translated as "liberty," "citizen," "democracy," "autocracy," "monarchy" or for that matter "politics," it has not been necessary for this investigation to become acquainted with them. But certain benefits to the pursuit of political studies can, it is suggested, be identified as arising from this short course in ancient Chinese philosophy. The idea that politics is a normative activity should be rather thoroughly grasped as a result of being made to consider a number of modes—ritual, language, tradition, discussion, authority,

[51] Fung, pp. 305, 307–8, 310–11; Dubs, pp. 283–84, 282–83, 289–90.

coercion—by which norms may be communicated. The character of language as a means of communication is brought out by comparing it with a non-verbal means of government like ritual. When tradition breaks down, it is seen, government and decision become crucial; in the absence of automatic compliance with norms, words must be increasingly used; and since words are inherently both ambiguous and controvertible, the choice between persuasion and coercion must be faced. Once words become the main medium of communication between ruler and ruled, the logic, grammar and dialectic with which they are used affects the character of the power exercised. One extreme heresy denies both the meaning of words and the necessity of power, thus emphasising that power is a consequence of the uncertainty of words; another divorces power alike from norms and their intelligible communication and discussion, thus demonstrating that power may be both non-moral and totalitarian—that is, divorced from any regard for human relationships as possessing a value. Language has been our theme throughout, and we have been employing a series of possible interpretations of Chinese political philosophy to give ourselves an intensive preliminary grounding in the social grammar of ethics, authority and power.

[3]

Civic Humanism and Its Role in
Anglo-American Thought

THE AUTHOR of this essay has been engaged in two related
lines of enquiry, out of which it has grown. The first, and
more historical, is an endeavour to find means of treating the
political thought of the post-medieval but pre-industrial West
as it was applied to the understanding of specific and particular
societies rather than to the problems of political society as an
abstract and universal concept. Italian readers, especially,[1] will
appreciate immediately that this presents itself as a study in
political thought considered as a form of historical consciousness. The second and more theoretical enterprise is an enquiry
into the way in which political societies generate concepts of
their existence in time, and encounter problems which necessitate increases in historical awareness and critical ability, as a
result of their efforts to legitimise and understand their existence as continuous political structures.

In the pursuit of these enquiries it has appeared, first—and

---

[1] This essay originally appeared in *Il Pensiero Politico*, a new Italian
journal of the history of political thought. It was enlarged from a paper,
"The Dimension of Time in Systems of Political Thought," delivered to
the 1967 convention of the American Political Science Association.

not surprisingly—that Florentine thought of the humanist and Machiavellian period offers a crucial case in the understanding of all these matters; but further, that ideas and problems from this source migrated from Italy to England and the American colonies during the second half of the seventeenth and the eighteenth centuries, where they exercised a profound effect on the self-understanding of these territorial, agrarian and commercial societies. Many interesting problems, both historical and theoretical, arise and can be studied in connexion with these phenomena. Among them is that of the relations existing between traditionalist, humanist and messianist-apocalyptic thought, and about this much work remains to be done. There is enough, however, to be worth putting forward as a report on work in progress.

If we now examine the character of European political thought towards the end of the medieval period, we find a culture with a very strong bias towards believing that only the universal, the unchanging and consequently the timeless, was truly rational. This raised in an acute form the problem, which could become crucial, of the intelligibility of the particular, the local, the transitory—and consequently of time considered as the dimension of transitory being. When we look for the conceptualised modes by which it was believed that the particular might be cognised and acted on, we find a rather restricted range of such modes available. In the first place, it was supposed that by syllogistic and other means, particular phenomena might be related to universal laws and subsumed under them. The way in which this was effected by scholastic methods, however, set limits to its satisfactoriness. In the second place, it was held that a faculty known as experience—intelligence operating on a low but effective level—empowered men to react to the particular situation or contingent happening, to remember their reaction and how it had turned out, and to react, when next the situation or one like it recurred, in a way fortified and enlightened by recollection. But it was difficult

81

for medieval theorists to develop modes of analysing and comparing particular situations, and consequently they could only represent usage and traditional action as based on the recollection that it had worked before, not on any understanding of the reasons why it had worked. What legitimated such an action was the weight of experience, the length of usage, behind it; and where alternatives presented themselves, the greater weight and the longer usage must prevail. An important consequence for medieval theorists was that laws and social norms must be represented as based either on timeless universals or on immemorial traditions (or at best some approximation to the latter). "Reason" and "experience," so conceptualized, did not allow for any systematic or methodical comparison or study of particular situations and how they came into being and passed away.

Knowledge of the particular was, as we have seen, largely coterminous with knowledge of time; but the means theoretically or conceptually available of attaining either were extremely scant. If there were no means of understanding the process of transition from one particular situation to another, it followed implicitly—and was often explicitly stated—that such transition or change was not intelligible or rational: that it represented a disruption of rationality, a move from order to disorder, which could only be dealt with, conceptually or practically, by restoring the order that had existed before it. Change in itself was not rational; yet such change was known to occur, and we are thus presented with a society whose theories of knowledge and action committed it to asserting that change was meaningless and irrational and consequently could not be controlled. Investigating further the political culture of such a society, we should next enquire what concepts it employed for expressing the idea that change was above merely human rationality.

In a monotheistic culture familiar with the idea of a divine will directing everything, it was possible to believe that God understood and directed the otherwise meaningless succession of particular happening to particular happening. "Providence" was the term applied to divine action as it directed this succession, though the constant stress laid on the inscrutability and mystery of providential action indicated that while human faith might be reposed in this aspect of divine wisdom, human knowledge might not expect to share it. We have at this point three faculties of the human mind, as medieval theory recognised them—reason, experience and faith—operating to explain the course of particular events and to legitimate political actions as based on understanding of that course. Christianity, like other monotheisms which depict God acting on the world by means of covenant, incarnation or prophecy, at a point in time, leaving the promise of his acts to be fulfilled at another point in the future, utterly transforms the nature of world and time. There now comes to be a cosmic past, present and future, constituted by divine acts which, because they are unique and unrepeatable, are particular and so constitute a time-scheme; time is the dimension of the particular, though these acts and the time they constitute are sacred rather than secular (in one of that word's meanings).

Consequences followed for the legitimation of particular actions and events. Because there was a scheme of prophecy in which divine actions in the past were linked to divine actions in the future and at the end of time, the course of providential action need not be thought of as entirely inscrutable. There was an eschatological scenario, available in many versions, into which the actions of providence could be fitted and assigned a significance. This scenario consisted of particular happenings, of the sort with which neither reason nor tradition could fully deal; and since it had been revealed by God to men through the mediation of prophets, it contained the notion of a mode of knowledge of a very special sort, which could be employed both to interpret events and to justify actions. We should beware of supposing that whenever in the study of Christian politics we meet with apocalyptic, eschatological and even millennial concepts, we are necessarily dealing with those chiliastic "religions of the oppressed" which are so much and so rightly studied.[2] Concepts of this order formed a vital and powerful element in the vocabulary of Christian society, one just as likely to be employed by members of the established power structure as by rebels against it; they were used to explain events and justify claims too dramatic and unprecedented to be dealt with in any other way, and the powerful as well as the powerless might find themselves needing to do this.

But the language of apocalyptic was thus widely employed because only a dramatised providence seemed capable of explaining secular and particular happenings when their particularity was so marked as to assume the character of sudden change. The secular intellect was not supposed to possess the means of understanding secular change, and in consequence such change was not supposed to be grounded upon any law accessible to that intellect. One might have faith in providence, and by faith in prophecy one might gain access to so much of the course of providential action as had been revealed to men; but should such faith fail one to the point where the process of change appeared a purely secular process, then that process became even more lawless and irrational than before. The unending succession of secular happenings might seem to be directed by a force neither rational nor divine, and such a force was de-

[2] V. Lanternari, *The Religions of the Oppressed* (English translation, New York: Knopf, 1963); Norman Cohn, *The Pursuit of the Millennium* (Fairlawn, New Jersey: Essential Books, 1957); Peter Worsley, *The Trumpet Shall Sound* (London: MacGibbon and Kee, 1957); Eric Hobsbawm, *Primitive Rebels* (New York: Praeger, 1963); and Sylvia L. Thrupp, ed., *Millennial Dreams in Action* (The Hague: Mouton, 1962), are the best-known works in English on this subject; but relatively little has till recently been done on the role of apocalyptic in the political thought of the Renaissance and Reformation. I take the warning against treating apocalyptic as necessarily the thought of the oppressed from William Haller, *Foxe's Book of Martyrs and the Elect Nation* (London: Jonathan Cape, 1963), especially pp. 61–62, 85; this is a key work in recent treatment of apocalyptic by historians of this period. See further William M. Lamont, *Godly Rule: Politics and Religion, 1603–60* (London: Macmillan, 1967), and essay 5 in this volume.

noted by the image, Greco-Roman in origin, of Fortune and Fortune's wheel. Blind, irrational and irresistible because unpredictable, Fortune was the atheist's version of providence, a medieval expression of the sense of the absurd. She—the symbol is feminine—stood for time as the dimension of contingency, when reduced to the last degree of the unintelligibility inherently attached to it in the medieval and Renaissance conceptual scheme; she was regularly invoked to "explain"—or to denote the inexplicability of—political change. The equation of time, of the "secular" in both senses of the word, and of the irrational was at this point complete.

If we now look for the first attempts to break free of this scheme, a plausible context in which to locate it is the civic humanism of Renaissance Florence, so powerfully if controversially analysed by Hans Baron.[3] Civic humanism denotes a style of thought—the controversial questions are when and why it emerged, and so need not detain us—in which it is contended that the development of the individual towards self-fulfillment is possible only when the individual acts as a citizen, that is as a conscious and autonomous participant in an autonomous decision-taking political community, the polis or republic. Now the republic—unlike the hierarchised cosmos of medieval imperial or monarchical thought—had to be conceived of as finite and localised in time, and therefore as presenting all the problems of particularity. The individual's prospect of fulfilling his moral and rational nature consequently depended on his ability to partake in political decisions within a particularised and secular framework; to be fully human, he must master the poli-

[3] Hans Baron, *The Crisis of the Early Italian Renaissance* (revised edition, Princeton University Press, 1966); Eugenio Garin, *Italian Humanism* (English translation, New York: Harper and Row, 1965). An energetic criticism of Baron's thesis has been put forward by Jerrold E. Seigel in "Civic Humanism or Ciceronian Rhetoric?," *Past and Present*, XXXIV (July 1966), 3–48, and Peter N. Riesenberg in "Civism and Roman Law in Fourteenth-Century Italian Society," *Explorations in Economic History*, VII, 1–2 (Fall/Winter 1969).

85

tics of time. Civic humanist thought strongly implied that the republic and its citizens were somehow capable of this mastery, but did not of itself offer an epistemological formula which could emancipate cognition of the particular from the medieval conceptual scheme. And if the individual as citizen should fail to master time through participation in political decision, he would find himself in the world of time neither understood, legitimised nor controlled. The failure of the republic was the triumph of Fortune. In fifteenth- and sixteenth-century Italy, where few republics could maintain themselves for long, it is observable that there was considerable interchange between the vocabulary of this philosophical problem and that of citizens striving to understand and manage an increasingly unmanageable world.[4] This language and its theoretical refinements, which reach a peak in the works of Machiavelli and Guicciardini, are essentially concerned with the intelligibility of the citizen's world and its extension in time.

The obvious solution was to adopt the Aristotelian formula of representing the republic as a polis, universal because self-sufficient and theoretically immortal because universal. Any republic could be presented as a paradigm of human association as such, in which all types of men combined to pursue all human goods, their nature being such that they could be pursued only in association. Since association was in itself a good, and intelligent activity another, it followed that the highest form of active life was that of the citizen who, having entered the political process in pursuit of his particular good, now found himself joining with others to direct the actions of all in pursuit of the good of all; the attainment of his private good was not lost but must take a lower priority. It was possible to distribute responsibility in decision-taking in such a way that each citizen was en-

---

[4] For a study of the language employed in the Florentine *pratiche*, see chapter 1, section III, pp. 28–45, of Felix Gilbert, *Machiavelli and Guicciardini: Politics and History in Sixteenth-Century Florence* (Princeton University Press, 1965).

abled to direct his activity and that of others—who in their turn directed his—towards the general good, while being subject to no lesser authority than that of all, in which he was himself participant. But if authority was maldistributed so that any one group was enabled to identify its particular good with the good of all, the republic would have failed of its purpose; both the ascendant group and those deprived of the opportunity of citizenship would now be attaining a lesser good than they might have attained. To lose one's due share of authority, or to have more than one's due, amounted to a loss of virtue, and since virtue consisted in a relation between equals its loss was not private but mutual. It might be thought of as coming about either when some became so strong that they could use others as their instruments, or when some became so weak that they could be so used. The republic could persist only if all its citizens were so far autonomous that they could be equally and immediately participant in the pursuit of the universal good.

It is characteristic of Renaissance thought that it presented the Aristotelian scheme in a form designed to emphasize the stability of the republic, as a particular form, in time, together with time as the dimension of its instability. Systems such as that of the Romanised Greek Polybius singled out the Aristotelian concept of injustice arising when the part substituted its good for that of the whole, and argued that when the one, the few or the many ruled unchecked, the virtue of the ruling part, precisely because it was a particular virtue, became corrupted, both in the obvious Actonian sense and in the sense that it prevented the development of virtue among the groups excluded from power. Only as a partnership in virtue among all citizens could the republic persist; if virtue were less than universal, its failure at one point must in time corrode its existence at all others. Each particular form of government, with its virtue, was doomed to that degeneration which Polybius depicted as a cycle of decaying forms; and the only form of government which could persist was that in which each group—classified as one, few and many—shared power with the others in such a way that none ruled exclusively and none was simply dependent on any other. In this form, moreover, the cause of degeneration, namely the monopoly of power by a particular agent, had been removed; universality and perfection had been attained and it was theoretically possible that the government might last forever.

In the Polybian "mixed government" we recognise the universality of the Aristotelian polis. We recognise also that the aim of politics is to escape from time; that time is the dimension of imperfection and that change must necessarily be degenerative. Since the imperfect, in politics as elsewhere, is still defined as the less than universal, it would seem that behind this manifestation of civic humanist thought there still reigns a conceptual scheme in which the particular is equated with the irrational. What is immediately important, however, is the political definition which equates particularity with corruption as the unchecked rule of some over others, or equally the unchecked dependence of some upon others. Where this exists the system has been set in change, and the direction of that change can only be towards disintegration. In such Renaissance theorists as Machiavelli—the Machiavelli of the *Discorsi*—and the Guicciardini of the *Dialogo e Discorsi* on Florentine government, the term "corruption" is used to mean three things: first, the degenerative tendency to which all particular forms of government are prone; second, the specific cause of that degeneration, which is the dependence of some men upon other men when they should be depending upon all and upon themselves; and third, the moral degeneration of the individual who, in these circumstances, is prevented from developing his virtue by identifying his particular good with the good of all. The climax of his corruption arrives when he finds his world controlled by an irrational Fortune instead of by the virtue of political man. Time, which cannot be conceptualised as qualitative change, is now in command.

Neither the moral autonomy of the individual, which renders him capable of relating himself to the good of all, nor the pattern of political relationships between individuals, which rests on and guarantees such an autonomy, can easily be conceptualised as undergoing change. One must be either autonomous or corrupt; there is no middle point and it is far easier to change in one direction than in the other. This comes about partly in consequence of the moral absolutism of the criteria employed; largely, also, because the personality and its independence are, in Aristotelian parlance, defined in teleological and ethical terms which do not change easily; and finally for a reason inherent in the distinction between a universal good, concern for which makes one a patriot, a citizen and an individual, and the multiplicity of particular goods, concern for which, if exclusive of the former, tends to corrupt one. The greater the number and diversity of particular goods available in a society, the greater the danger of corruption in which it stands. Both Machiavelli and Guicciardini considered a Spartan rejection of private satisfactions the necessary guarantee of civic virtue; Guicciardini as a young man was as eager to "burn the vanities" as Savonarola, though he identified himself with Lycurgus rather than Jeremiah in advocating it.[5] The idea of a society grown luxurious through trade was as near as either Florentine came to the idea of a society impelled by economic growth towards increasing productivity and diversification, but they would have distrusted the latter, as Rousseau was to do,[6] for exactly the same reasons as made them distrust the former. Such a society offered an increasing number of opportunities to the individual to prefer private goods to the *res publica* and so

[5] In the *discorso di Logrogno*; see *Dialogo e Discorsi del Reggimento di Firenze* (ed. Palmarocchi, Bari, 1932), pp. 257–59.
[6] For a demonstration which makes it excitingly clear how far Rousseau's thinking was anchored in the civic humanist tradition, see Judith N. Shklar, *Men and Citizens: A Study of Rousseau's Social Theory* (Cambridge University Press, 1969). See also Elizabeth Rawson, *The Spartan Tradition in European Thought* (Oxford University Press, 1969).

89

to corrupt by his weakness the strength of those who did not. The doctrine that the integrity of the polity must be founded on the integrity of the personality, and that the latter could be maintained only through devotion to universal, not particular goods, had committed both ethical and political theory to a static ideal. The concept of the citizen or patriot was antithetical to that of economic man, multiplying his satisfactions and transforming his culture in a temporal process: it encouraged the idea that change and process were entropic and that only a Spartan rigidity of institutions could enable men to master the politics of time.

The theory of classical republicanism required an ethos of extreme personal autonomy—a requirement, it is interesting to note, which a feudal ethos of honour and a Puritan ethos of self-respect seem to have been equally capable of meeting. It is in the late seventeenth and the eighteenth century that the paradigms of civic humanism may be observed under challenge from the development of human relations with the material environment, and the history of how this came about tells us much about the role in the history of ideas of the concept of corruption. In post-Civil War England a need seems to have existed to define the political community rather more as a polity and rather less as a hierarchy than had been the case before, and this formulation had to go on in the context of a rather highly governed agrarian society where the relation between legal property—outstandingly in land—and governing authority was the central question of politics. In the forty or so years between Harrington and Locke—and affected during its subsequent history, I believe, more by the former—there can be seen emerging a concept of politics which constitutes a distinctively English, or rather Anglo-American, brand of civic humanism.[7] True to the main Aristotelian tradition, this declared that

[7] For fuller study of Harrington's thought and his role as the principal English civic humanist, see the next essay in this volume and "The Onely Politician: Machiavelli, Harrington and Felix Raab," *Historical Studies:*

the individual as citizen might be known by the autonomy of his participation in politics, but it was peculiarly concerned with the material basis of that autonomy. The function of property was to render the individual independent, and the ideal paradigm—though not, by any means, the only form—of the property which did this was an inheritable freehold in land. To Ireton and Harrington, the English polis was a community of freeholders; the latter attempted to depict it in the form of a classical and Polybian republic, and even after 1660 his successors applied his ideas to the problem of relating English property to a still quasi-independent executive.

The point about freehold in this context is that it involves its proprietor as little as possible in dependence upon, or even in relations with, other people, and so leaves him free for the full austerity of citizenship in the classical sense. Other forms of property—and these are many—are regarded with distrust in proportion as they are easily alienable. "Lightly come, lightly go," says Harrington (unnoticed by C. B. Macpherson) of property in the market sense; [8] but his attitude is ambiguous—he does not deny that mobile property confers independence and the capacity for citizenship, and only questions whether the owner of such property can be trusted to keep it, and his po-

---

Australia and New Zealand, XII, 46 (April 1966), pp. 165–96. The last-named is a review article centering around Felix Raab, *The English Face of Machiavelli* (London and Toronto: Routledge and Kegan Paul, and University of Toronto Press, 1964).

In developing the thesis of an Aristotelian and humanist attitude to property, dominant in the social and political thought of the eighteenth century, I do not here enter into controversy with C. B. Macpherson, *The Political Theory of Possessive Individualism* (Oxford: Clarendon Press, 1962), who has argued that the era of Hobbes and Locke gave rise to the political theory of a market society. It seems to me that both classical and bourgeois concepts of property and power are to be found in the eighteenth century, and are to be found dialectically related, but that Harrington's place is rather with the former tradition than with the latter, where Macpherson would locate him. I hope to deal further with this problem in an edition of Harrington's works, now in process.

[8] John Toland, ed., *The Oceana and Other Works of James Harrington* (London, 1774), p. 227.

litical freedom, as long as the inheritor of land. The point was slow to arise that the possessor of market property is defined by his exchange relationships with other men, and may therefore be said to lack the entrenched autonomy of the freeholder. In the evolution of agrarian civic humanism the essential antithesis is not that between the manor and the market, but rather that between an unspecialised agrarian and a specialised rentier-bureaucratic society; and the reason for this is that the concerns of thinkers in this tradition were unvaryingly civic and political.

The function of property is to guarantee the citizen his independence. The dependence from which it must save him is the political dependence upon others which constitutes corruption, and the modes of economic being which it is important to avoid are those in which property and political dependence go hand in hand. A feudal society in which the proprietor is someone's vassal is a case in point, and Harrington saw the disappearance of tenurial subordination as the restoration of civic virtue, but his successors were able to persuade themselves that the world of lords and vassals had never even existed.[9] The merchant, whatever reservations one might have about him, was not involved by his exchange relationships in political subordination, and a prejudice against the entrepreneur is far less common in eighteenth-century agrarianism than is supposed. What increasingly frightened the humanists of that age was the apparition of modes of economic being which involved dependence upon the public power. If the end of property was independence, the end of independence was citizenship and moral personality. Only the autonomous man could have those relationships with authority which constituted citizenship, and under monarchical and executive government this meant that independence must above all be independence of public authority. Anything which made the proprietor—or worse still, his property—dependent on government constituted the worst

[9] See below, pp. 120, 135-37, 138-39, 141-42.

kind of corruption, for it not only lessened his citizenship but perverted government itself from a public authority into a private interest. A citizen who took bribes from men in power was not only corrupt in the common sense of the word, but corrupt in the classical; he was liable to become dependent on that source of supply and, like the soldiers of the late Roman Republic, to degenerate from a citizen into a client.

But there were social types appearing about 1700 whose very mode of existence constituted a graver source of corruption than the mere venality of knaves. These were, first, the rentier or stock-holder, whose property consisted in funds which he had lent to government in the expectation that government would provide him with an income; second, the military or civilian office-holder, subsisting on the possession of a skill—sometimes not even that—which only government would adequately reimburse. These were, in a sense, Aristotle's banausic men, less than citizens because they had specialised in the development of only one capacity; but to be banausic was also to be potentially or actually corrupt. The social crime of these individuals was that their being was definable in terms of their dependent relationship to government, whereas that of the citizen—the only truly virtuous and indeed human being—was defined in terms of his independence of the government in which he participated. But although classical thought provided the paradigms in which the rentier, the officer and the bureaucrat could be defined and denounced as beings below the level of the political animal, in their economic reality they struck the mind of the eighteenth century with the force of new historical phenomena. From the middle years of Charles II's government, through the foundation of the Bank of England and the National Debt, the South Sea crisis and the intellectual opposition to Walpole's regime, and forward in later American history to the successive epochs of the Revolution, the opposition to Hamilton and the United States Bank, one can trace the mounting fear that people of this kind were becoming increasingly common, that they were being intruded into government where they could only have a corrupting effect, that they were being used by men in power with a deliberate design of corrupting the body politic.[10] An unmistakably paranoiac note is sounded at times, and seems to reveal the existence of a genuine crisis in the relations between the age's political norms and paradigms and its awareness of social realities. The crisis appears most clearly when we consider the eighteenth century's attitude to the question of historical change.

The civic humanist concern with the personal autonomy of the citizen had led to the selection of freehold land as the form of property best defining and protecting that autonomy. For reasons that lie within the history of European and English scholarship, it was possible for theorists at the end of the seventeenth century to look back on a medieval period in which landed property had been the sole determinant of social relationships. The relation of lord to vassal being as far as possible eliminated from the picture, the feature of feudal—or as they termed it "Gothic"—society on which many eighteenth-century theorists seized was the performance by the landowner of the military, judicial and administrative functions performed in their own day by specialised servants of government. It was this that in their minds equated the "Gothic" freeholder with the classical citizen, and it was of course the independent heritability of his fief or freehold that guaranteed his political person-

[10] The most comprehensive studies of such thought in eighteenth-century England are: Caroline Robbins, *The Eighteenth-Century Commonwealthman* (Cambridge, Massachusetts: Harvard University Press, 1959), and Isaac F. Kramnick, *Bolingbroke and His Circle: The Politics of Nostalgia in the Age of Walpole* (Harvard University Press, 1968). There are useful materials in Jeffrey Hart, ed., *Political Writers of 18th-Century England* (New York: Knopf, 1967), David L. Jacobson, ed., *The English Libertarian Heritage* (Indianapolis: Bobbs-Merrill, 1965), and John F. Naylor, ed., *The British Aristocracy and the Peerage Bill of 1719* (New York: Oxford University Press, 1968). For the American context, see the following notes, and J. R. Pole, *Political Representation in England and the Origins of the American Republic* (London: Macmillan, and New York: St. Martin's Press, 1966).

ality. Nor is it accident that the term "Gothic" should have been one of high praise in the language of politics, while remaining a synonym for barbarism in the language of cultural history and aesthetics; there was implicit in the creed of civic humanism a real doubt whether citizenship and culture were not at least partly incompatible—the "Spartan" image at work once more. Those who applauded the liberty and lack of specialisation of "Gothic" politics had to account for the presence in their world of many features, both cultural and political, not to be found in medieval agrarianism. Not infrequently they constructed an explanation in terms of the increased diffusion of wealth and culture at the end of the Middle Ages; this had on the one hand enabled individuals to rise above the cultural level of a thirteenth-century baron, but on the other hand encouraged freemen to specialise in pursuits which left them no time to be soldiers, judges or participants in government; and the surrender of these functions to salaried experts and servants of the king had opened the way to the professionalised society which was virtually synonymous with corruption.

There is an important ambivalence in such a pattern of historical explanation. On the one hand, it seems to present economic, social and cultural change as explicable in terms of historical process, but to insist that the political community, being by definition a perfectly structured set of relationships between perfectly autonomous personalities, is incapable of any change other than corruption and disintegration. But on the other hand, those processes of change which are explicable are expressed very largely in terms of a movement of diversification and specialisation, leading away from the primitive equality of classical citizens and away from the primitive agrarian freehold which was its economic base. Explanation and non-explanation seem here to be in a close and complex relationship, and the important development for the student of social theory is the disjunction between political and cultural values revealed in the ambivalence of the term "Gothic." From this growing fear that liberty and culture might prove to be incompatible springs, needless to say, a great deal of the thought of the age of Rousseau; but the contribution of civic humanism to the origination of this problem, and to the formation of the classical period of American political thought, has not yet been intensively studied. The foundations of such a study are, however, being laid.[11]

In a remarkable sequence of recent publications,[12] Bernard Bailyn and Gordon S. Wood have investigated the ideology behind the movement towards the American Revolution and have brought out most clearly the extraordinary hold which the concept of corruption, and the vocabulary generated by the movements of opposition to government in eighteenth-century England, had over the articulate mind of colonial America. They raise the question: what role in the preparation of men in this age for revolution should we ascribe, not to a newly-enlightened belief in progress, but to their possession of a conceptual vocabulary, Renaissance in origin, which made it very hard for them to conceive of certain changes except as "corruption," or to conceive of corruption as anything but total, involving the necessary disintegration of the political and moral fabric as a whole? Giuseppe Giarrizzo's analysis of the historical thought of David Hume[13] indicates that after employing the

[11] For the classical and Renaissance elements in American political thought, see Howard Mumford Jones, *O Strange New World* (New York: Viking Press, 1964); H. Trevor Colbourn, *The Lamp of Experience: Whig History and the Intellectual Origins of the American Revolution* (Chapel Hill: University of North Carolina Press, 1965); Hannah Arendt, *On Revolution* (London: Faber and Faber, 1963), chapters 4 and 5; Edmund P. Willis, ed., *Fame and the Founding Fathers* (Bethlehem, Pennsylvania: Moravian College, 1967), especially the contribution of Douglass Adair.

[12] Bailyn, *Political Pamphlets of the American Revolution*, vol. I (Cambridge, Mass.: The Belknap Press of Harvard University Press, 1965); *The Ideological Origins of the American Revolution* (Belknap Press, 1967); *The Origins of American Politics* (New York: Knopf, 1968); Wood, *The Creation of the American Republic* (Chapel Hill: University of North Carolina Press, 1969).

[13] G. Giarrizzo, *David Hume, Politico e Storico* (Turin: Einaudi, 1962).

contemporary vocabulary concerning the relations of property, politics and culture with a sophistication far beyond his age, Hume in the last years before his death in 1776 became convinced that England was threatened with imminent corruption by the inescapable growth of the National Debt and the political influence of stock-holders. If any doctrine could drive the mind of Hume into prophetic despair, it is evident that we have to take its effects very seriously.

American thought became to a high degree permeated with the idea that Europe was already corrupt through the loss of Gothic liberty, that England, after escaping corruption through the survival of parliamentary institutions, was sinking into it at last, and that the Revolution was the necessary and triumphant struggle of America to escape that same corruption. The concept of corruption came to form part of the American vocabulary, and in a sense remains so to this day; and the values which it helped to reinforce there were the values of an agrarian humanism. From the social critics of eighteenth-century England, observers in Massachusetts, Pennsylvania and Virginia took over the image of a "Gothic" world where freeholders had been citizens because they were warriors, but which had been progressively destroyed after 1500 by the encroachments of government and luxury, bureaucracy and standing armies. The fathers of the Revolution—Dickinson, Adams, Jefferson—feared that English rule was seeking to perpetuate this corruption in America; and, the Revolution once achieved, Jefferson and his heirs continued to dread that government, great cities, banks, concentrations of finance capital and professionalised armies and navies—the "military-industrial complex" of President Eisenhower in our own time—would corrupt the farmers of the West for the profit of the urban East.

We may detect the humanist origins—or rather the origins in that conceptual world of which humanism was the child—of Jeffersonian mythology by reading, as it were in sequence, Bailyn's *Ideological Origins of the American Revolution*, Henry

Nash Smith's *Virgin Land: The American West as Symbol and Myth* [14] and Ernest Tuveson's *Millennium and Utopia* [15] and *The Redeemer Nation: The Idea of America's Millennial Role*.[16] If freehold land is the guarantee of virtue, of moral and political personality, and if corruption is any social change which tends to displace it as the material base of human relations, then the myth of the American frontier, of the farming West, that all but inexhaustible reservoir of arable land which Nash Smith has found denoted by such nineteenth-century terms as "the garden of the world" and "the fee-simple empire," takes its place in the history of civic humanism. The West, that "last best hope of earth," was to be the last stronghold of virtue as Spartans, Romans and Goths had in turn known and realised it. "Westward the course of empire takes its way," Bishop Berkeley had written long before the Revolution; [17] it was a humanist commonplace that dominion was founded in liberty and had been exercised and lost in turn by Romans and Goths, as they had possessed and lost the virtue which was the foundation of liberty and the material independence which was the foundation of virtue. Roman virtue had been undermined when the warrior farmer had been replaced by the client soldier, the professional legionary and the praetorian; in contemporary Europe—and in the American East?—the last strongholds of Gothic virtue were falling before the same combination of credit and professionalisation. Machiavelli, we see, is a father of American populism.

In the "fee-simple empire" virtue and dominion were to be reborn, and were to liberate Asia by providing a world market for its trade; [18] but we ought to notice the extent to which Berkeley's language was apocalyptical if not millennarian. "The

---

[14] New York: Vintage Books, 1950.

[15] Berkeley and Los Angeles: University of California Press, 1949.

[16] Chicago and London: University of Chicago Press, 1968.

[17] "Verses on the Prospect of Planting Arts and Learning in America," written in the 1720's and discussed at length by Tuveson and Nash Smith.

[18] Nash Smith, especially Book 1, chapters i–iv.

four first acts" of empire were "already past; a fifth shall close
the drama with the day; Time's noblest offspring is the last."
America was to be the Fifth Monarchy; but Ernest Tuveson,
whose earlier work has been devoted to studying the transformation of millennium into utopia, has recently stressed [19] that
Berkeley is appealing rather to the tradition of *translatio imperii*
than to that of the thousand-year reign of Christ and his
saints, and that his language is elegiac rather than millennarian.
But there may be an explanation of this within the framework
which we are employing.

The formal dilemma of the humanist republic had been that
it attempted to realise a universality of virtue within a particular, and therefore finite and mortal, political form. In Savonarola's sermons we may clearly read [20] the realisation that the republic is possible only if all men are virtuous, and that all men
can be virtuous only if they deserve, and receive, the divine gift
of grace. But the idea that a special gift of grace was to descend
on the secular entity, Florence, at the point in time 1494, could
be expressed only in eschatological terms. These Savonarola had
drawn on the tradition of heterodox preaching to provide,[21] and
it seems wholly legitimate to interpret Machiavelli's and Guicciardini's grim insistence on the supremacy of Fortune in terms
of their unspoken recognition that the "fifth age of the
Church," of which the Friar had spoken, was not to be. If the
republic was not to be aided by grace, it must confront Fortune;
and an orthodox Christian might continue to hold that only
saints, in the sense of the elect, could truly be citizens. Yet the
Polybian and Venetian imagery of balanced government pro-

[19] *The Redeemer Nation*, pp. 92–95.
[20] I have employed the edition of F. Cognasso, *Prediche Italiane ai
Fiorentini. I. Novembre-Dicembre 1494* (Perugia-Venezia: La Nuova
Italia Editrice, 1930).
[21] Donald F. Weinstein, "Millenarianism in a Civic Setting: the Savonarola Movement in Florence," in Thrupp, ed., *Millennial Dreams in
Action* (already cited); and "The Myth of Florence," in N. Rubinstein,
ed., *Florentine Studies: Politics and Society in Renaissance Florence* (London: Faber and Faber, 1968).

vided an apparent means of making republics stable, and men therefore virtuous, through the adjustment of constitutional machinery unaided by grace. There seems a certain significance, though one hard to fix with historic precision, in the circumstance that Harrington's *Oceana*, in which Englishmen are shown as the citizens of an immortal commonwealth, appeared —in 1656, a year beloved of apocalyptic numerologists—at the moment when the Puritan attempt to make England a community of the elect was on the point of final failure.

But Harrington had made the possibility of Polybian stability contingent on an equal distribution of freehold land. In America, where millennial modes of thought were longer associated with the political vision than they were to be in England, the "virgin land" of the West had held out the promise of a preservation of virtue into a future so indefinite as to aid in the transformation of millennium into utopia. But however huge the reservoir of western land, it was known to be exhaustible in the end, and Berkeley's language, of the "westward course" and the "drama" that must "close with the day," had unmistakably confined the American geopolitical utopia within a closed circle of world history. From Jefferson to Frederick Jackson Turner and beyond, it was a commonplace that sooner or later the frontier would be closed, the land filled, and the corruptions of history —urbanisation, finance capital, "the cross of gold," "the military-industrial complex"—would overtake America. Here are the origins of American historical pessimism.[22] There is a historical irony about the way in which the university city bearing Berkeley's name on the Pacific coast has become a focus of the ideological discontents of an American intellectual Left still deeply populist.

If there is reason to think that American messianism envisages not so much a Hegelian transformation of history as a Polybian escape from it, we can explain this by locating its

[22] Nash Smith, especially chapters xviii–xx.

roots in a pre-modern or Renaissance conception of history. The humanist scheme, according to which history consisted of the integrity of the political personality and its decay in a series of cycles, belonged to the same conceptual world as that which evoked apocalyptic dramas to explain a history which it lacked the equipment to reduce to concepts of secular process. The humanism of the eighteenth century suffered, often consciously, from the same inadequacy, and this can be explained by stressing that its political norms were based on a concept of the political personality, and the economic and social conditions necessary to it, which did not admit of change and so could only expect decay. But here we must ask the question: what other concept of the social and political personality was then possible? There is in fact evidence of a continuing attempt throughout the eighteenth century to explain how the individual of an urban and commercial society could be a citizen, free, virtuous and above all uncorrupt—or, as Tocqueville was to put the question, how the Americans could be free when they were not, in the classical sense, virtuous. Montesquieu and Franklin are only two among many who evoked a pre-Weberian image of the thrifty accumulator to explain how the trading bourgeois could meet the classical requirement that he subordinate his private satisfactions to the public good.[23] But in that crucial generation which preceded the American and European Revolutions, the most systematic and penetrating attempt to find a substitute for humanist moral and political economy was made in the schools of Glasgow and Edinburgh, by Adam Ferguson, Adam Smith

[23] This seems clearly implicit in Edmund S. Morgan, "The Puritan Ethic and the American Revolution," *William and Mary Quarterly*, 3rd Series, Vol. XXIV (1967), though Morgan does not underline the classical element in such thinking. See further, Wood, *op. cit.*; Gerald Stourzh, *Alexander Hamilton and the Idea of Republican Government* (Stanford University Press, 1970) and Melvin K. Richter, "The Uses of Theory: Tocqueville's Adaptation of Montesquieu," in Richter (ed.), *Essays in Theory and History: An Approach to the Social Sciences* (Cambridge, Mass.: Harvard University Press, 1970).

and John Millar.[24] In place of the rigorous identification of property and personality they set up a historical scheme of modes of production—hunter, shepherd, farmer, trader, manufacturer—through which mankind moved according to a law of increasing specialisation and division of labour. They were able furthermore to relate the historisation of property to the historisation of social personality; as man moved through these successive phases of relationship with his environment, his social, political and cultural needs and aptitudes, and with them his intellectual and imaginative capacities, changed accordingly. A historical science of culture now seemed possible: "President Montesquieu is the Bacon of this branch of philosophy," wrote Millar; "Dr. Smith is the Newton." [25]

But it is of the highest significance that all the leaders of Scottish social science employed the humanist concept of the personality's integrity as a normative control upon their scheme of historical development, and employed it on the whole pessimistically. In the three I have named—in Ferguson and Millar particularly, since few of Smith's teachings on this point have survived—we find the idea that once a certain point in social specialisation has been passed, the personality begins to suffer, since its capacity to participate in social pursuits is now being impoverished. And both Ferguson and Millar employ a political definition of the optimum point in this development: they select man's capacity for citizenship, for concerning himself with the determination of the common good, as marking that point; they locate in the past the moment at which political capacity was attained and began to be lost—Ferguson is inclined to locate it in warrior tribes, to which cultural level he assimilates

[24] Adam Ferguson, *Essay on the History of Civil Society* (ed. Duncan Forbes, Edinburgh University Press, 1966); David W. Kettler, *The Social and Political Thought of Adam Ferguson* (Columbus, Ohio: Ohio State University Press, 1965); W. C. Lehmann, *John Millar of Glasgow* (Cambridge University Press, 1960).

[25] *A Historical View of the English Government*, 4th ed. (London, 1818), II, 429–30.

the society of the city-state Greeks—and for the subsequent
process they both employ the term "corruption." [26] It is evident
that the humanist analysis was still operative, and that behind
the Scottish discovery of economic man doubts remained as to
whether his history worked to the advantage of man as a political and therefore a moral animal. The Scotsmen were systema-
tising the same insights as Rousseau, and employing a much less
intensely focussed, but not less authentic image of man as citizen; and it is clear at this point that it was the civic humanist
ideal which provided the point of departure for the concept of
alienation.[27] The undistracted, unspecialised man—hunter in
the morning and critic in the afternoon—whom Marx and
Lenin hoped to restore to his universality is in the long view an
Aristotelian citizen, participant in all the value-oriented activities of society, and his history is in large part the history of
civic humanism.

[26] See Forbes's introduction to his edition of Ferguson's *Essay*, and, in
general, vols. III and IV of Millar's *Historical View of the English
Government*.
[27] Shklar, *op. cit.*

[4]

Machiavelli, Harrington and English Political Ideologies in the Eighteenth Century

T HE STUDY of past political ideas is an activity which may be undertaken for at least three methodologically distinguishable types of reason. For the historian it is primarily, I think, the study of the language used in a particular society to discuss political problems, and of the light thrown, often inadvertently, by the use of that language upon the character of that society and the events taking place in it. For the political scientist it is —somewhat more abstractly—the study of the rise and the role of an organized political language in a society's political activity, or in the political activity of society in general. Lastly, the political philosopher studies the ideas of the past with a view to seeing which of them are worth using, rephrasing, criticizing, or employing as the foundation of other propositions in the making of statements about politics abstractly considered.

It is in the first of these characters, that of the historian, that I wish to appear in this paper. I aim at saying something about a current of political discourse that ran through the life of the English-speaking peoples in the eighteenth century, and at eliciting from the relevant material a few propositions about the social and intellectual world in which those peoples, and especially the English themselves, may be said to have lived. It should be clear already that I shall be dealing with that vexed yet favorite topic of the relation of ideas to social reality, but I shall be doing so in tones of extreme caution. The slogan that ideas ought to be studied in their social and political context is, it seems to me, in danger of becoming a shibboleth; too many of those who pronounce it assume, often unconsciously, that they already know what the relations between ideas and social reality are, and this can lead to much coarse and uncritical thinking. Most commonly it takes the form of a rather crudely applied correspondence theory; the ideas under study are assumed to be characteristic of some faction, group, class, or type to which the thinker allegedly belonged, and it is then explained how the ideas express the interests, hopes, fears, or rationalizations characteristic of that group. The danger here is that of arguing in a circle. It is in fact often very difficult to identify without ambiguity the social membership of an individual, still harder that of an idea—consciousness being the contradictory thing it is—and one tends to buttress the assumptions one is making about the social position of the thinker with the assumptions one is making about the social significance of his ideas, and then to repeat the procedure in reverse by a thoroughly deplorable perversion of critical method. All this flows, if we analyze it, from the making of unacknowledged assumptions about the relation of ideas to social reality; and it is precisely because that relation is a real and important one that we ought not, as it seems to me, to be making assumptions about it so much as hypotheses. Empirically speaking, the more I reflect about the possible relations between a society's ideas and the different facets of its structure and activity, the more complex, two-faced, and contradictory those relations seem to me to become; and if we are to go in for the sociology of ideas we ought surely to do so as scientifically as possible, making as few assumptions as we can that are not capable of being tested. But before we need embark on this difficult exercise there is, fortunately perhaps, another kind of inquiry that can be carried on: and that is to ascertain, by normal critical interpretation, what the ideas were that were in use at a particular time, what in fact they said and implied, and on what commonly accepted assumptions and methods they were based. To embark on a sociology of ideas without an accurate and extensive knowledge of the ideas' primary meaning and secondary implications is a dangerous venture, even if we believe that only the sociological approach will bring us to their true significance; and assuredly, a systematic survey of the ideas used for certain purposes in a certain period can be peculiarly destructive of the clichés of intellectual history. There is a Namierism of the history of ideas as there is of the history of Parliament, and it consists of identifying the concepts, assumptions, and languages actually involved in given periods and areas of human life. These birds can be as crook-talon'd as any other fowl that come to the historian's net, and I have sometimes thought that it would be fun to challenge the profession with a work entitled "The Structure of Political Ideas in the Eighteenth Century," for it is meaningful to say that there was one.

What I propose to do is investigate the significance in the eighteenth century of a current of ideas that stems mainly from James Harrington, but can be traced additionally to the seventeenth-century theorists studied years ago by Z. S. Fink under the name of the "classical republicans." [1] These men—Milton, Andrew Marvell, Algernon Sidney, Harrington himself, and a number of lesser figures—were impressed by the stability of Venetian constitutional forms and through them by the Greek and Renaissance Italian theorists of mixed government, of whom Polybius was the most representative among the ancients

---

[1] Z. S. Fink, *The Classical Republicans: An Essay in the Recovery of a Pattern of Thought in Seventeenth Century England* (Evanston, 1945).

and Machiavelli—the Machiavelli of the *Discourses*—among the moderns. The English "classical republicans" have reappeared in more recent research as the key figures of Caroline Robbins' *The Eighteenth-Century Commonwealthman;* [2] only here, it is important to note, they bear a new collective name, that of "the Whig canon." The great value of Professor Robbins' book is that it illustrates, with much learning, how regularly recourse was made, throughout the century, to a group of writers essentially the same as Fink's Venetian theorists. These were the classics presented by Boswell to Paoli, studied by John Adams in Massachusetts, and praised by Wordsworth in a famous sonnet as "the elder Sidney, Marvell, Harrington, young Vane and others who called Milton friend." Young Vane, I suspect, owes his place in the sonnet largely to the exigencies of meter; Henry Neville, Andrew Fletcher, John Trenchard, or—little as Wordsworth might have cared for the idea—John Toland the deist, all had a rather better claim as transmitters of the tradition. But Professor Robbins has documented so fully the continuity of classicism in the Whig mind from the end of republicanism to the beginnings of democratic radicalism that from her work alone it is clear that the textbook account of Augustan political thought as *Locke et praeterea nihil* badly needs revision. Her big book suffers, I will suggest, from only two real deficiencies. Because she identifies the ideas she studies with a chain of intellectual groups arising to the left of Whig statesmen and constantly criticizing them in the name of their own official ideals, she does not take account of the role in the history of these ideas of men like Bolingbroke, and so does not see that they can often better be understood in a Court-Country context than in a Tory-Whig or a Whig official-Whig intellec-

---

[2] Caroline Robbins, *The Eighteenth-Century Commonwealthman: Studies in the Transmission, Development, and Circumstances of English Liberal Thought from the Restoration of Charles II Until the War with the Thirteen Colonies* (Cambridge, Mass., 1959). For her comment on criticisms such as mine, see her preface to the Atheneum paperback edition (New York, 1968).

tual one. Secondly—again perhaps because she is mainly concerned with the transmission of these ideas from one group to another—she does not do all that might have been done to study their assumptions or consider them as a commentary on English politics which entailed certain intellectual consequences for those who adopted it. Something can be done, I believe, to remedy these deficiencies, if we go back to the fountainhead— that is, if we go back to Harrington, who is in a special sense the central figure among the "classical republicans" of "the Whig canon," and trace from his time the descent of certain ideas, the uses that were made of them, and the changes which they consequently underwent. That is what I propose, in a cursory way, to attempt; but to engage in the interpretation of Harrington is to become involved in recent academic controversy, and I fear I must say a word about that first.

Because Harrington declared that a shift in the social distribution of power had made its effects felt in his time, he has always been a target for the interpretations of those interested in relating ideas to contemporary social "reality"; and there has been a natural tendency to try and connect Harrington's ideas about what was happening in the seventeenth century with the views on the same subject held by the historian who is seeking to interpret Harrington and the seventeenth century simultaneously. Perhaps because the general interpretation of the seventeenth century is not a task I have ever presumed to attempt, this has always seemed to me a rather dangerous proceeding. I should prefer to find out what Harrington thought was happening and then to compare it with what I think was happening, though there is of course no harm in testing to see whether elements of one's interpretation are present in Harrington's thought, as C. B. Macpherson has lately done.[3] Anyway, there are three recent interpretations of Harrington to which I must now allude; one is Macpherson's and a second, I am afraid, is my own. But

[3] C. B. Macpherson, *The Political Theory of Possessive Individualism: Hobbes to Locke* (Oxford, 1962), chap. 6. See especially pp. 182–88.

the first that must be mentioned is that of Professor Trevor-Roper in his renowned essay on *The Gentry*.[4] Here, of course, he presented Harrington as embodying the consciousness of the declining mere gentry, cut off from office and so from wealth and power, and as writing *Oceana* in 1656 in order to provide his fellow *hobereaux* with the consoling myth that "the gentry have all the lands." This seems to me incorrect, both as regards what Harrington actually said and as regards his motives for saying it, but I mention this interpretation for the interesting reason that I shall shortly be pointing to a time, some forty years after Harrington wrote, when his ideas were actually used in much the way that Trevor-Roper describes, but had to be somewhat sharply modified in order to be so used. Trevor-Roper's interpretation, furthermore, while almost Marxian in its insistence on viewing Harrington's ideas as a piece of class-consciousness, did raise in arresting language the question of what class Harrington was attached to, and thus made possible the radical suggestion that he was not attached to any class with such psychological completeness that his ideas were a simple rendering articulate of their collective social unconsciousness. I therefore found that Trevor-Roper's contentions had a really liberating effect when I came to put forward my own interpretation of *Oceana*,[5] which was based not on Harrington's place in the social structure, but on his use of the intellectual vocabulary of his times. I contended that Harrington saw the "changes in the balance of property," which he said had begun in England with the advent of the Tudors, not so much in terms of the transfer of land ownership in consequence of buying and selling and other forms of economic activity, as in terms of changes in the legal obligations of land tenure; and that what he was interested in was the transition from a broadly

---

[4] H. R. Trevor-Roper, *The Gentry, 1540–1640* (London, 1953).
[5] J. G. A. Pocock, *The Ancient Constitution and the Feudal Law: A Study of English Historical Thought in the Seventeenth Century* (Cambridge, Eng., 1957), chap. 6.

feudal pattern, in which the typical freeman was the military tenant of some lord and obliged to fight in his quarrels, to a pattern of independent tenure, in which he was a freeholder who need fight in no one's quarrel but the public's. From this I concluded that Harrington was not much interested in economic activity and that the power whose distribution in society he was trying to chart was essentially the possession of land that gave a man independence, this independence being in the last analysis measured by his ability to bear arms and use them in his own quarrels. Harrington's democracy was a republic of freeholders owning their own lands and weapons—"Englishmen with swords in their hands."

The third interpretation is that of C. B. Macpherson: he argues that English economic and consequently social relationships were in the mid-seventeenth century becoming increasingly founded on entrepreneurial activity, and that Harrington discerned enough of this transition to make it possible to say that, in the last analysis, he depicted the relationships between men as relationships of the market. Macpherson concedes that Harrington did not see very much of this, but contends that he saw enough of it to bring him under the rubric of Marxist interpretation; so that Macpherson's argument tends to consist of an unending retreat upon previously-prepared positions. It is expressed partly in the form of a correction of my own earlier interpretation of Harrington; and there is no doubt that he does succeed in showing that Harrington knew that land might be farmed for profit, that there was such a thing as a land market, that a cottager might prefer to sell his labor for wages rather than seek to enlarge his exiguous holding, that the growth of towns provided a market for the produce of the land, and so on—all things which my desire to emphasize the tenurial aspect of Harrington's thought may have led me to suggest did not figure in his theories. But the point is not whether Harrington knew that these things were going on—why should he not?—but whether he founded any of his key ideas upon them; and Macpherson's attempt to show that Harrington's system will not work unless entrepreneurial behavior in landowners is presumed to be at its basis really comes down to his interpretation of a single passage—that in which Harrington says that even in the unlikely but possible event of his agrarian law bringing all the land into the permanent possession of five thousand proprietors, it would not be in their interest to "exclude the people," whatever exactly that may mean. Macpherson argues that this passage only makes sense if we presuppose that the five thousand would be anxious to maintain an open market in land, and thus, he says, we find that at bottom Harrington's landowners form an entrepreneurial community to whom the value of land is what it will fetch at market. But assuming Macpherson's interpretation to be correct here—I am not sure of this—there is still a great deal of Harrington's thought which he has not shown to be grounded on assumptions of entrepreneurial behavior, and has more or less conceded not to be so grounded. I think these aspects of Harrington can be interpreted in line with my previous analysis, and with Macpherson's concessions to that analysis, so that to a large extent his interpretation and mine are not so different as might appear.

In the first place, Harrington's notion of the power which the man who has property exerts over the man who has none does not entail any particular description of the economic relations between the two men, or of the economic process in which the two are engaged. All that is necessary to know is that the one is independent and the other dependent on him; the one is master and the other servant, and the only image of the English political economy which Harrington need have had in order to express his theory of power is one which showed it as consisting of households or families, themselves polarized into masters and servants.

We may observe this by considering the following propositions from his posthumously-published *A System of Politics,* in which he digested his theory in the form of aphorisms.

I, 13. The man that cannot live upon his own must be a servant; but he that can live upon his own may be a freeman.

I, 14. Where a people cannot live upon their own, the government is either monarchy or aristocracy; where a people can live upon their own, the government may be democracy.

I, 15. A man that could live upon his own may yet, to spare his own and live upon another, be a servant; but a people that can live upon their own cannot spare their own and live upon another, but (except they be not servants; that is except they come to a democracy) they must waste their own by maintaining their masters or by having others to live upon them.

I, 16. Where a people that can live upon their own imagine that they can be governed by others and not lived upon by such governors, it is not the genius of the people; it is the mistake of the people.

II, 4. If a man has some estate he may have some servants or a family, and consequently some government or something to govern; if he has no estate he can have no government.[6]

The important consequence is that Harrington's economics and his politics were alike essentially Greek, and that all he knew about English agrarian society was at the service of a fundamentally Aristotelian theory of citizenship. Like the Athenian analysts, he saw the citizen as the head or potential head of a household, and the non-citizen or servant as he who lacked that potentiality. The danger to a commonwealth from its servants, he said, was external rather than internal; human society consisted first of the commonwealth, the citizens, those

[6] John Toland, ed., *The Oceana of James Harrington and His Other Works* . . . (London, 1737), pp. 496–97.

whom possession of property had made independent and capable of having dependents—just as the Aristotelian citizen qualified for public power by his capacity for exercising private power within his household—and secondly, of those whom lack of property rendered incapable of independence and so of citizenship. But if Harrington was as conservative as Henry Ireton in his insistence that property was the prerequisite of political rights, he was also as democratic as Thomas Rainborough in his willingness to extend citizenship to the poorest that was not a servant. A cottager who keeps himself above the subsistence level by laboring for wages is not excluded by any property qualification from appearing at the muster of Oceana.[7] The employer–wage-earner relationship is not a determinant of power or of rights until it becomes a relationship of independence and dependence, of master and servant; and it is not thought of as being that in itself.

Harrington's citizen may or may not be an entrepreneur, but he is primarily a freeholder. One of many reasons why land, not trade, is the necessary background to Harrington's thought— why he is unable to give a convincing account of how master-servant relationships determine the distribution of power in Holland or Venice [8]—is that his ideas hinge so greatly on the contrast between an England in which the ordinary proprietor

[7] Such a person is described, *ibid.*, p. 166, where he is clearly not a servant, and the argument is that he will not use his political power to bring about a complete leveling of estates. However, he is not to be altogether trusted in war (p. 84). It is now generally argued that the Levellers would have excluded servants and other dependents from the parliamentary franchise.

[8] It is never quite clear to what degree the power of the Venetian nobility consists in their land (*ibid.*, pp. 105, 137). Holland and Genoa are the only states where money is acknowledged to be more important than land (pp. 245–47), but though there is an account of the relation of Amsterdam to agriculture in the Dutch economy (pp. 300–1), neither Dutch nor Genoese government is ever considered in detail, nor is there any account of the relation of master to servant, aristocracy to democracy, in a mercantile economy. It seems probable that Harrington thought the only difference between a landed and a business household was that the former was the more stable and the easier described.

was the military tenant of a feudal magnate and one in which he is free to bear arms in his own or the commonalty's quarrel. The right to bear arms, and the propertied independence enabling one to provide one's own, become the tests of citizenship in Harrington's England as they had been in Athens or Rome; *Oceana* is a dispersed *polis*, or rather a dispersed *comitia centuriata*, in which the county assemblies are at once assemblies of the electorate and musters of the militia; the citizens are exercising by their ballots the freedom they manifest in their arms, and casting their votes in the course of their military drill.[9] In this manner Harrington conveys what was to be perhaps his chief gift to eighteenth-century political thought: the discovery of a means whereby the county freeholder could equate himself with the Greco-Roman *polites* and profess a wholly classical and Aristotelian doctrine of the relations between property, liberty, and power. This was to make Harrington—I shall further suggest later—a major figure (if a very late one) in English political humanism.

If Harrington's doctrine of social power did not entail any particular theory of economic activity, there was the less need for him to explain any major shift in the distribution of power as the result of a shift from one mode of economic activity to another. This accounts for the ambiguity—or what appears to us the ambiguity—of his description of the change from an aristocratic to a popular balance in English history. He describes this as the result, in the first place, of Tudor legislation which emancipated the various classes of tenant from feudal dependence on their lords, but at the same time he emphasizes that the lords in consequence began to sell their lands and that the dis-

---

[9] See the speech of Hermes de Caduceo, *ibid.*, p. 99: "We have this day solemnized the happy nuptials of the two greatest princes that are upon the earth or in nature, *Arms* and *Councils*; in the mutual embraces wherof consists your whole *Commonwealth*; whose councils upon their perpetual wheelings, marches, and countermarches, create her armys; and whose armys with the golden vollys of the Ballot at once create and salute her councils."

solution of the monasteries greatly increased the amount of land open to what he calls "the industry of the people." A wave of intensified land-selling therefore helped bring about a redistribution of land and power, but this does not mean that Harrington meant us to infer that there was at the same time a change to a mode of land exploitation in which buying and selling were of an importance they had not hitherto reached. Macpherson seems to concede this, and looks elsewhere for evidence of Harrington's awareness of the pervasiveness of market relationships between men—and by "elsewhere" I mean outside Harrington's cardinal contentions and deep down in what I am tempted to call their subconscious implications.

But I have dwelt on this point for a particular reason. I am proposing to trace the use and development of Harrington's ideas after Harrington, and we shall come to a time when his view of English history did provide the basis for an increased awareness of the growing importance of monetary relationships —but, as we shall see, in a somewhat unexpected way and only after they had been so sharply modified, as compared with what he had meant by them, as almost to merit the use of the term "stood on their head." In fact, Harringtonian doctrine had to be partly transformed before it could be used in the way Trevor-Roper says it was used at its inception, and before it could mean at least one of the things it ought to mean before Harrington can occupy his proper place in a neo-Marxist scenario. The men who carried out this transformation of Harrington I shall call neo-Harringtonians.

The restatement of Harrington's doctrines began about 1675 —in many ways an interesting date in the history of English ideology—and the point at which it began was located in the immediate vicinity of the first Earl of Shaftesbury. That statesman's intellectual activities, like most things about him, are difficult to analyze in detail, but it is known that he was a patron of political intellectuals, including at this time Locke, and something of one himself; and it is striking to find, so close to these two great men, the beginnings of so many of the characteristic themes of opposition ideology for the next century and longer. The sources on which I base this claim are: Shaftesbury's speech in the House of Lords upon Shirley *v.* Fagg, dated October 20, 1675; the tract called *A Letter from a Person of Quality to his Friend in the Country*, of which a copy is said to have existed in the handwriting of John Locke; one or two other lesser tracts of the same tenor and date (all these are printed in the *State Tracts in the Reign of Charles II*); and two years later, in 1677, Andrew Marvell's *Account of the Growth of Popery and Arbitrary Government in England*. To take Shaftesbury's speech first, it opens with a dramatic assurance to the Lords that "our all is at stake," and a little later we find the following passage:

> My Lords, 'tis not only your Interest, but the interest of the Nation, that you maintain your Rights; for let the *House of Commons*, and *Gentry of England*, think what they please, there is no Prince that ever Governed without *Nobility* or an *Army*. If you will not have one, you must have t'other, or the Monarchy cannot long support, or keep itself from tumbling into a *Democraticall Republique*. Your *Lordships* and the *People* have the same cause, and the same Enemies. My Lords, would you be in favour with the King? 'Tis a very ill way to it, to put your selves out of a future capacity, to be considerable in his Service. . . .[10]

Now the opening sentences of this image of the Lords as a *pouvoir intermédiaire* are straight Harringtonian doctrine—or are until we start looking beneath the surface. Harrington's entire theory of monarchy can be reduced to two propositions: first, that the King's agents and servants must be supported

---

[10] *State Tracts . . . in the Reign of Charles II . . .* (London, 1693), p. 59. K. H. D. Haley, *The First Earl of Shaftesbury* (Oxford, 1968), pp. 390–96, has dealt with the composition of this speech and the *Letter from a Person of Quality.*

either upon the land, as a feudal aristocracy, or about his person, as praetorians or janissaries; second, that whichever of these methods is adopted, relations between the military class and the King will be so prone to tensions that monarchy can never be a stable form of government.[11] The actual passage in *Oceana* to which Shaftesbury seems to be alluding is one in which Harrington says that once Charles I found that the House of Lords had collapsed as a political support—a collapse which Harrington explains in the long-term historical context of changes in landownership—he had no recourse but to try and govern through an army, but had no better fortune with this for much the same historical reasons.[12] But to regard this as a direct source for Shaftesbury's argument raises in acute form the question: what was Shaftesbury doing quoting Harrington to the House of Lords in 1675? His author had still a year or two to live, though he was by now much enfeebled in body and mind and had been a state prisoner for some time in 1662. But not only might the Lords have regarded him as a dangerous subversive; according to the doctrines of *Oceana*, neither they nor their House should have existed any longer, or been a political force if they had. The choice should indeed have lain between a "democratical republic" and military government—something very far removed from what Shaftesbury was saying. It is easy to make the obvious reply that Shaftesbury no doubt assumed that few if any of their lordships had read *Oceana* or would recognize the source of his ideas; but he must have thought they would be receptive to the ideas he was trying to put across, and of these we already know, first, that they required to be expressed in Harringtonian concepts, second, that they entailed a view of the state of England in 1675 in some respects the antithesis of Harrington's predictions. What exactly was Shaftesbury trying to convey? Part of the answer may be found slightly later in the same speech:

[11] See, *e.g.*, Toland, *Works*, pp. 52–53, 70–72 (*Oceana*).
[12] *Ibid.*, p. 70.

The King governing and administering Justice by his House of Lords, and advising with both his Houses of Parliament in all important matters, is the Government I own, am born under, and am obliged to. If ever there should happen in future Ages (which God forbid) a King governing by an Army, without his Parliament, 'tis a Government I own not, am not obliged to, nor was born under.[13]

And if we turn to the *Letter from a Person of Quality*—a pamphlet so close in thought to Shaftesbury's speech that it certainly emerges from the same stable—we find this:

. . . it must be a great mistake in Counsels, or worse, that there should be so much pains taken by the Court to debase and bring low the House of Peers, if a Military Government be not intended by some. For the power of *Peerage* and a *Standing-Army* are like two Buckets, the proportion that one goes down, the other exactly goes up, and I refer you to the consideration of all the Histories of ours, or any of our neighbour Northern Monarchies, whether standing forces, Military, and Arbitrary Government came not plainly in by the same steps, that the Nobility were lessened; and whether whenever they were in Power and Greatness, they permitted the least shadow of any of them. . . .[14]

The thought is plainly the same. Here we are in at the birth—with Harrington playing at least an umbilical role—of that concept or bogey of the standing army which was to figure so prominently among the political ideas of the next century. I put the birth of the bogey in 1675, rather than under the Protectorate or at the Restoration, for a reason; but first let me underline how paradoxical it was that it should have been Harrington whom both Shaftesbury and the Person of Quality

[13] *State Tracts in the Reign of Charles II*, p. 60.
[14] *Ibid.*, p. 55.

employed to father their concept of the standing army's baleful role in politics and history. For though Harrington was certainly author of the doctrine that kings must govern either through a nobility or through an army, and though he made Olphaus Megaletor—the Cromwell-figure of *Oceana*—renounce all thought of ruling through a permanent military force, he had little real conception of the standing army as the later seventeenth century was coming to understand the term. What he had in mind was praetorians and janissaries—whom he thought incompatible with any stable monarchy—not a permanent professional force maintained by the administration and supplied out of the public exchequer. His notions of public finance, so far as they can be discovered, simply did not admit of the idea that the state could organize itself so as to bear this burden, or make the upkeep of a professional army anything but pure loss. "A bank never paid an army," he wrote, "or paying an army, soon became no bank" [15]—words true enough of Renaissance government, but which Michael Godfrey was to die to prove obsolete. Harrington did not think that an army could be planted on any permanent footing other than land; it must either be quartered on the people—which meant a choice of tyranny or rebellion—or settled on the land, which meant the establishment of military colonies (in conquered territories) or of a feudal knighthood (in domestic government). [16]

The establishment of military rule, he thought, would be fatal to liberty, but also fatal to authority; it could not lead to any stable system of government at all. [17] Consequently, he can never have ascribed to it the historical role which the Person of Quality assigns to the standing army when he talks of it rising upon the ruins of the nobility in "our neighbour Northern Monarchies" and threatening to do the same in England. The reference to "neighbour Northern Monarchies" is a plain allu-

[15] Toland, p. 243 (*The Prerogative of Popular Government*).
[16] *Ibid.*, pp. 71–72 (*Oceana*).
[17] *Ibid.*, p. 521 (*Political Aphorisms*, nos. 95–100).

sion to the idea of a common "Gothic" pattern of free government, which had been or was being subverted everywhere but in England, and the standing army is seen as the historical agent of that subversion. But Harrington, though he believed in a common "Gothic" pattern, did not see it as either free or stable. He considered it an uneasy alliance between monarchy and feudal aristocracy, a perpetual prey to disorder and civil war; and because he thought it inherently unstable, he had no need to assign sophisticated historical causes to its ultimate disappearance. It had abolished itself; the Tudor kings had brought about a redistribution of land in order to undermine their nobility, and in so doing had undermined themselves. A question which Harrington glanced at was why it seemed to be lasting longer in France.[18] But the Person of Quality has to explain its disappearance, and present the standing army as an agent of historical change, because he looks on the "Gothic model" as free, stable, and natural. To him it is not the disorderly feudalism of Harrington, but the ancient free government of England by King, Lords, and Commons, in which all but a few *esprits forts* —such as Harrington—firmly believed. He is dwelling on the Lords as a threatened essential of this system, but it could just as well have been the Commons, and was to be, repeatedly, in thought of this order. In short, Harrington did not believe in the Ancient Constitution, but Shaftesbury and the Person of Quality, twenty years later, did. They chose, however, to present their ideas in Harringtonian form, and the essence of neo-Harringtonianism lies in the drastic revision of Harrington's historical doctrine which this necessitated.

So far as one can see, the appeal of Harrington's doctrine to them was that it was admirably suited to the expression of ideological opposition to the idea of a standing army, even though the construction of such an ideology had been no part of Harrington's intentions. The standing army—though little

---

[18] *Ibid.*, pp. 271–75 (*The Prerogative of Popular Government*).

more than a bogey in political reality, at any rate after 1689—
is one of the seminal historical and political ideas of the period;
and it is relevant to the present inquiry to raise the problem of
the bogey's origins. The textbook account of the matter gives
the obvious explanation, that it lay in the painful memories of
Cromwellian rule; and so plausible does this seem that I
would not attempt to deny that there must be much truth in
it somewhere. But there are some inconvenient bits of evidence;
and though by mentioning them I raise a problem I cannot
solve, it will nevertheless illuminate my theme if I do so. Let
us glance back to the Person of Quality. He says that he cannot
believe that the King himself meditates military rule: "he is
not of a temper Robust and Laborious enough to deal with such
a sort of Men or reap the advantages, if there be any, of such a
Government; and I think, he can hardly have forgot the treatment his *Father* received from the Officers of his Army . . ."
and here we might expect rehearsal of the calamitous events at
Holmby House, Hampton Court, Carisbrooke, and Whitehall.
But the sentence goes on "both at *Oxford* and *Newark;* 'twas
an hard, but almost an even choice, to be the Parliament's
Prisoner, or their *Slave*" [19]—words which can only allude to the
angry scenes between Charles I and Prince Rupert's officers
which followed the surrender of Bristol; there is nothing about
the experience of Cromwellian rule in the rest of this pamphlet.
Now it would certainly be possible, by treating this as a *pièce
d'occasion,* to find local and particular reasons why the Person
of Quality should have wanted to present the standing-army
threat as emanating from the King's courtiers and ministers,
conspiring against his relations with his Houses of Parliament;
and we could point to these as showing how the fear of a standing army remembered from Cromwell's days became transferred
to the image of a standing army serving the King. There may
well be something in this; but the fact remains that the memory

[19] *State Tracts in the Reign of Charles II,* p. 55.

of Oliver, his colonels, his purges, his major-generals, received curiously little emphasis in the first forty years or so of standing-army doctrine—of which there is a great deal. In 1698, it is true, the third volume of Ludlow's very anti-Cromwellian memoirs [20] was published with a preface linking it to the current controversy over William III's guards; but that controversy was already in full swing and well provided with its familiar concepts, among which that of Cromwellian rule was far from dominant. By about 1714, the debate about renewing the Mutiny Bill, which enlivened almost every year of an eighteenth-century parliamentary session, began to see Cromwellian precedents brought forward in force; but there is not much of it earlier. An elaborate ideology grew up about standing armies, and generally speaking it is based, not on allusions to the Cromwellian experience, but on the idea already expressed for us by the Person of Quality and seen to be the foundation of neo-Harringtonian doctrine: namely, that standing armies appear in history about the end of the fifteenth century and are one of the instruments whereby absolute monarchies subverted ancient Gothic free government. Into this highly generalized picture it was hard to fit Cromwell and the New Model, and one may wonder whether it arose merely out of the memory of them. The reason why we invariably meet the standing army in this guise, however, is a simple one: it invariably appeared as the Person of Quality presented it, as a danger emanating from the court, a conspiracy of evil counselors and corrupt ministers against the happy relationships of King, Lords, and Commons. The standing army was a bogey intended for country gentlemen, part of a hydra-headed monster called Court Influence or Ministerial Corruption, whose other heads were Placemen, Pensioners, National Debt, Excise, and High Taxation. The

---

[20] *Memoirs of Edmund Ludlow, Esq; Lieutenant General of the Horse, Commander in Chief of the Forces in Ireland, One of the Council of State, and a Member of the Parliament Which Began on November 3, 1640 . . . , 3 vols.* (Vivay, 1698–99).

term linking all these was "Court," and while it may be, as Trevor-Roper has argued, that country gentlemen about 1656 saw the Protectorate as a form of court rule, to post-Restoration audiences it appeared anomalous, atypical, a usurpation representing nothing in the workings of the traditional constitution. If you wished to denounce the court there was little reason to denounce the Protectorate as part of it; and there was a well-established terminology for denouncing the court, in which allusions to the Protectorate played no great role. Of that terminology the standing army was part, and there is consequently a discontinuity between the memory of actual rule by an army—a memory which I agree must have been present—and the way in which the concept of rule by an army was actually used. There may be ways of bridging that discontinuity, but I shall not attempt to find them here,[20a] since my concern is with the further history of the neo-Harringtonian ideology.

That this was an ideology intended to make country gentlemen discontented with the court is evident from the whole story of its development. Shaftesbury's speech and the *Letter from a Person of Quality* are both aimed at the Lords rather than the Commons, and are concerned with an alleged plot by evil counselors to substitute military for parliamentary rule; but if we turn to Marvell's *Growth of Popery and Arbitrary Government* (1677), a work of comparable political standpoint, we find ideas aimed at the Commons backbencher and his constituents, in which the threat from the court is one of corruption rather than dictatorship. Marvell paints a clear picture [21] of the three elements of a Namier-type Parliament as seen through the eyes of a disgruntled independent member. There are the placemen, including military officers, whose allegiance is to their

[20a] See further "James Harrington and the Good Old Cause: A Study of the Ideological Context of His Writings," *Journal of British Studies,* Vol. X, No. 1 (November 1970), pp. 30–48.

[21] Andrew Marvell, *An Account of the Growth of Popery and Arbitrary Government in England* . . . (London, 1677), pp. 74–81.

employer the Crown rather than to Parliament and whose sole business is to support the increase of government expenditure and "the depression of civil authority." There are the office seekers, into whose ranks honest country members are constantly drawn, and who are both exposed to court corruption and a source of corruption to others. Their crime in Marvell's eyes is that they are loyal to their factions and leaders rather than to Parliament as a whole, and in a passage interesting to the student of Harringtonian ideas he compares them to the retainers of the fifteenth century: "they lift themselves streightways into some Court faction, and it is as well known among them, to what Lord each of them retaine, as when formerly they wore Coats and Badges." Last of all there is the "salt . . . that hath hitherto preserved this gross body from putrefaction," the independent gentlemen proof against corruption and loyal only to the country, one another, and themselves. But it is characteristic of the opposition "Country" ideology which Marvell is helping to found that he believes that only short and frequent parliaments can preserve these men of worth from corruption, whether by place, place seeking, or too much familiarity with one another, so that they too become a faction in their own right. There was to be much writing on this theme of the need for frequent parliaments, and a recurrent note is the necessity to keep the independent member politically virgin by isolating him from too much contact with power, its exercise, its pursuit, or even its opposition. "All power corrupts" might have been a Country motto, and the barrenness of Country ideology came from its insistence on regarding Parliament as a collection of men who had no more to do with power than exercise a jealous suspicion of it.

If we now summarize the main outlines of the "Country" vision of English politics as it appears in a multitude of writings in the century that follows 1675, we may attempt to see what is Harringtonian, or rather neo-Harringtonian, about it. Society is made up of court and country; government, of court and

Parliament; Parliament, of court and country members. The court is the administration. The country consists of the men of independent property; all others are servants. The business of Parliament is to preserve the independence of property, on which is founded all human liberty and all human excellence. The business of administration is to govern, and this is a legitimate activity; but to govern is to wield power, and power has a natural tendency to encroach. It is more important to supervise government than to support it, because the preservation of independence is the ultimate political good. There exists an ancient constitution in England, which consists in a balance or equilibrium between the various organs of government, and within this balance the function of Parliament is to supervise the executive. But the executive possesses means of distracting Parliament from its proper function; it seduces members by the offer of places and pensions, by retaining them to follow ministers and ministers' rivals, by persuading them to support measures—standing armies, national debts, excise schemes— whereby the activities of administration grow beyond Parliament's control. These means of subversion are known collectively as corruption, and if ever Parliament or those who elect them—for corruption may occur at this point too—should be wholly corrupt, then there will be an end of independence and liberty. The remedy for corruption is to expel placemen, to ensure that members of Parliament become in no way entangled in the pursuit of power or the exercise of administration, and to see to it that parliaments are frequently elected by uncorrupted voters.

The standing army appears in this context as an instrument of corruption rather than of dictatorship. Army officers in Parliament are placemen, and they encourage the growth of a military establishment outside parliamentary control. The threat of rule by the sword is there, but it is muted. But fortunately the independent polity possesses in itself a counterpart to the standing army, which should render it forever unnecessary. The essence of the standing army is its long-service professionalism, which is what makes it a sinister interest and a potential uncontrolled branch of government. But there is an ancient institution known as the militia, whereby the public defense is exercised directly by the independent proprietors appearing in arms at their own charge. If the armed force of the nation is embodied only in this form, there can be no threat to public liberty or the public purse; and the proprietor's liberty is guaranteed as much by his right to be the sole fighter in his own defense as by his ultimate right to cast a vote in his own government. To defend the militia against a standing army is the same thing as to defend Parliament against corruption. Here are two passages from Shaftesburian tracts printed in 1675, which might be duplicated from many later publications:

> A *standing Parliament* and a *standing Army* are like those *Twins* that have their lower parts united, and are divided only above the Navel; they were born together and cannot long out-live each other.[22]

And:

> The same might be said concerning the only Ancient and true Strength of the Nation, the *Legal Militia*, and a *standing Army*. The *Militia* must, and can never be otherwise than for *English Liberty*, because else it doth destroy *itself*; but a *standing Force* can be for nothing but *Prerogative*, by whom it hath its *idle living* and *Subsistence*.[23]

Now if we look for what is most purely Harringtonian in all this, we shall find it, I think, in the associated ideas of propertied independence and the militia. Harrington's theory of citizenship, I contended earlier, was that property conferred two things: independence, and power over those who depended on

[22] *Two Seasonable Discourses*, in *State Tracts in the Reign of Charles II*, p. 68.
[23] *A Letter from a Parliament Man to his Friend*, ibid., p. 70.

one's property for their subsistence; and the citizen displayed his independence, and exercised it, by appearing in public with those arms which were his own and which he need use only in his own or the public quarrel. In Harringtonian thought, then, the commonwealth and the militia were one and the same; but where Harrington contrasted the republic of armed proprietors with the feudal combination of monarchy and aristocracy, the neo-Harringtonians contrasted it with the professional army maintained by the executive power. (In these terms, of course, the New Model was not a standing army; it never found an executive power capable of maintaining it.) But whether in 1656, 1675, or later, the ideal of citizenship is the same. It is, as I have said, essentially Greek; and from this point of view, what Harrington contributed to English thought was an intellectual device whereby the county meeting, which looked so similar whether its purpose was to elect knights of the shire or to take sides in a civil war, could be equated with a Greek or Roman civic assembly—*comitatus* with *comitia*—and be robed in all the dignity of classical citizenship. Harrington helped create the political mood of the eighteenth century in a number of ways. With his emphasis on the role of property, he helped create the ideal of the independent man, which was one of the few subjects on which the age allowed itself to become fanatical —"I am the man," said the seditious undergraduate to the Oxford proctor, "that dare say God bless King James the 3d and tell you my name is Dawes of St. Mary Hall. I am a man of independent fortune and therefore am afraid of *no one* or *no man*" [24]—and by equating the freeholder with the *polites* or *civis*, he helped make the eighteenth century what it notoriously is, the most classical-minded of English centuries. In political thought, indeed, I should like to suggest that the humanist Renaissance came late to England, and that it was Harrington and the neo-Harringtonians who gave it its true form. Tudor

[24] W. R. Ward, *Georgian Oxford: University Politics in the Eighteenth Century* (Oxford, 1958), p. 170.

political thought is Christian, medieval, and slightly Machiavellian; Puritan political thought is a battleground between the apocalyptic and the secular; but once the medieval hierocracy was smashed and the Puritan impulse exhausted, and the *communitas* needed a new vision of itself in radically secular terms, then Renaissance humanism could perform its true function of holding up the classical mirror, in which could be perceived what was enduringly human in a world of instability and disorder. Harrington performed this task, proclaiming the return to England of what he called "ancient prudence," and this is what I meant by describing him as among the first of English political humanists. There seems to me a close parallel between the story of Harrington and the neo-Harringtonians and the story traced by Hans Baron in his study of the Florentine Renaissance. In a time of crisis, the Florentine humanists urged their city to find strength and assurance in embracing directly the classical model, even if this involved a repudiation of the medieval past; and so did Harrington. But as the immediate crisis passed, it was found that pure classicism did too much violence to the image of the city's continuity, and the classical ideals had to be rephrased to make room for the great writers of the *trecento*; just so, I suggest, did the neo-Harringtonians rephrase their doctrine to bring it into line with that idealization of medieval law and government we call the ancient constitution.

But the classicizing influence of Harringtonian ideas upon English thought was not exerted solely through the identification of freeholder with citizen. To understand their effect more fully, we need to look into the implications of the idea that by preserving their independence against the court, Parliament and its extension the country were preserving what was called "the balance of the constitution." The idea of mixed or balanced government in England was of course not new; one has to think only of the Answer to the Nineteen Propositions, with its doctrine of sovereignty vested in a kind of equipoise between King, Lords, and Commons; but older than any expression of this doctrine in English constitutional terms, and present by implication, in some degree, whenever such an expression was formulated, was the Polybian doctrine of the mixed constitution, which the Renaissance had revived and Machiavelli transmitted to the many countries where he was read. According to this doctrine, each of the three pure forms of government, monarchy, aristocracy, and democracy, would if existing alone be destroyed by excess of its own qualities; it would be replaced by its own perverted form and that by one of the pure forms, itself doomed to excess and replacement; and so on in an unending cycle. Only a mixed or balanced constitution, combining the qualities of all three forms, could hope to escape the doom of degeneration through excess; but as excess was in this model the only cause of change in political systems, it was seriously contended that a perfectly balanced combination of monarchy, aristocracy, and democracy ought to last forever. The immense prestige of Venice among some theorists of this school was based on their belief that she had attained this immortal equilibrium; that was the meaning, to them, of the epithet Serenissima. But most admitted that even the most perfect equipoise could only be maintained through human care and attention, and since that was fallible, some theoretical attention had to be paid to the cause and cure of degeneration in the balanced constitution. In Machiavelli, the most influential of the Renaissance transmitters of Polybius, the technical term for this sort of degeneration is "corruption." It arises when the balance is disturbed, typically through the encroachment of one of its three constituents upon the others; and since, in Machiavellian thought, stability in the political system is a precondition of morality in the individual life, corruption is a moral as well as a political phenomenon. But as it is the degeneration of what would otherwise be perfect, the remedy is a return to first principles, a redefinition of the balance in its original rigor; for such is the only kind of reform possible on a static-cyclical view of history.

Ideas of this kind were in use in England, and applied to the

English constitutional system, well back into the sixteenth century. But if Machiavelli was the chief transmitter of Polybius, Harrington was the chief translator of Machiavelli into English political, legal, and historical terms. He admired Venice and thought Machiavelli the greatest of post-classical political theorists; the constitution of *Oceana* is meant to be the constitution of an "immortal commonwealth"; but in his doctrine of the agrarian—the need for the distribution of power to be proportioned to the distribution of land—he supposed that he had hit on the principle which made the Polybian cycle historically intelligible and showed how it might be applied to the successive phases of West European and English history. This involved treating English history as a record of instability and successive degenerations, but also showed how this instability might be escaped for the future. The neo-Harringtonian contribution was to reverse this image, and reconcile Harrington with the historical complacency of the English, by arguing that the ancient constitution was itself an example of the Polybian-Harringtonian mixed constitution.[25]

The ideas earlier expressed in the Answer to the Nineteen Propositions [26] became increasingly important in the reign of William III: that is, the idea of the constitution as a sharing of power between King, Lords, and Commons, and the idea that its underlying principle was that of a balance between these three. Since Polybian concepts were already common, we do not need to invoke Harrington to explain for us why King, Lords, and Commons were identified with monarchy, aristocracy, and democracy, and the balance of the English constitu-

---

[25] The key work here is Henry Neville's *Plato Redivivus* (London, 1681). Neville carried out the formal task of refurbishing Harringtonian theory and bringing it into line with ancient-constitution doctrine, and Professor Robbins has traced his influence on her "Commonwealthmen"; but the borrowing of Harrington's ideas for country-party purposes began earlier, and in the way I have described. See also Robbins, ed., *Two English Republican Tracts* (Cambridge, 1969), an edition of Neville's *Plato Redivivus* and Walter Moyle's *Essay on the Roman Government*.

[26] See Corinne C. Weston, *The House of Lords and English Constitutional Theory* (London, 1965).

tion with the balance of Sparta, Rome, or Venice; when Disraeli, long after, talked about a "Venetian oligarchy" he was criticizing Whig England in its own terms and using a language as old as the Civil War or older. Nor do we need Harrington to explain for us why it was that the King in this model balance became identified with executive power, the Commons with legislative authority, and the Lords with the bridge between the two, thus launching English constitutional theory on the slippery slope which led from Polybius to Montesquieu. But the neo-Harringtonian contribution was that country ideology whose beginnings we have studied in 1675; and it was here that Harrington was caused to exert his significant influence on eighteenth-century thought.

The central Harringtonian idea is that property confers independence, and the central idea of the Harringtonian balance is that power must not be so distributed that it encroaches on the independence of property. In neo-Harringtonian hands this was transformed to read: the English constitution consists of an ideal balance between the powers of the Crown and those of Parliament, which stands for property and independence. But the Crown has not only a tendency to encroach, but a means of doing so. This particular means is what we collectively term influence, but its enemies, corruption; and it is important to realize that the word "corruption" in the eighteenth century is very often being used in its Machiavellian sense, as well as in the vulgar sense of bribery. That is, it is used to denote a disturbance of the balance of the constitution, with the demoralization of individuals and the public that is supposed to go with it; and the gloomier critics of public morality found it easy to suppose that the nation as a whole might soon be corrupt, and to ask with Machiavelli whether there was any way out. But the Crown would have been precipitating corruption even if it had "influenced" Parliament by means other than the suborning of individuals—not that the "Country" critics envisaged any other way of doing it—because, in "Country" theory, the balance of the constitution depended on the complete separation of Parliament and administration. It was for the Crown to govern, and for Parliament to exercise a jealous surveillance of government; "corruption" would follow if the Crown discovered any means at all of attaching members of Parliament to it in the pursuit of its business. Both Court and Country, in eighteenth-century constitutional debate, believed that the constitution consisted in the balance maintained between its parts; but the "Country" theory maintained that the balance was to be preserved by preserving the parts in independence of each other, while the "Court" apologists—nearer as they usually were to constitutional reality—contended that the balance was between parts that were interdependent and must be preserved by keeping the interdependence properly adjusted. Both schools of thought, true to their Machiavellian premises, believed that when there was corruption it must be dealt with by a return to the original principles (or original balance) of the constitution, but the Country pamphleteers were of course usually to be found in the posture of insisting that there was corruption and that it ought to be reformed forthwith, and it is consequently they who are responsible for importing into eighteenth-century thought the notion that the basic principles of the constitution—held to consist of some kind of balance or separation of powers—were known, as well as ancient, and that recourse could and should be made to them whenever there was need. This had some interesting intellectual consequences; and in exploring them, we shall be able to see more clearly just what it was that was Harringtonian, as well as Machiavellian, about the Country ideology.

Seventeenth-century ideas were to a significant extent oriented around the conception of the ancient constitution—that is to say, the conception that the existing constitution was ancient and perhaps immemorial. I have tried to show in another place [27] that this belief arose because the constitution was

[27] Pocock, *The Ancient Constitution and the Feudal Law*, chaps. 2 and 3.

identified with the common law and the common law with custom, which was by definition immemorial; and I have also tried to show that there was a philosophy of custom—a view of institutions as based purely upon immemorial usage and experience, with no conscious beginnings and nothing more to justify an institution than the presumption that, being immemorial, it must on innumerable occasions have proved satisfactory—which was expressed in detail by seventeenth-century lawyers and, a century later, powerfully affected the thought of Edmund Burke.[28] This philosophy of custom lay at the back of belief in an ancient constitution, though it was not necessarily entailed by every expression of that belief. However, the ancient constitution was supposed to be immemorial, and its merit consisted in the antiquity of its usage rather than in any rationalization of its principles. Now the essence of neo-Harringtonianism lay in its reconciliation of Harrington's vision of a balanced commonwealth of proprietors with the older English vision of the ancient constitution, and one result of this somewhat uneasy marriage was the importation of Polybian and Machiavellian ideas into the way in which Englishmen thought about their constitution. The seventeenth century saw the constitution as ancient; the eighteenth, as ancient and balanced. Those eighteenth-century Englishmen who were dissatisfied with their constitution and wanted to reform it typically presented their proposed reforms as involving a return to the constitution's original principles—a doctrine not characteristic of opposition thought under the first four Stuarts and involving attitudes rather fundamentalist than prescriptive, rather reactionary than conservative. The pamphlets and politicians who made use of the Country ideology were adopting the posture of a radical right; but their terminology and ideas were extensively borrowed by the radical left when one began to appear in George III's reign.

[28] See essay 6, below.

Mr. Robert Shackleton has argued [29] that Montesquieu obtained much of his doctrine of the separation of powers from Bolingbroke, when the latter was at the height of his press campaign against Walpole. Sir Herbert Butterfield has commented on the Machiavellian elements in Bolingbroke's ideology, notably in his call for a return to the original principles of the constitution.[30] But I know of no study which emphasizes the extent to which Bolingbroke was the most spectacular of the neo-Harringtonians,[31] though in his writings of the *Craftsman* period—in both the *Dissertation on Parties* and *Oldcastle's Remarks on the History of England* [32]—may be found a full-dress interpretation of English politics and history from the neo-Harringtonian point of view, with both its plausibility and its contradictoriness strongly brought out. The term "neo-Harringtonians" may be best employed to denote specifically the group of intellectuals who were active around and after the year 1698. They included Henry Neville, an intimate of Harrington himself, who may have had a hand in the original *Oceana* and who lived till 1694; Andrew Fletcher of Saltoun, the Scot who had been out with Monmouth and ended his days opposing the Union; Walter Moyle, nearly the only one of all these idealizers of the country gentleman who had English estates and spent some of his time on them; John Toland, the Irish deist through whom we can link the neo-Harringtonians with the circle round Robert Viscount Molesworth in Dublin; John Trenchard and his younger collaborator, Thomas Gordon, who was active till nearly 1750.[33] Trenchard and Gordon were responsible in the

[29] Robert Shackleton, "Montesquieu, Bolingbroke, and the Separation of Powers," *French Studies*, III (1949), 25–38; and *Montesquieu: A Critical Biography* (Oxford, 1961), pp. 296–301.

[30] Herbert Butterfield, *The Statecraft of Machiavelli* (New York, 1956), pp. 135–65.

[31] This has since been provided by Isaac F. Kramnick's *Bolingbroke and His Circle: The Politics of Nostalgia in the Age of Walpole.*

[32] Both these appeared in serial form in the *Craftsman—Oldcastle's Remarks* in 1730–31 and the *Dissertation* in 1733–34.

[33] Professor Robbins gives a valuable account of them all.

1720's for two periodicals, the *Independent Whig* and *Cato's Letters*, through which the ideas of this school passed to the American colonies; [34] it is the deist rather than the neo-Harringtonian aspect of their influence that has been studied in America, but the Country language was spoken on both sides of the Atlantic, as has been amply demonstrated by Bailyn, Wood and Colbourn.[35]

Now the essential difference between Harrington and the neo-Harringtonians was that Harrington dismissed medieval politics as incoherent and saw his commonwealth of freeholders as coming into existence only after 1485, while the neo-Harringtonians identified it with the ancient constitution. When they sought to convert Harrington's language to their own uses, therefore, there were bound to be clashes between the two diametrically opposed versions of history involved, and this is particularly noticeable when the neo-Harringtonians permit themselves to speak as if there had been a relatively recent transfer of effective landownership into gentry hands—a view of course incompatible with the antiquity of the House of Commons. It is this idea that "the gentry have all the lands" which led Trevor-Roper to say that Harrington was supplying consolatory myths to a gentry starved by exclusion from office. Now certainly *Oceana*—that extended city-state, as I have called it—presents a vision of a republic of proprietors governing themselves without permanent officeholders living at their expense; but if Harrington had been a simple dreamer of dreams for the country in its opposition to the court, one would have expected to find something about the court in his works—about its expense and corruption, about how it ceased to be a historical necessity—and there is not nearly enough. He regarded pre-

---

[34] Clinton Rossiter, *Seedtime of the Republic: The Origin of the American Tradition of Political Liberty* (New York, 1953), pp. 141–46, 492.

[35] P. 96 above, notes 11 and 12; and see Stanley G. Katz, "The Origins of American Constitutional Thought," *Perspectives in American History* (1969), pp. 474–90.

Civil War England as an unstable monarchy governing through a landed aristocracy, and no more; "office" in his works is a French phenomenon. But the neo-Harringtonians were Country ideologists in the full sense of the term, avowed enemies of a court which they denounced for governing through influence and standing armies and for boosting the expenses of government in the form of high taxation, national debts, and (yet again) influence and corruption. In short, they seem to fit the Trevor-Roper pattern a good deal better than Harrington does; only the court they denounce is not the overdeveloped but underfinanced Renaissance court of the Crisis in Government, but a mercantilist court rapidly advancing in the arts of administrative bureaucracy and government credit and finance—things which Harrington not only did not denounce but was certain could not exist.

The neo-Harringtonians, furthermore, were making an open attempt (as Harrington had not) to win support from country gentlemen discontented with the progress of court government. But in order to do this the first ideological necessity was to abandon Harrington's radical revision of accepted English historiography and restore to its central place among their concepts that ancient constitution in which all country gentlemen believed; for, as Ireton had shown himself aware at Putney, the antiquity of the constitution was the antiquity of their titles to estates and position. If Harrington had been a simple Country ideologist he might have done this for himself, instead of leaving it to Shaftesbury, Neville, and the Person of Quality; but the neo-Harringtonians, down to and including Bolingbroke, were entangled in some interesting dilemmas by their determination to make this revision. They presented the medieval period of English government in terms of the commonwealth of independent freeholders envisaged by Harrington—this was in line with the established belief that the House of Commons was older than the Conquest—and this exposed them to the attacks of those who knew, like Harrington and the Levellers on the far left or Robert Brady and his friends on the far right, that medieval government had been an affair of feudal aristocracy. But on the other hand it compelled them to present those things to which they were hostile—finance, bureaucracy, the standing army—as corruptions of an original balance, and so as historical innovations occurring at the end of the Middle Ages. They had to find causes for these innovations, which led to the paradoxical consequence that the reactionary neo-Harringtonians were in several respects more original historians than the radically independent Harrington; and since the innovations for which they had to account all added up to the single concept of government by money, the antithesis I have just drawn seems to me to tell against Macpherson's thesis that Harrington was importantly aware of the rise of the market.

To take the second of these two aspects of their thought first, I have argued that in order to explain Harrington's conception of power and citizenship, it is unnecessary to take account of economic relationships more complex than those of master and servant, independent and dependent. A fairly strong case can be made for holding that this was all that the neo-Harringtonians either found it necessary to envisage or regarded as desirable, which is more than I would say of Harrington; that is, that their scheme of social preferences was pre-capitalist in the sense that it stopped short at the master-servant household economy and did not envisage a society of investors and wage-laborers. Fletcher of Saltoun proposed [36] to deal with the poor of Scotland by a scheme of legally-regulated servitude, to forbid any proprietor to buy more land than he could work with his own servants and to compel those who farmed less to sell the profits of their land for a fixed sum to those who farmed up to the stated maximum—which hardly sounds like a scheme for capitalist agriculture. Admittedly, Fletcher was a Scot and it is well to regard eighteenth-century Scotland as a land foreign to Eng-

[36] *The Political Works of Andrew Fletcher, Esq.* (London, 1732), pp. 121–75 ("Second Discourse Concerning the Affairs of Scotland").

land; but Trenchard and Gordon, in their vehement and re-peated objections to Church of England charity schools, are voicing hostility both to High Church educational activity and to social mobility; they want the children of the poor left in the servant class where they belong.[37] These are indications—I would not put it more strongly—of a neo-Harringtonian prefer-ence for an economy of masters and servants, defined mainly in agrarian and traditional terms, which would go neatly with their general program of conceiving eighteenth-century Britain as an Aristotelian polity (a democracy of the independent, an aristoc-racy of the leisured and well-born, a fixed hierarchy of the inde-pendent and dependent). But whatever their social preferences —and I repeat that most of these idealizers of propertied inde-pendence were coffeehouse intellectuals living by their wits—their theory of political power, and the version of history to which it gave rise, were neither feudal nor capitalist, but hu-manist and Aristotelian.

Their Harringtonian interpretation of the ancient constitu-tion led them to present the "Gothic" political structure of England and Europe in the Middle Ages—playing down its aristocratic aspects—as a freeholder's commonwealth in which every man owned the means of his independence and fought for his own liberty, and the King had to seek the consent of the freeholders or their representatives in assembly. But this had visibly ceased to be true of most of Europe and was supposed to be in danger in England, and the theory of the corruption of an original balance compelled them to present those things to which they were hostile—that is to say, all that was symbolized by the terms "Court" and "corruption"—as historical innova-tions, and to date and explain them. When we turn once more to Andrew Fletcher, we find that in a work of 1698 entitled *A Discourse of Government with relation to Militias*, he gave the following four causes for the decline of Gothic government:

[37] See *Cato's Letters, passim.*

the revival of learning, the invention of printing, the invention
of the compass, and the invention of gunpowder. (None of
them is in Harrington.) In fact, it seems to have been Fletcher
and writers like him, about 1700, who established what I am
tempted to call the schoolbook interpretation of the end of the
Middle Ages. Why did they do so? To account for the decline
of Gothic liberty at the hands of the court, or—as the schoolbook calls it with approximately equal penetration—the rise of
absolute monarchy. Of Fletcher's four causes, three are supposed to explain the spread of tastes that could be satisfied only
by spending money and the rise of a commercial prosperity that
provided the money to spend, and the fourth—gunpowder—
symbolizes the rise of the standing army, the means, that is to
say, whereby the King could govern by spending money on professional soldiers and need not rely on the support of the free
armed proprietors who were his subjects. (Once again, we see
that the standing army was conceived as a bureaucratic rather
than a Cromwellian phenomenon.) In short, he is talking of the
rise of government by money, the thing Harrington believed impossible. The framework of his thought is neo-Harringtonian; he
is opposing the administrative bureaucracy of the court to the
independent and virtually ungoverned freeholders of the country; but his interpretation of European political history—for all
its preconceptions and naïveties—represents an advance, in
terms of historical explanation, over anything of which Harrington was capable. Fletcher really is talking about the rise of the
modern state and the effect of money upon society; but he is not
doing so out of a bourgeois consciousness, or out of an increasing awareness of the "market" or "entrepreneurial" element in
social relationships. What moves him is an increasing—and
hostile—awareness of the importance of money in government:
of public finance, of the professionalization of army and bureaucracy, of the inducements which a well-financed court bureaucracy can offer the subject to co-operate. And this awareness
grows out of an ultimately mythical idealization of the role in

politics of propertied independence, a kind of radical Aristotelianism which is Harringtonian.

Awareness of what was called the Court—what we might
term mercantilist government—and a theory of its role as a
"corruption" or historical innovation, can be found growing on
both sides of the Court-Country dichotomy among early eighteenth-century pamphleteers. If writers like Fletcher emphasized
the rise of government by money because they regarded it as
corrupting the earlier balance of the constitution, writers at the
other end of the lists emphasized it too, because they wanted to
argue that the old "Gothic" mode of government was no longer
possible. Charles Davenant, for instance, whose usual place is
in histories of economic thought, though he became a furious
Country pamphleteer, did at one moment engage in a defense
of standing armies, and is to be found contending that the days
are gone when one army defeated another because it was braver
or more patriotic; nowadays, that army wins whose financial resources enable it to stay in the field longest, and so there must
be permanent military establishments and a system of finance
to pay for them.[38] Both Fletcher and Davenant accept the same
historical scheme: first the Gothic commonwealth of freeholders, then finance, the standing army, and their governmental
consequences; but what Fletcher rejects as corruption, Davenant
accepts as the foundation of a new order. There are clearly
grounds for the hypothesis that it was awareness of the changing
role of government, not awareness of the role of the market in
shaping social relationships, that brought increased awareness of
the role of commerce and finance as historical determinants; a
Marxist might say that this was a mercantilist rather than an
entrepreneurial consciousness, if that were not probably revi-
sionism.

[38] Charles Whitworth, *The Political and Commercial Works of That
Celebrated Writer Charles D'Avenant* . . . (London, 1771), I, 13–16.
This was written about 1695. For comment on the above interpretation,
see Kramnick, *op. cit.*, pp. 237–43, 309.

But, if only because Davenant accepts historical change where Fletcher desires to reverse it, his consciousness of history is one degree more sophisticated. The same can be said, and said with interesting implications, of those Court writers who defended against the Country ideologists, notably Bolingbroke, the idea of the Crown's exerting a lawful influence over Parliament and thus preserving the interdependence of the parts of the balance. Their work seems to occur late in the history of neo-Harringtonianism and its opponents, and after the effective termination of Bolingbroke's political career: between 1741, when there appeared *A Letter from a Bystander to a Member of Parliament*; 1743, when the Earl of Egmont published his *Faction Detected by the Evidence of Facts*; and 1748, when Bishop Samuel Squire produced *An Historical Essay upon the Balance of Civil Power in England*. The argument of these three writers is in one major respect the same: that under the Gothic mode of government the King possessed an influence over the conduct of Parliament men which arose from his being supreme feudal landlord, and which he exerted either immediately or through the mediation of tenants in chief, but that this has now disappeared with the abolition of feudal tenures and must be replaced by influence of another character if the balance is to work smoothly. The Civil List thus becomes historical successor to the feudal prerogative, and is justified in thoroughly Harringtonian terms. But it is to be observed that in pleading this case the Court writers have reverted from neo-Harringtonianism to the ideas of Harrington himself; they are presenting the medieval period as one of feudal government in which the King ruled with an aristocracy, and power was exercised through the binding force of dependent tenure upon every man. Such a view of history was of course incompatible with the idea of an ancient, independent House of Commons, that is to say with the idea of the ancient constitution itself, and the Court writers were perfectly well aware of this. As far back as the 1730's—to go no further—the authors waging battle with Bolingbroke—Lord Hervey, for instance, in his *Ancient and Modern Liberty Stated and Compared* (1734) and the editorial writer of the *London Journal,* the paper sponsored by government to oppose the *Craftsman*—had shown themselves ready to revive the feudal interpretation of medieval history, drawing both on Harrington and on Robert Brady and the Spelmanist writers of the 1680's, and to argue with them that there had been no ancient constitution and that the whole "principle of reference to antiquity" (as Burke was to call it), whether in search of the precedents of immemorial law or in Machiavellian quest of the original principles of the constitution, was intellectually baseless. Liberty and the balance of the constitution, they said, were modern, not ancient; rooted in nature, not history; the discoveries of reason, not usage. And government, they were further inclined to argue, was a matter of implementing certain obvious necessities; there must be authority, just as there must be liberty; and in opposing the idea of necessity to that of elaborate classical principle, they drew near to, and at times drew upon, the notions of the *de facto* Tories of the immediate post-Revolution years, who had seen in the doings of 1688 not the assertion of principle but (as one of them put it) "utmost necessity, and these are terrible things." [39]

To find the conservative party repudiating history, and the opposition appealing to it, sounds rather strange to our Burkean ears. But these were pre-Burkean conservatives and pre-Jacobin reformers. The conservative, it is worth remembering, defends things as they are—in the present tense. When the adversary by whom he is faced is a fundamentalist reactionary, advocating a return to things as (he says) they once were, it is not surprising that the conservative should argue, first, that things in the past were not as the adversary supposes, second, that the whole idea of appeal to the past is out of order. He can achieve the former

[39] For further treatment, see Kramnick, *op. cit.,* chap. 5. The "Court" version of English history was energetically stated as late as 1781, by Josiah Tucker in his *Treatise of Civil Government.* Its role in the making of Hume's historical thought should also be borne in mind.

by means of historical criticism, which is just as likely to be a conservative as a radical technique. The latter he can achieve in either of two ways. Like Hooker and Burke, he can appeal to tradition, to the constant and continuous transformation of past into present, and to the principle of *plus ça change*; or he can have recourse to a hard-headed empiricism, which scouts the whole notion of history as a court of appeal and insists that in any situation you need pay attention only to what your own hard head tells you are the permanent necessities of any situation. These two arguments are not as different as they might appear. The ancient Chinese philosopher Hsun Tzu tried to unite them,[40] and in that Oakeshotten isle of Albion they are, of course, found in many combinations. But if we may look on the constitutional debate of eighteenth-century England as a dialogue between a Country interpretation which blended Machiavelli and Harrington with the ancient constitution and a Court interpretation addicted to historical criticism and *de facto* empiricism, then it is strange to see, standing at the end of the spectrum, that figure of many complexities, Edmund Burke. For Burke was neither Court nor Country; he thought the British government, in its attitude on the American question, as insensible to history as the parliamentary reformers of 1780–84 with their demand for a return to the original principles of the constitution; and against both pragmatist Court and fundamentalist Country he marshaled a traditionalism which rested directly on, and appealed openly to, that philosophy of custom which ultimately underlay the concept of the ancient constitution. Though Burke's interpretation of the events and ideas of 1688 has elements of *de facto* Tory thought about it, he is in large and significant degree the apologist of the ancient constitution in something like the seventeenth-century sense of the idea; and it is only because the history of eighteenth-century ideology has not yet been studied in depth that we do not really know

[40] See pp. 72–73, 248, 262–66 in this volume.

how far back he had to go in order to do this, or how unfamiliar his language on this head was to his hearers.

The effect of the material I have reviewed must, I think, be subversive of some widely accepted and some vigorously argued views on the character of English political thought between the revolutions—between, that is to say, about 1675 and 1776. The period between Locke and Hume—even, to narrow it down, the period of the first two Georges—was not, as is sometimes thought, a period of contented silence in political and constitutional speculation. There was much noise in Grub Street and the coffeehouses, and the debates of Court and Country, even if they had much about them which was fictitious from the point of view of the practical politician and his practical historian, were expressed in a highly individual language and recorded a highly individual view of English politics and English history, replete with awareness of historical change. Nor was this period one in which Locke's *Two Treatises* were deemed to have said the last word on all political questions and to have annulled constitutional antiquarianism and the appeal to the past. If one follows out the history of Professor Robbins's "Whig canon," it is often hard to see how the prestige of Locke stood in relation to that of Milton, Marvell, Sidney, and the rest of them; and if one follows out the history of neo-Harringtonian ideas and their opposites, it is remarkable to observe how much could be said by their aid which did not necessitate reference to Locke at all. Though Locke supplied a theoretical background to the constitution, he did not write or think within the changing framework of commonly accepted ideas about the constitution, and it is arguable that in the eighteenth century he was a writer largely for those who were situated somewhat outside the established order and wanted to appeal against its practice to its somewhat remotely perceived principles—Anglo-Irishmen, Americans, Dissenters.[41] Nor again, does an unhistorical atti-

[41] See John Dunn, "The Politics of Locke in England and America in the Eighteenth Century," in John W. Yolton, ed., *John Locke: Problems and Perspectives* (Cambridge, Eng., 1969).

tude to politics occur, in this perspective, at all where we should expect to find it; if it is Whig it is Court Whig; its bias is conservative, not radical. The thought of the Country school makes both a medievalist and a classicist appeal to the past, and we must wait until perhaps the 1780's for a radicalism we can call either Lockean or unhistorical; and it may not be fully representative of its time even then. But the political ideas of the age governed most fully by the Revolution settlement belong to the Renaissance more than to the *Aufklärung;* if Bolingbroke and his friends taught Voltaire to take no interest in English medieval precedents, that was at most their esoteric doctrine, perhaps even less than that; in public they were neo-Harringtonians, participating fully in the common language of an age which saw the high-water mark in England of the political thought of classical humanism, uniquely blended with antiquarian medievalism. It was a well-watered soil on which the ideas of Montesquieu fell, and out of which some of them grew.

Late in George III's reign we could doubtless detect great changes in English political language. Price and Priestley distilled a Lockean oxygen out of the stream of ideas that had come down to them. The writings of Bentham's first maturity represent a systematic and deeply thought out rejection of nearly everything I have been talking about. Paine rejected both the constitution and its history, though in a manner so reminiscent of Lilburne and Walwyn that one wonders whether he did not belong to the tradition even in his rejection of it. Perhaps more important, there would surely be found a steady if slow decline of the agrarian ideal of propertied independence and the Aristotelian ideal of citizenship founded upon it. But as against that—more precisely, as part of it—there can be traced a major movement of Country ideas into the radical-democratic tradition; not only much of the Chartist program, but a good deal of its ideology as well, can be shown to possess a history continuous since the days of Shaftesbury. There is room only for one or two corroborative details. James Burgh's *Political Disquisitions,* which link the Wilkesite movement with the Yorkshire Association, are full of quotations from Bolingbroke, centering around the concept of corruption. The Society for Constitutional Information disseminated the writings of Bolingbroke, Fletcher, and Molesworth along with those of the "Whig canon," Locke and the seventeenth-century antiquarians. John Thelwall taught English workmen democracy by lecturing to them on Roman history, using the works of Walter Moyle as a text. And Major Cartwright's ideal of English democracy was founded, to the end of his long and active life, on an ideal of the English militia.[42]

These are not intellectual curiosities, but key points in the long continuous history of a political language and its concepts. Thelwall and Cartwright were eccentric because they expressed central ideas with naïve simplicity. In the same way, the myth of the standing army, the Gothic society of free landed proprietors, and the rise of luxury and bureaucracy, was both the worn coinage of tediously insincere parliamentary debate and one of the seminal ideas of eighteenth-century English historiography. How much of Gibbon's analysis of the Decline and Fall is based on the Machiavellian-Harringtonian antithesis between the free peasant-proprietors and citizen-soldiers of the Republic and the mercenary armies of the Empire, and is not this part of what he meant when he said that the captain of Hampshire militia had not been useless to the historian of the Roman Empire? The great achievement of the Scottish school of sociological historians was the recognition that a commercial organization of society had rendered obsolete much that had been believed about society before it; and the underlying themes of Scottish thought include a constant debate between commerce and corruption.[43] Lastly, let anyone who knows the

---

[42] See his *The English Constitution Produced and Illustrated* (London, 1823), and his correspondence with Thomas Jefferson on the subject in 1824. F. D. Cartwright, ed., *The Life and Correspondence of Major Cartwright* (London, 1826), II, 265–78.

[43] See pp. 101–03 above.

neo-Harringtonian version of English history consider the context in which Macaulay sets the seventeenth-century civil wars, and he will find it there: the rise of standing armies, replacing the feudal array of landowning volunteers, set off a struggle between kings and estates for control of the taxation by which these armies were maintained. What I have called neo-Harringtonianism was, then, an important element in the ideas and symbols by which eighteenth-century society set forth its awareness of itself and its history.

Time, History and Eschatology
in the Thought of
Thomas Hobbes

The change from the medieval interpretative gloss on a passage of Scripture to the new grammatical analysis of the passage brought forth an entirely new question in theology. The rhetorical commentaries of the earlier period, generally concerned with delineating the intention of a phrase and never questioning any matter of textual integrity, gave way to the disquisitiones philologicae *in which all instances of textual corruption were investigated, and the whole emphasis placed upon exact rendition. The older query, so to speak, of "What does God mean here?" became the far more arresting question, "What has God said here?" Allegory, mystic paraphrase, tropology and the whole formal literature of interpretation were uncompromisingly attacked as doctrinal irrelevancies by syntax and lexicography. Grammar, not speculation, became the greatest heresy of the*

> *Christian world, and unhappily no fires could be kindled to consume the* rudimenta linguae *of Hebrew and Greek.*
>
> George Newton Conklin, Biblical Criticism and Heresy in Milton (*New York: King's Crown Press, Columbia University, 1949), pp. 1–2*

THE ASSERTION that Hobbes's political philosophy is "unhistorical," though often made and in some senses correct, is neither economical nor elegant. There are simply too many ways in which a man's thought can be said to be "historical," and too many ways of negating each one of these statements, for the epithet alone to have any very obvious meaning. Hobbes, as is generally known, declared that you could not ground a philosophy of politics on the study of human experience as recorded in history because, as he put it, "experience concludeth nothing universally." [1] But this did not prevent his being interested in history; the thought even of his later years can be observed keeping pace with some of the sharpest and most advanced historical perception of his time.[2] On matters of English tenurial and Parliamentary history, he profited by his friendship with Selden [3] and went beyond that great but elusive scholar in some respects. Again, his famous characterization of the papacy as "the ghost of the deceased Roman Empire, sitting crowned upon the grave thereof," [4] like his interpretation of the Cluniac campaign for clerical celibacy,[5] could only have come from a

[1] Hobbes, *Elements of Law,* I, iv, 10 (ed. Tonnies, repr. ed. London, 1969, p. 16).
[2] Pocock, *The Ancient Constitution and the Feudal Law,* ch. vii.
[3] Selden's *Titles of Honour* (1614 and 1631) is almost the only contemporary work mentioned with respect in *Leviathan* (i, 10; Oakeshott edition, Oxford: Basil Blackwell, p. 62).
[4] *Leviathan,* iv, 47 (Oakeshott, p. 457).
[5] In *Behemoth;* Hobbes argues that this was designed to separate the kingly office from the priesthood (*English Works,* VI, 180–1). The interpretation may not be correct; what matters is the quality of the thought that produced it.

149

vivid and freely ranging historical imagination. The epithet "unhistorical," then, is not immediately justified and needs clarification; and this has been sensibly and acceptably provided by, for instance, M. M. Goldsmith.[6] But it should be observed that what has happened illustrates the lack of economy arising from historians' use of the rhetoric of common speech. An appropriate-seeming term occurs to someone and is used; it wins enough acceptance to become part of the conventional wisdom. But in conventional use it is discovered to bear too many possible meanings to be uniformly applicable to the evidence, and the community of historians is saddled with the necessity of discovering the sense or senses in which it can be used so as to mean something.[7] Professor Goldsmith has shown that there are indeed ways in which Hobbes's thinking may accurately be termed "unhistorical," but the very success with which he does so inevitably if unintentionally carries the implication that he has vindicated the original adoption of the term and its use by his predecessors; and the way in which it has come into use remains uneconomical and has involved an excessive deployment of what Hobbes himself memorably termed "insignificant speech." [8]

Historians are condemned to this sort of thing, and it is not intended to suggest that they have any alternative to using common speech first and refining it afterwards.[9] But specialized techniques may be developed as means of cutting corners in this process and rendering it more economical, and it is part of

[6] M. M. Goldsmith, *Hobbes's Science of Politics* (New York: Columbia University Press, 1966), pp. 232–42, 251–52.

[7] The language used here is intended to give some indication of my debt to Kuhn's *The Structure of Scientific Revolutions*.

[8] "I say not this as disproving the use of universities; but because I am to speak hereafter of their office in a commonwealth, I must let you see, on all occasions by the way, what things would be amended in them; amongst which the frequency of insignificant speech is one." *Leviathan*, i, 1 (Oakeshott, p. 8). See also i, 8 (Oakeshott, pp. 51–52).

[9] On this see J. H. Hexter, *Reappraisals in History* (London, 1961), and my review article in *History and Theory*, III, 1 (1963).

the intention of this essay [10] to assert that one technique exists which may be applied to the question whether or not a man's thought is "historical." Instead of applying an epithet and then debating its use until some precise meaning for it is discovered, it should be possible to institute a critical enquiry aimed at discovering what, if any, elements that may be termed "historical" a man's thought contained. There is, of course, one obvious difficulty in the way of such a proceeding. It may seem necessary to establish in advance canons of what constitutes "historical" thinking, and this can all too easily lead to the sort of academic high-jump contest beloved of Hegelian and Crocean scholars, in which the bar of true historicity is raised again and again until only the fortunate candidate succeeds in leaping it. But we are not obliged to engage in such sterile olympiads. It can be shown that the language even of pre-historicist social and political thinkers carries a constant tissue of statements, explicit and implicit, about the time-structures in which society and the political order were thought of as existing, and that these consisted mainly of statements about the occurrence, recurrence and continuity of the modes of human action and cognition held to constitute social and political behaviour, as well as the divine actions and utterances which in monotheist contexts were indispensable to its understanding. Time so conceived differed from the time of the physicist or the metaphysician in being filled with—indeed, composed of—a rich texture of the acts, words and thoughts of personal and social beings; and in stating the continuities, recurrences and occurrences of which it consisted theorists frequently encountered problems which com-

[10] An earlier version was read to the Midwest Conference on British Studies, at the University of Kansas on 26 October 1968, and at a University of Wales colloquium at Gregynog Hall on 14 March 1969. M. M. Goldsmith, Steven Schwarzschild, Quentin Skinner and William M. Lamont have helped me by criticism at various stages in its preparation; and I owe a special debt to discussion and correspondence with Patricia Springborg during the preparation of her unpublished master's thesis (Patricia M. McIntyre, "Authority, Ecclesiastical and Civil, in Hobbes's *Leviathan*," University of Canterbury Library).

pelled them to recast their thoughts in terms of process, change and discontinuity.[11]

At this stage in the analysis, it becomes in principle possible to show how specific thinkers and traditions of thought have encountered problems of this kind, how they have dealt with them and what further problems have arisen in consequence of their responses; and in doing so, modes of thought may be met with which approximate to what we mean when we use such terms as "historical." At the cost of some looseness, we may employ such terms in exploring these intellectual developments, and to do so has the great advantage of being positive instead of evaluatory. Instead of trying to determine whether a man's thought was or was not "historical" according to some preconceived criterion, we can trace the ways in which—rather than the extent to which—his thought had become involved in questions and answers of the kind to which such a term may possibly be illuminatingly applied; and we can concern ourselves with the substance rather than the epithet, with what his thought was rather than with what it may not have been.

The problem, then, becomes that of discerning the languages, explicit or implicit, concerning time of which Hobbes made use, what he did with them and in what ways he turned them to his characteristic purposes. There were a number of modes in which it was possible for men of his day to conceptualize society's existence in time and time itself as the dimension of social existence,[12] and of two of these at least Hobbes made significant use. It must be remembered, not only that these modes of conceptualization seem remote and primitive to minds of the twentieth century, but that they imposed cramping limi-

[11] For two attempts to state the theory of this kind of time-awareness, see "The Origins of Study of the Past: a Comparative Approach," *Comparative Studies in Society and History*, IV, 2 (1962), and essay 7 in this volume.

[12] I have tried to particularize them more fully in "The Onely Politician: Machiavelli, Harrington and Felix Raab," *Historical Studies: Australia and New Zealand*, XII (1966), 46. See also above, pp. 80–85.

tations against which minds of the seventeenth can be seen struggling, often in vain. It was, that is to say, difficult for the contemporary intellect to conceive of the sequence of events and problems in time except in terms which suggested that these were accidental and irrational, that few and limited means existed whereby the human mind could understand and control them and that the means of maintaining a political system as a structure of intelligent behaviour existing in time, foreseeing its emergencies and maintaining its own stability, were correspondingly limited and the prospects of success small. One entire rhetoric, of Greco-Roman and Florentine origin—that of fortune and innovation, cycle and equilibrium—was available for the dual purpose of stressing the instability of politics in time and suggesting means by which recurrent disorder might after all be controlled; but Hobbes made little or no use of it. Instead, his thought stresses in the first place—in order to reject or minimize later—that very ancient doctrine of man's ability to understand and control the accidents of time, which was based on the concept of experience. The human mind, it was held, dealt with secular happenings by recollecting one's previous encounters, and those of other men, with phenomena resembling them and by trading on the assumption that likes recurred in like circumstances, so that responses appropriate on former occasions would prove appropriate on what appeared to be occasions of recurrence. Only further experience could test this presumption, and of that experience, even if the test were passed, only the memory would remain, so that the whole procedure would have to be gone through again on the next encounter with a similar phenomenon;[13] but a sufficiently lengthy accumulation of similar experiences would equip us with a tradition of usage looking

[13] A classical statement of this position was coined in reply to Hobbes's *Dialogue of the Common Laws,* by Sir Matthew Hale. See Holdsworth, *History of English Law* (London and Boston, 1924), V, 499–513: and Pocock, *The Ancient Constitution and the Feudal Law,* pp. 170–81, and the next essay in this book.

back to its own antiquity—the doctrine of custom evolved by English common lawyers is the classic instance of this—while the individual, operating on his own experience and that which he shared with other men, might at least develop in the present the quality called "prudence," which was in the individual and his moment what custom was in institutionalized antiquity.

It was of this Hobbes declared "experience concludeth nothing universally." He was not being particularly striking or original when he used those words; his philosophical radicalism lay in his ideas about how memory did operate to point to universal conclusions. It was a commonplace that since experience and use were based on nothing but presumption, they could never provide rational demonstration that the consequences they predicted would follow, or explanation of why they did so; and to all but the most drastic innovators, the demonstrable and the universal were interchangeable terms. But it is worth studying attentively the language in which Hobbes points out the limitations of experience and prudence, both because it indicates clearly how far secular political understanding was seen as the understanding of events in time and because it demonstrates how closely Hobbes's own views on this matter were still tied to the medieval trinity of reason, experience and faith:

> But this is certain: by how much one man has more experience of things past than another, by so much also he is more prudent and his expectations the seldomer fail him. The present only has a being in nature; things past have a being in the memory only; but things to come have no being at all, the future being but a fiction of the mind, applying the sequels of actions past to the actions that are present, which with most certainty is done by him that has most experience, but not with certainty enough. And though it be called prudence when the event answereth our expectation, yet in its own nature it is but presumption. For the foresight of things to come, which is called provi-

dence, belongs only to him by whose will they are to come. From him only, and supernaturally, proceeds prophecy. The best prophet naturally is the best guesser, and the best guesser he that is most versed and studied in the matters he guesses at, for he hath most signs to guess by. . . .

As prudence is a presumption of the future, contracted from the experience of time past, so there is a presumption of things past, taken from other things, not future but past also. For he that hath seen by what courses and degrees a flourishing state hath first come into civil war and then to ruin, upon the sight of the ruins of any other state will guess the like war and the like courses have been there also. But this conjecture hath the same uncertainty almost with the conjecture of the future, both being grounded only upon experience.[14]

Particular events, Hobbes is saying, take place in time and we have only sense and memory to tell us of their occurrence. If we attempt to think diachronically, to reason from occurrence at one point in time to occurrence at another, we shall be compelled to rely on the presumption that one event will be attended with circumstances like those attending another which resembles it. This presumption can only be tested by experience, and we can draw no general conclusions from it. Therefore the most we can do, so long as we continue to think in this manner, is to accumulate more remembered data and more cases in which the event has confirmed the presumption. In this way the individual acquires prudence and—Hobbes could have added— society builds up traditions and customs; but the process is a quantitative and actuarial one, in which the probabilities of successful prediction grow ever greater while never attaining certainty. Certainty of prediction, or prophecy, or providence—the

---

[14] *Leviathan*, i, 3 (Oakeshott, p. 16). In extended quotations, I have sometimes modified Hobbes's punctuation in ways that seem to me to make the sequence of ideas plainer to a modern eye.

terms are used interchangeably—belongs only to God, because he is not an observer of events, but the author of them.

It is the time-bound nature of human intelligence which renders it incapable of predicting occurrences and events with any certainty. "Signs of prudence are all uncertain, because to observe by experience, and remember all circumstances that may alter the success, is impossible." [15] We inhabit a flux in which there is more going on than can be observed at one moment, and too much change to permit of our recollections remaining valid for long; it is an indication that Hobbes took a relatively stable, customary society for granted that he dealt with this problem in terms of the limitations of experience, where Machiavelli had seen it in terms of the difficulty of innovation in a world controlled by chance.[16] But we can escape from the flux, and enter a world of scientific certainties, if we abandon our insistence on thinking diachronically and, instead of seeking to argue from moment to moment, occurrence to recurrence, reason from premise to consequence. This will liberate us from Plato's cave, from the world of phenomenal time:

> No discourse whatsoever can end in absolute knowledge of fact, past or to come. For as for the knowledge of fact, it is originally sense and ever after memory. And for the knowledge of consequence, which I have said before is called science,[17] it is not absolute but conditional. No man can know by discourse that this or that is, has been or will be, which is to know absolutely; but only that if this be, that is; if this has been, that has been; if this shall be, that shall be; which is to know conditionally, and that not the consequence of one thing to another, but of one name of a thing to another name of the same thing.[18]

[15] *Ibid.*, i, 5 (Oakeshott, p. 30).
[16] See in particular chs. ii, vi and xxiv–xxv of *The Prince*.
[17] *Leviathan*, i, 5 (Oakeshott, pp. 29–30).
[18] *Ibid.*, i, 7 (Oakeshott, p. 40).

Hobbes does not even mention the possibility of knowing that if this is, that shall be; so determined is he to separate the world of logical from that of temporal consequence, the world of rationally perceived necessary consequence from the world of facts observed by sense and memory as they occur in time. Knowledge of the former world he terms "science" or "philosophy," knowledge of the latter "history." [19] From this point in the analysis we are constructing, he may be seen going on to show how knowledge of premise and consequence brings knowledge of cause and effect, knowledge of the universe of consequences knowledge of the universe of motions. Through extension of this kind of knowledge, we discover the laws of nature that bind our consciences; we discover the necessity for a representative sovereign and are led to perform the acts which set him up; we conclude that God exists and is all-powerful, and that the normative laws which our reason discovers must be also his commands. This complex process of making discoveries and acting upon them takes place in time—there is no action or motion in Hobbes's world which does not—but has no history; it is synchronic, observable as taking place at any and every moment, and does not necessitate that any civil society, or mankind at large, possess a past, present or future in which the stages of its development may be observed. Hobbes has followed the pattern, very common in the history of Western philosophy, of removing from the domain of political time into that of political space,[20] a removal usually carried out for precisely the reason which he gives: the sequence of events in time cannot be known with certainty sufficient to be termed "philosophical."

[19] *Ibid*, i, 9 (Oakeshott, p. 53). Professor Oakeshott, arguing that a distinction between science and philosophy is emergent in Hobbes's thought, agrees (Introduction, p. xxi) that he uses the terms synonymously.

[20] The very valuable terminology is that of Sheldon S. Wolin, *Politics and Vision* (New York and London, 1961), *passim*. See also John W. Gunnell, *Political Philosophy and Time* (Wesleyan University Press, 1968).

Only by abandoning diachronic for philosophical thinking can we understand scientifically how political authority must come into being, or erect a system of authority on a foundation of rational certainty.

We have now uncovered and clarified a sense in which it can very properly be said that Hobbes's political philosophy is un-historical. He distinguished between philosophy and history as two modes of knowledge and ascribed scientific or rational demonstrability only to the former. But we must be careful not to suppose we have proved too much, or to fall into this error by using the words "philosophy" and "history" loosely and anach-ronistically. Since Hobbes uses "philosophy" as the name of one of two modes of knowledge, it clearly does not follow that phenomena which are known historically do not exist or have no relevance to politics. A more subtle error would be to sup-pose that "history," which Hobbes uses to denote the world of phenomena sensed and remembered as occurring in time, de-notes each and every way in which human existence in time is known or important. It may seem natural to suppose that the temporal sequential phenomena which become apparent to our perceptions embrace the totality of human history, though a philosopher of history would probably find this supposition naïve; but even the debate which we might hold with him would not save us from the anachronism of supposing that what Hobbes meant by "history" embraced every way in which the seventeenth-century intellect saw human existence as carried on in time and marked by its stages. All that we have considered so far consists of Hobbes's responses to the assertion that man's temporal existence was known to him through experience; yet it is quite certain that contemporary thought saw man as having another history, known in another way. The anachronism of re-fusing to recognize this accounts for the extraordinary neglect and inattention paid to Hobbes's text by the whole tradition of modern scholarship.

Leviathan consists of four books, with an introduction and a conclusion. Books I and II contain the doctrine to which attention has already been given and the rest of Hobbes's political philosophy, properly so called; and the interest of philosophers and historians of philosophy has quite rightly been focused upon them. But at midpoint in the whole work, at the end of book II and the outset of book III, Hobbes embarks on a new course. He states quite plainly [21] that human existence, knowledge, morality and politics must be thought of as going on in two distinct but simultaneous contexts: the one of nature, known to us through our philosophic reasoning on the consequences of our affirmations, the other of divine activity, known to us through prophecy, the revealed and transmitted words of God.

> . . . there may be attributed to God a twofold kingdom, *natural* and *prophetic*: natural, wherein he governeth as many of mankind as acknowledge his providence, by the natural dictates of right reason; and prophetic, wherein having chosen out one particular nation, the Jews, for his subjects, he governed them, and none but them, not only by natural reason, but by positive laws, which he gave them by the mouths of his holy prophets.[22]

The change in mid-sentence from present to past tense indicates the major and significant alteration that has begun to occur. The Christian God operates in time, and our knowledge of prophecy is our knowledge of the time-frame and scheme of events within which he does so. There are two ways in which this comes to be the case: first, God performs acts, including acts of revelation to prophets, at various points in time; second, the words by which we have knowledge of his acts are revealed

---

[21] *Leviathan*, ii, 31 (Oakeshott, pp. 232–34) and iii, 32 (Oakeshott, pp. 242–43).

[22] *Ibid.*, ii, 31 (Oakeshott, pp. 233–34). The formal link is that men must hear God commanding them directly before they can in the full sense be obliged to obey him. This kind of obligation is not universal, but peculiar to the chosen or elect.

to prophets at specific moments in time, and are subsequently transmitted through tracts of time by the authority, religious or civil, on which the prophets and their words are taken to be authentically God's. Actions and words, both divine and human, prophetic and civil, join to constitute a time-scheme which is not only that within which Christian thought is inescapably conducted, but is actually that of which the Christian has knowledge. Our knowledge of God is knowledge of his acts, gained through his words, both of which are performed in time and schematize it. Hobbes therefore affirms the existence of a sacred history, which does not appear in the scheme of philosophical and historical knowledge set out in book I, chapter 9, but which does constitute virtually the whole of the subject-matter of books III and IV. In these books Hobbes sets forth his perceptions of the Christian religion, or as he significantly calls it "the prophetic kingdom of God," as a system of belief in past acts and utterances of the deity, and of expectation of future acts which those utterances foretell. Following the orthodox scheme, in short, his exposition of the Christian faith concluded with an eschatology; following certain less orthodox schemes, it is very nearly reducible to one.

The two books in which Hobbes expounds Christian faith and its sacred history are almost exactly equal in length to books I and II;[23] yet the attitude of far too many scholars towards them has traditionally been,[24] first, that they aren't really there, second, that Hobbes didn't really mean them. For this obviously unsatisfactory state of affairs various reasons can be

[23] In the first edition of *Leviathan*, the Introduction plus bks. i and ii total 193 pages, bks. iii and iv minus the Review and Conclusion 192. I am indebted to Professor Goldsmith for pointing this out.

[24] Exceptions to this all too general rule may be found in the writings of A. E. Taylor (Keith C. Brown, ed., *Hobbes Studies*, Harvard University Press, 1965, pp. 35, 50, 54n.), Willis B. Glover (Brown, *op. cit.*, pp. 141–68), Oakeshott (Introduction, pp. xliv–l, lxi–lxiv) and Goldsmith (*op. cit.*, pp. 217–27, and "A Case of Identity" in King and Parekh, eds., *Politics and Experience: Essays Presented to Michael Oakeshott* [Cambridge University Press, 1968]).

suggested. In the first place, the history of thought has been too much left in the hands of philosophers, historians of philosophy and scholars who have assumed that the history of thought can be subsumed under the history of successive philosophic systems. Since Hobbes was a major philosopher, and books III and IV of *Leviathan* are manifestly not philosophy, it has seemed simplest to leave them out; and on grounds like these scholars feel justified in producing students' editions of *Leviathan* from which books III and IV, and of *De Cive* from which chapters XVI and XVII, are simply omitted. In the second place, for historical reasons inclusive of that just given, scholarship has suffered until recently from a fixed unwillingness to give the Hebrew and eschatological elements in seventeenth-century thought the enormous significance which they possessed for contemporaries. In the third place, Hobbes's readers since his own lifetime have found reason to doubt if he was a man of deep personal piety and even to affirm that he was an atheist; and even the recent revival of interest in the possible role of God in his thought[25] has focused upon the theory of natural law, which forms part of his philosophy, and not upon his doctrines of prophecy and eschatology, which do not.[26] It has thus come to be a near-orthodoxy that he did not believe what he wrote in the unread half of *Leviathan*, and that consequently these books have no meaning, though the fallacy should be evident of affirming that the sincerity of a man's belief in what he

[25] See Brown, *op. cit., passim*; Howard Warrender, *The Political Philosophy of Hobbes: His Theory of Obligation* (Oxford, 1957), F. C. Hood, *The Divine Politics of Thomas Hobbes* (Oxford, 1964) and Quentin Skinner, "Hobbes's *Leviathan*," *The Historical Journal*, VII (1964), 321–33. Some of these writings—notably Hood's—make a serious attempt to show that the thought of bks. iii and iv is implicit in i and ii, but do not focus on the analysis of prophetic content.

[26] Prophecy cannot, of course, be the object of philosophical knowledge as Hobbes understands the latter; nor does he include sacred history in his classification of the modes of that branch of knowledge (i, 9), presumably because it is not an object of sense-knowledge. His theory of knowledge determines the status of our belief in prophecy, but cannot determine the content of what we believe.

says suffices to determine the content of what he says or its impact upon others. Although esoteric reasons have been suggested why Hobbes should have written what he did not believe,[27] the difficulty remains of imagining why a notoriously arrogant thinker, vehement in his dislike of "insignificant speech," should have written and afterwards defended sixteen chapters of what he held to be nonsense, and exposed them to the scrutiny of a public which did not consider this kind of thing nonsense at all. The only recourse open to the historian is to examine, not Hobbes's sincerity of conviction, but the effects which his words seem designed to produce, reconstructing the meanings which their contents would appear to have borne, first, in the thought-patterns characteristic of the time, secondly, in the thought-patterns characteristic of their author. If the effect or the intention of books III and IV was to reduce the Christian revelation to insignificance, this will be discovered not by making prior assumptions about Hobbes's beliefs when he wrote them, but by paying attention to what he actually wrote. And, further, if we are to conclude that he esoterically intimated that Christian eschatology was nonsense, we must begin by ascertaining the ways in which it was conventionally held to make sense.

Prophecy and eschatology—to which Hobbes in effect reduces the whole body of revealed religion—were not merely a system of dogmas for believers, but a highly important component of the conceptual equipment possessed by Christian Europe. They constituted an intellectual scheme of a distinctive kind, known by an intellectual faculty unlike any we have so far considered. The greater part of their content consisted of acts which God was said to have performed in the past, or which it had been promised that he would perform in the future; and

---

[27] The classic instance is that of Leo Strauss (Brown, *op. cit.*, p. 27, n. 43). It is odd that Strauss seems to speak of the view that Hobbes meant what he said as constituting a "prevalent practice"; belief in his theistic sincerity has surely been a minority opinion.

each statement of which prophecy consisted had itself been uttered by God or his prophets at a distinctive moment in time. In two ways, therefore, prophecy constituted a sacred history, and if "prophecy" and "revelation" were taken as interchangeable terms, it must follow that knowledge of the Christian revelation was in a sense historical knowledge. But the question must arise of how the events of this history were to be known. It would be common ground to Hobbes and a scholastic thinker that they were not accessible to reason, since they were not consequences to be inferred or deduced from a premise, and that they were equally inaccessible to experience, since their content (as distinct from their verbal utterance) did not belong to the realm of phenomena which the individual sensed and remembered for himself. They were statements, made on specific occasions and transmitted through subsequent time, which we accepted either as true or as authoritative—it was on this point that the schools divided—by means of a faculty of the mind known as faith. Faith was distinct from either reason or experience, and this must be why sacred history, to which so large a part of *Leviathan* is devoted, does not figure in the scheme of knowledge set out in chapter 9 and divided into modes of philosophy and modes of history. Experience and prudence, forms of thought appropriate to the study of natural and civil history, have no part to play in the study of revealed history.

Books III and IV, then, form in a sense Hobbes's contribution to the study of faith, both as a system of revealed truth and as a faculty of the mind. But at a much earlier point in *Leviathan*, immediately after drawing his distinction between experiential knowledge of facts and logical knowledge of the consequences of verbal affirmations, he had turned his attention to the question of what faith was; and it will aid our study of his eschatology if we keep in mind what he there said:

> When a man's discourse beginneth not at definitions, it
> beginneth either at some other contemplation of his own,

and then it is still called opinion; or it beginneth at some saying of another, of whose ability to know the truth and of whose honesty in not deceiving he doubteth not; and then the discourse is not so much concerning the thing as the person, and the resolution is called BELIEF and FAITH: *faith* in the man, *belief* both *of* the man and *of* the truth of what he says. So that in belief are two opinions, one of the saying of the man, the other of his virtue. . . . But we are to observe that this phrase, *I believe in* [and its Greek and Latin equivalents] are never used but in the writings of divines. Instead of them in other writings are put, *I believe him* [etc.] . . . [and] this singularity of the ecclesiastic use of the word hath raised many disputes about the right object of the Christian faith.

But by *believing in,* as it is in the creed, is meant not trust in the person, but confession and acknowledgement of the doctrine. For not only Christians, but all manner of men do so believe in God as to hold all for truth they hear him say, whether they understand it or not; which is all the faith and trust can possibly be had in any person whatsoever; but they do not all believe the doctrine of the creed.

From whence we may infer that when we believe any saying, whatsoever it be, to be true from arguments taken not from the thing itself or from the principles of natural reason, but from the authority and good opinion we have of him that hath said it, then is the speaker or person we believe in or trust in, and whose word we take, the object of our faith; and the honour done in believing is done to him only. And consequently, when we believe that the Scriptures are the word of God, having no immediate revelation from God himself, our belief, faith and trust is in the church, whose word we take and acquiesce therein. And they that believe that which a prophet relates unto them in the name of God, take the word of the prophet, do honour to him and in him trust and believe touching the

164

truth of what he relateth, whether he be a true or a false prophet. And so it is also with all other history. . . . If Livy say the Gods made once a cow speak and we believe it not, we distrust not God therein, but Livy. So that it is evident that whatsoever we believe, upon no other reason than what is drawn from authority of men only and their writings, whether they be sent from God or not, is faith in men only.[28]

The last conclusion that we should draw from this passage is that Hobbes is declaring God to be non-existent or irrelevant. If we can only believe that God spoke on the authority of men who speak to us subsequently, we believe that he spoke once we accept their authority, and in so believing we invest him as well as them with the authority that comes with speaking. What Hobbes is doing is historizing faith in a new way, one of the highest relevance to politics. Faith is reposed in a system of statements and in the authors who transmit them through time, and whether we stress the statement or the author as the object of our faith, a large part of the content of the statements made and transmitted by every author, saving God himself, consists of statements about previous authors. Since once we accept that an author spoke, whether directly or on the authority of another, we invest that speaker with an authority of divine origin, it follows that the whole body of our faith is reducible to the construction of a system of authors and of authority, existing through time and resting on the statements they transmit, our opinion of the authority they have as transmitters, and the authority of the previous speakers, back to God himself, whom we accept as authors in the act of accepting any one of them. This system of authority constituted by faith differs from the system of authority constituted in the erection of the civil sovereign in that historicity is of its essence; it rests upon the transmission of words through time, words which constantly reiterate

[28] *Leviathan*, i, 7 (Oakeshott, pp. 41–42).

statements about previous utterances of the same words; and the individual believer becomes involved in this history as he validates and perpetuates it through faith.

There exist then in *Leviathan* two structures of authority, one as a-historical as the other is historical, and they will come into direct and potentially competitive coexistence once the commonwealth constituted in books I and II becomes "a Christian Commonwealth"—words which, including the article, form the title of book III. The civil sovereign is set up by the a-historical processes of civil philosophy and natural reason, which among other things declare that God exists and commands obedience to the laws of nature which the sovereign also enjoins. He now finds himself faced by a new system of authority, resting upon what are accepted to be utterances of the same God, made in a past and concerning a future, but in no way deducible by the reason which set him up and validates his authority. The sovereign, and the student of civil government, must pay urgent attention to the content as well as the transmission—which, again, forms a large part of the content—of the body of revelation on which rests the structure of religious authority; the inhabitants of the a-historical world of reason must enter the historical world of faith. Since faith is reposed in the content of revelation as well as in its authors and transmitters, and since on the other hand the content of the statement transmitted affects in many ways the sort of authority possessed by those involved in its transmission, the whole content of revealed religion is potentially of concern to the civil magistrate. We shall see that this is particularly true of revelation's eschatological component.

The one thing which scholars do generally know concerning Hobbes's doctrine of prophecy is that God does not speak to us direct but mediately, through the utterances of men—the prophets and Christ in his human nature—to whom or in whom he reveals himself; and that whether God has indeed spoken direct to any man is a thing past any man's capacity to determine,[29] so that the belief we repose and publicly own in the prophets is grounded either on our opinion—which is never our knowledge—of their authenticity, or on the command of the civil sovereign once he is constituted and requires us in the name of civil peace to accept this man as prophet or this doctrine as the word of God.[30] And on the supposition, which there is no need to contest here, that Hobbes did not show that anything except the needs of civil peace bound the will of the sovereign in decreeing matters of this sort, it is usual to drop the subject, leaving it to be inferred that the revealed prophetic word means nothing but what the sovereign ordains that it shall mean, and that the domain of prophecy has been successfully reabsorbed by that of nature, by the unhistoric rationality of the civil order and its sovereign.

But that is not how Hobbes proceeds, and if it is what he really meant then he meant something other than what he said. The history of God's prophetic word, and the future prophesied by that word, constitute the sacred history of mankind, and if Hobbes had meant that sacred history had no meaning of itself and that the sovereign might rewrite it to suit the permanent or passing needs of society, he would hardly have written chapter after chapter of exegesis with the proclaimed intention of arriving at the truth about it. Yet this is what he did, and hav-

---

[29] *Ibid*, i, 7 (Oakeshott, p. 42); i, 12 (Oakeshott, pp. 77–80); i, 14 Oakeshott, p. 90); ii, 26 (Oakeshott, pp. 186–88); iii, 32 (Oakeshott, pp. 243–46); iii, 34 (Oakeshott, pp. 254–55); iii, 36 (Oakehott, pp. 277–85); iii, 37 (Oakeshott, pp. 286–91); Review and Conclusion (Oakeshott, p. 465).

[30] *Ibid*., ii, 26 (Oakeshott, p. 188); iii, 32 (Oakeshott, p. 246); iii, 34 (Oakeshott, pp. 254–55); iii, 38 (Oakeshott, pp. 290–91); iii, 42 (generally, but in particular Oakeshott, pp. 327–30 and 340–41). Since some Jewish and all Christian kings have ruled in times when direct prophetic inspiration was in suspension or at an end, their opportunities for sitting in judgment upon true prophets have been limited. The interesting case, with which Hobbes does not deal, is that of Elisha, who conveyed the Lord's command to Jehu, authorizing him to overthrow King Joram and take his throne (in 2 Kings ix). Jehu must have exercised his own judgment as to the authenticity of this revelation by one who was already an accredited prophet.

167

ing once acknowledged the existence of prophecy he could hardly have done less or more. The magistrate may be the supreme and unchallenged interpreter of God's word, but that is not at all the same as being its author—either in the sense of being God himself or of being one of those acknowledged as uttering that word at God's direct or even mediated command. The authority by which the sovereign interprets the prophetic word is clearly distinct from the authority by which the word is uttered; and since the word, its content, its transmission and its authors constitute a history, the secular ruler finds himself inhabiting a history which he did not make—it does not owe its being to the natural reason which produced him—and which indeed looks forward to a time when his authority will be exercised by the risen Christ. The word and the history it connotes are given him, and his authority as interpreter begins only from acceptance of it as *datum*. Hobbes therefore, as a private man, a subject and (so he tells us) a Christian, inhabiting the same history, finds it desirable to pursue an accurate interpretation of the same data, and does not wait in mindless quiet for the sovereign to interpret it to him.

The prophetic word of God constitutes the past, present and future of mankind. At moments in the past, God spoke to prophets, who relayed his word to his peculiar people—the Jews first and the Christian elect later; it was his word commanding them, and their acceptance of him and his prophets as uttering it, which constituted the peculiar kingdom of God over them, and a peculiar kingdom thus differs in kind from a natural civil kingdom. After the deaths of the various prophets, there were —as there still are—periods of time in which the people continued to accept their word as God's and to remember them as having received and given it.[31] Sacred time, thus far, consists of moments of divine revelation and continua of human transmission. But a prophet may be a *prolocutor* who speaks in

[31] *Ibid.*, i, 7 (Oakeshott, p. 40); i, 12 (Oakeshott, p. 78); iii, 36 (Oakeshott, pp. 282–85); iii, 40 (Oakeshott, p. 312).

God's name—all revelation is prophecy in the sense that it is mediated through such men—or a *predictor* who foretells what is to come.[32] Some part of the content of prophecy is prediction in that it foretells a future, composed of divine actions, including the action of foretelling it, in which we believe and which we expect. The present, consequently, is a time of remembering past prophecies and expecting the future which they foretell.

But all these subdivisions of sacred history, including the future, are also subdivisions of the history of political authority. In the synchronic, a-historical world of natural civil authority, there is movement from a phase in which we know by reason what are the laws of nature and that they are also the commands of God, but are obliged by this knowledge only in conscience and *in foro interno*,[33] to a phase in which our wills and actions are lawfully obliged because there is now one Leviathan whom we have constituted with power to command us. But in the diachronic world inhabited by God's peculiar people, this purely natural movement does not take place, because God is active from the time of Abraham,[34] commanding men directly, not only through reason and experience, but through his word which is spoken by the prophets. Political authority is present from certain moments and it has a history—including a recorded commencement—because the prophetic word has a past, present and future and entails different modes of authority at different times.

For two reasons, the authority which God exercises over his peculiar people is a civil or political authority in the full sense of the term: first, because God is literally present and commanding the people through positive laws, peculiar to themselves, issued through his prophets; second, because the people

[32] *Ibid.*, iii, 36 (Oakeshott, pp. 275–76).

[33] *Ibid*, i, 15 (Oakeshott, p. 103).

[34] *Ibid.*, ii, 26 (Oakeshott, pp. 187–88); iii, 35 (Oakeshott, pp. 266–67); iii, 40 (Oakeshott, pp. 307–8). The covenant with Abraham is relatively little emphasized as compared with that with Moses.

have covenanted, at Sinai and on other occasions,[35] to obey him through his prophets, acknowledged as uttering his laws. The term "covenant" is used here in a variant of the full Hobbesian sense. In the natural world the covenant sets up Leviathan, the mortal god, a man or men bearing the person of all other men composing the community. In the prophetic world the people covenanted with Moses to speak with God for them, and so obliged themselves to accept as God's word all that Moses told them for such.[36] Does this mean that Moses as representative sovereign constituted Israel a people in a manner no different from that of other Leviathans? Not if we accept, as there is no sign that Hobbes did not, that God spoke to Moses, for then Moses was in the prophetic world and not simply in the natural. We cannot know that God spoke to him; the authority on which we accept this must be largely his own; the faith by which we acknowledge it must be largely faith in Moses; but once we accept it Moses becomes the lieutenant of God in a way in which the civil sovereign can never be, since in the natural world God rules through reason and not through positive and peculiar command.

God exercised direct political authority—that is to say, he was king—over Israel from the time of Moses to that of Samuel. He ruled, it is true, through lieutenants of two kinds: a constituted succession of priest-kings in the line of the heirs of Aaron, and—given the people's frowardness and constant demands for signs of his will—an extraordinary and occasional succession of judges and other prophets, recognized by a far from infallible popular opinion as speaking with his voice.[37] But with the death of Eli the line of the ruling high priests ended, and the misdeeds of the children of Samuel caused the people to lose faith

[35] A renewal of the covenant took place under Esdras, at the return from the Captivity, but did not constitute a new civil sovereignty. *Leviathan*, iii, 40 (Oakeshott, p. 315) and iii, 42 (Oakeshott, p. 342).

[36] *Ibid.*, ii, 20 (Oakeshott, p. 134); ii, 26 (Oakeshott, p. 188); iii, 35 (Oakeshott, pp. 267–78, 270); iii, 40 (Oakeshott, pp. 308–11); iii, 42 (Oakeshott, pp. 340–41).

[37] *Ibid.*, iii, 40 (Oakeshott, pp. 311–12).

in the prophetic succession in a way that proved irrevocable.[38] Samuel—who was soon to pronounce the old law at an end [39]—presided over that most controversial moment in pre-Exilic history as seen through seventeenth-century Christian eyes, the election of Saul to be king in the manner of the Gentiles. Innumerable were the emphases which could be selected in interpreting this event, and Hobbes's treatment can be seen as it were suspended between two of them: emphasis that it constituted a "rejection" and "deposition" of God from his direct kingship over Israel, and insistence that this nevertheless occurred with his permission and consent, so that the authority of the kings was not merely natural, but had his express and positive sanction.[40] But if we compare the works on politics

[38] *Ibid.*, i, 12 (Oakeshott, pp. 78–79); iii, 35 (Oakeshott, p. 268); iii, 39 (Oakeshott, p. 314).

[39] *De Cive* (*English Works*, II, 245). Hobbes gives St Jerome as authority for this.

[40] *Elements of Law* (Cambridge University Press, 1928), Pt. I, ch. 7, sec. 5, pp. 127–28: no distinction drawn between high-priests and kings. *De Cive*, xvi (*English Works*, II, 245): "the kingdom of God by way of priesthood (God consenting to the request of the Israelites) was ended"; "new priesthood and new sovereignty . . . founded in the very concession of the people." *Leviathan*, i, 12 (Oakeshott, p. 79): "faith also failed; insomuch as they deposed their God from reigning over them." ii, 20 (Oakeshott, p. 134): "when the people heard what power their king was to have, yet they consented thereto, and say thus . . . *we will be as all other nations.* . . . Here is confirmed the right that sovereigns have. . . ." ii, 29 (Oakeshott, p. 213—passage deals with "the infirmities of a commonwealth"): "And as false doctrine, so oftentimes the example of different government in a neighbouring nation disposeth men to alteration. . . . So the people of the Jews were stirred up to reject God, and to call upon the prophet Samuel for a king after the manner of the nations." iii, 35 (Oakeshott, pp. 268–69): "after the Israelites had rejected God, the prophets did foretell his restitution; as . . . I will reign over you, and make you to stand to that covenant which you made with me by Moses, and brake in your rebellion against me in the days of Samuel and in your election of another king . . . it were superfluous to say in our prayer, *Thy kingdom come*, unless it be meant of the restoration of that kingdom of God by Christ, which by revolt of the Israelites had been interrupted in the election of Saul." iii, 38 (Oakeshott, p. 294): "they rebelled." iii, 40 (Oakeshott, pp. 313–14): "cast off by the people, with the consent of God himself. . . . And yet God consented to it. . . . Having therefore rejected God, in whose right the priests governed, there was no authority left to the priests, but such as the king was pleased to allow

which Hobbes is known to have composed before the outbreak of the Civil War—the *Elements of Law,* written in 1640, and *De Cive,* published in 1642—with the language published in *Leviathan* in 1651, we shall notice an important difference of emphasis and an extension of the argument into new fields of relevance.[41] The stress in *Leviathan* falls very heavily indeed, in ways not paralleled in the earlier works, upon the idea that the supreme purpose of Christ's mission is to restore the literal and political kingdom of God upon earth that existed from Moses to Samuel; that, since the Jews have rejected Christ's invitation to re-enter this kingdom, it is now to be exercised over a new peculiar people, the Christian elect; and that through the death, ascension and promised return of Christ, the second kingdom of God is to begin only at his return and at the resurrection of

---

them; which was more or less, according as the kings were good or evil. . . . (p. 314) And afterwards, when they demanded a king after the manner of the nations, yet it was not with a design to depart from the worship of God their king . . . they would have a king to judge them in civil actions, but not that they would allow their king to change the religion which they thought was recommended to them by Moses. So that they always kept in store a pretext, either of justice or religion, to discharge themselves of their obedience, whensoever they had hope to prevail" [!]. There follows on p. 315 a confused account of the dealings of the later kings with the prophets after Samuel; Elijah and Elisha are not mentioned. iii, 41 (Oakeshott, pp. 318–19): Christ to restore the kingdom "cut off by rebellion," but only to proclaim its future coming; Pilate accepts his claim to be king of the Jews as not contrary to the laws of Caesar. iii, 42 (Oakeshott, p. 376): "Before the people of Israel had, by the commandment of God to Samuel, set over themselves a king, after the manner of other nations, the high-priest had the civil government, and none but he could make or depose an inferior priest. But that power was afterwards in the king. . . . Kings therefore may in like manner ordain and deprive bishops, as they shall think fit for the well-governing of their subjects." It would on the whole appear that a kingdom of men legitimized by nature exists only in an interlude of sin and rebellion against God. The king reigns in God's absence, but that absence is caused by the king's election.

[41] Chs. xvi and xvii of *De Cive* should be carefully compared with bk. iii of *Leviathan,* and the relation between the two texts considered. If we conclude that Hobbes's interest in eschatology sharply increased between 1642 and 1651, this must have occurred during his residence at Paris, in a *milieu* not usually considered eschatologically minded.

the saints, which is to end this world and inaugurate a new one. Where in the first kingdom God reigned in his representatives Moses and the prophets, he will reign in the second kingdom in the person of Christ risen in his human nature and his human body; and the identity of Christ's kingship with that of Moses is insisted on so strongly that it impels Hobbes to one of the only two occasions in *Leviathan* on which he resorts to the typological mode of argument, in which Christ and his precursors are presented as reiterating and perfecting a common figurative pattern.[42] If the sole purpose of Christ's mission is to restore the immediate civil rule of God over his peculiar people which ended with the election of Saul, it might almost seem as if that event constituted a second fall of man, something which the whole process of redemption exists to undo. Hobbes does not go to these lengths, since he wishes to maintain the legitimacy of Davidic kingship over the peculiar people; though in common with the general trend of Christian interpretation of later Jewish history, he does not attempt to assign post-Exilic forms of political power a distinctive role in the history of prophetic authority, and the emphasis falls by default on the utterances of the Exilic prophets in foretelling Jesus as the Messiah.[43] But the fact remains that his history of prophetic authority has been projected into an eschatological future. His

[42] *Leviathan*, iii, 41 (Oakeshott, pp. 316–17): the sacrificed goat and the scapegoat both "types" of Christ; pp. 320–21: the "similitude with Moses"—twelve princes and twelve apostles; seventy elders and seventy disciples; circumcision and baptism; the washing of lepers a "type" of baptism. "Seeing therefore the authority of Moses was but subordinate, and he but a lieutenant of God, it followeth that Christ, whose authority as man was to be like that of Moses, was no more but subordinate to the authority of his Father."

[43] *De Cive* (*English Works*, II, 248) and *Leviathan*, iii, 40 (Oakeshott, p. 315) make the point that post-Exilic history is too confused to be of authority. iii, 36 (Oakeshott, p. 280): "after the people of the Jews had rejected God, that he should no longer reign over them, those kings which submitted themselves to God's government were also his chief prophets," in the *prolocutor* sense presumably. iii, 42 (Oakeshott, pp. 341–42): the problem of when the Exile prophecies became canonical.

173

politics have taken on a messianic dimension, just as the messianism they entail is almost brutally political.

As Hobbes's thought enters the domain of eschatology, it begins to make use of apocalyptic: both that part of the content of acknowledged revelation which had to do with the acts of God promised for a future, and the doctrines and speculations, for historical reasons largely heterodox or heretical, which had been built up around it. He insists unremittingly on the literal and physical nature of Christ's return, the literal, physical and political character of his kingdom after the resurrection of the saints. It is to be exercised on earth,[44] and indeed from Jerusalem,[45] since "salvation is of the Jews (*ex Judaeis*, that is, begins at the Jews)"; the speculation is of the same order as that which represented the conversion of the Jews as a necessary preliminary to a millennial *regnum Christi*. Formally, Hobbes is not a millennialist, or at least a pre-millennialist, since his kingdom of Christ follows and does not precede the end of this world; [46] but as the allusion to Jerusalem shows, his "world to come" so closely replicates this world that the distinction tends to disappear. On an earth indistinguishable from this one, Christ in his risen human body is to reign for ever over the elect in theirs, and "for ever" has no other meaning than that time as we know it in this life is prolonged *ad infinitum*.[47] The risen saints will neither beget nor die; since Hobbes refuses to accept eternal torment, or any evil greater than personal death, he has the damned resurrected to face the certainty of a second and eternal death, not to be suffered before they have begotten children in the state of damnation, who will continue to all

[44] *Leviathan*, iii, 38 (Oakeshott, pp. 292–96).
[45] *Ibid.* (Oakeshott, pp. 301–3). On p. 294 it seems that the conversion of the Jews must precede the second kingdom.
[46] *Ibid.*, p. 303; also p. 295.
[47] *Ibid.*, iv, 44 (Oakeshott, pp. 411–12); the damned to be renewed "as long as the kind of man by propagation shall endure, which is eternally," *Answer to Bishop Bramhall* (*English Works*, IV, 299): "*God's mercy endureth for ever*, and surely God endureth as long as his mercy; consequently there is duration in God, and consequently endless succession of time."

eternity the generations of men doomed to perish utterly without help from the God who visibly and humanly reigns over them.[48] Since Hobbes could as well have extinguished the damned without allowing them to breed, his theory of damnation is gratuitous; and since he knew more clearly than most men that damnation consists in the deprivation of hope, it appears more than usually abominable. Its importance, however, is that it underlines both the material and the temporal nature of his hereafter. Salvation and damnation both happen in the world of matter and of time. As Hobbes denies that eternity is a *nunc-stans* or "eternal now," and will permit it only to be an infinite prolongation of the time we know,[49] so his "heaven" is located in no spiritual and (until we ask where God is now) hardly any spatial realm, but essentially in time—in the infinite future of the material world.[50] It is this which links his hereafter to the millennium of the Protestant sects; Gerrard Winstanley had already shown that Christ's resurrection could be described exclusively in terms of a transformation of this world's conditions. Again, Hobbes's determination to acknowledge no processes outside the world of matter, space and time led him to follow many radical sectarians and much contemporary higher criticism [51] in propounding the doctrine of mortalism, according to which the soul could have no existence apart from the body, but must perish with it at death and enjoy immortality only with it on resurrection.[52] This too was an apocalyptic heresy: immortality did not consist in the soul's

---

[48] *Leviathan*, iii, 38 (Oakeshott, pp. 296–300); iv, 44 (Oakeshott, pp. 410–12).

[49] *Ibid.*, iv, 46 (Oakeshott, p. 443). *Of Liberty and Necessity* (*English Works*, IV, 271). *Answer to Bishop Bramhall* (*English Works*, IV, 298–300).

[50] *Leviathan*, iii, 38 (Oakeshott, p. 294–95).

[51] G. H. Williams, *The Radical Reformation* (London, 1962), *passim*. George Newton Conklin, *Biblical Criticism and Heresy in Milton* (New York: King's Crown Press, Columbia University, 1949). Nathaniel H. Henry, "Milton and Hobbes: Mortalism and the Intermediate State," *Studies in Philology*, XLVIII (1951), 234–50.

[52] *Leviathan*, iii, 38 (Oakeshott, p. 292); iv, 44 (Oakeshott, pp. 407–12).

existence outside time, but was a gift to be received by the elect in an infinite future. Clearly, what is going on is a conjunction of some kind between Hobbes's philosophical materialism and the apocalyptic and millennialist speculation reaching a high-water mark in England about the time that *Leviathan* was published, a conjunction occurring at the point where salvation could be presented as a temporal, a historical and even a millennial process; and we have to understand this conjunction if we are to understand Hobbes's political eschatology.

Among the radical sects—one has only to mention *Man's Mortalitie*, usually ascribed to the Leveller Richard Overton [53] —such a heresy as mortalism could go hand-in-hand with chiliasm and enthusiasm; the paradox of the doctrine is that it could flourish among mystics whose belief in the primacy of the spirit was so absolute that they saw spirit as immanent in matter to the point where it could by no means be separated from it. Man's spirit was his body and his body his spirit; the resurrection of the one was the resurrection of the other, and it was blasphemy to try to separate the two. Along these lines it was perfectly possible for a devout and even mystical Christian to be a systematic materialist. A hundred years after Hobbes, Joseph Priestley was to combine materialism with millennialism,[54] and in his own day one has but to think of Gerrard Winstanley to be reminded of a cluster of sects subscribing to varieties of materialist pantheism. Hobbes does not share the outlook of these men; it can quite conclusively be shown that his thought does not rest on belief in the primacy of the spirit, but on denial of this belief, but he has to be understood as living in the same

[53] John Canne's edition, giving the author as "R.O.," was dated from Amsterdam in 1649. See W. Haller, *Liberty and Reformation in the Puritan Revolution* (New York, 1955), pp. 175–78; and for doubts about the authorship, Henry, *loc. cit.*, n. 51, above.

[54] See, as introductory to an extensive literature, "Institutes of Natural and Revealed Religion" and "Disquisitions Relating to Matter and Spirit," in *Theological and Miscellaneous Works of Joseph Priestley*, ed. J. T. Rutt (London, 1825), II and III. For the relations of science and millennialism in the eighteenth century, see Ernest Tuveson, *Millennium and Utopia* (Berkeley and Los Angeles, 1949).

world and belonging to the same context in intellectual history. We do not profit by treating him in isolation or by treating him in the light of ideas about materialism and atheism which belong properly to the nineteenth century.

Christianity is a prophetic religion, which cannot wholly escape from depicting the salvation of men as an event taking place in the future; and its insistence on the resurrection of the body imparts a bias towards depicting this event as taking place in the material and even social environment of human life, and therefore in the future of that environment. But these tendencies have always been combated, for reasons which are of vast importance to political thought because they have affected the views men hold of the nature and authority of the Church. St Augustine, and Catholic tradition after him, discouraged thought focused on the idea of a future collective redemption of mankind in time or at its end, and stressed that we were not told much of these things and that what we did know was better interpreted as figurative of the individual soul's redemption and ascent to God. The effect was to divert attention from the diachronic to the synchronic presentation of God's relation to men; instead of human salvation being brought about by a succession of acts performed by the eternal upon the world in time, it appeared rather in terms of the passage of numbers of souls through time to eternity—a passage performed through the actions of pure grace upon the individual's spirit, which however were usually thought of as institutionalized in the sacramental and other channels provided by the organizational Church, exercising in the world of time an authority derived from the eternal. The medieval Church thus rested largely upon the minimization of the eschatological perspective and the diversion of attention from the historical to the institutional; its philosophy correspondingly dealt in terms of the intelligibility of timeless universals in which part of God's reality was accessible to human reason.

As a tactical consequence of this, late-medieval heresy and both the magisterial and the radical Reformations, all bent on undermining the foundations of the institutional Church, commonly adopted arguments which pressed Christian thought back towards the eschatological perspective and its apocalyptic and millenarian forms. (That Calvin himself is an exception is a momentous fact in the history of English Puritanism.) If salvation came through grace, not reason, or through faith, not works, the Christian community might appear not a body of pilgrims ascending the Church's institutional ladder through time into eternity, but a body of faithful situated in time, reading God's word given in the past, commemorating Christ's passion suffered in the past, and reposing faith in a promise which was very largely an undertaking that he would return in the future. Salvation came through this expectation and not through Christ's real presence in the immediate now of the sacramental union; but it followed both that salvation could only come about in time and that Christ himself was seen as operating diachronically. He had come in the past and would return in the future; and salvation itself might be seen as a historical process. Joachim of Calabria, or perhaps rather the Spiritual Franciscans who had adapted his teachings,[55] had depicted the three persons of the Trinity as operating through successive ages to make history a process of the reunion of man with God. In this and other ways, it happened that every statement to the effect that salvation was to be expected in time became a blow struck at the sacerdotal enemy. Eschatology, prophecy and even millennialism became weapons in the armoury of Protestantism, whether the Protestant community was seen as a secular nation organized under its prince or as a gathered congregation separated from his obedience; and scholars have remarked [56] that several sixteenth-century princes took a deep—and, remotely and vaguely, Joachite—interest in the

---

[55] Gordon Leff, *Late Medieval Heresy* (2 vols., Manchester, 1967), I, 68–83.

[56] Frances A. Yates, "Queen Elizabeth as Astraea," *Journal of the Warburg and Courtauld Institute*, X (1947), 27–82, esp. 78–79.

idea that the authority of the Holy Spirit differed somehow from that of the Vicar of Christ. Certainly, a secular prince who had encouraged his subjects to believe that the Kingdom of God or the Age of the Spirit was at hand might live to regret it; such an expectation, especially when couched in millennial terms, might inconveniently underline the transitoriness of his authority, and his divines might make haste to preach that the Son of Man came as a thief in the night and none knew the hour of his coming. But it was the temporal (and so the transitory) nature of his authority which had led him to encourage such ideas in the first place. Prophecy and eschatology formed a device for drawing the process of salvation more fully within the world of time, and so subjecting its outward organization to temporal authority; history (and especially sacred history) was the instrument of the secular power. The adjectives "secular" and "temporal" themselves indicate the primacy of time, and even the apocalyptic of Patmos or Calabria was to a surprising degree a means to secularization.

We are now in a better position to see what Hobbes was about when he made use of the rhetoric of eschatology and apocalyptic. He does not employ the language of Patmos—there are only five references to the Book of Revelation in *Leviathan* and three to the Book of Daniel, none of them very important [57]—but he is engaging in traditional anti-Papal strategy when he reduces the Christian religion to a system of prophecy. All that has happened is that God has pronounced, through the mouths of prophets, certain words in time; the occasions of these pronouncements, together with other happenings to which they refer, constitute a series of divine acts in past time; we believe that these acts were performed by believing the authors and the words which they have relayed to us; these words include foretellings and promises of a resurrection

[57] Oakeshott, pp. 275, 278, 293, 297 (2), Revelation; 263, 299, 365, Daniel.

and a world to come; by believing these among other words, we ensure to ourselves a reward which will be only then, in that future. All is *logos,* and *logos* is a system of communications through time. Since salvation and even eternity are entirely temporal, there can be no Church in the sense of a spiritual institution communicating between time and an eternal now; and Hobbes denies not only purgatory, to do which was orthodox Protestantism, but the separate existence of the soul between the death and resurrection of the body, to do which was less orthodox though intellectually somewhat fashionable, in order to deny that there is a process of salvation occurring outside historical and political time, over which the Church exercises a separate authority that must be obeyed in the here and now.

Neither the use of apocalyptic in *Leviathan,* nor its mortalism and materialist literalism, suffice to place Hobbes outside the mainstream of Protestant thinking. Protestantism was the religion of the word, and the word not only consisted in large measure of a system of prophecies concerning future time, but in its character as a series of utterances required men to think in terms of a time-scheme which it was necessary to express in an eschatological language.[58] But Hobbes's thought is antisectarian as well as anti-Papal, and it is here that his role in the Protestant tradition becomes visibly enigmatic. He set himself to counter the sin of Korah, Dathan and Abiram, who had rebelled against Moses on the ground that "all the congregation are holy, every one of them." [59] If Protestantism was the religion of the word, it was also the religion that exalted the primacy of faith, and the story need not be rehearsed here of how in Puritan thinking the life of faith had become a realm of direct spiritual experience, in which the individual might, and regularly

[58] For the classical modern study of this, see W. Haller, *Foxe's Book of Martyrs and the Elect Nation* (London, 1963). Michael Fixler, *Milton and the Kingdoms of God* (London, 1964), should also be consulted.
[59] *Leviathan,* iii, 40 (Oakeshott, p. 310).

sought to, feel himself the subject of direct action by the will and redemptive mercy of God; or how the word became the vehicle of the spirit, and the spirit—moving rather in the individual than in the congregation or the church—the means of interpreting the word. By 1651, when *Leviathan* appeared, every possible challenge implicit in this development was being publicly articulated and the collision between private inspiration and the authority of the civil magistrate had become a staple of political debate. The far greater attention paid to apocalyptic in *Leviathan* than in *De Cive* may perhaps be a consequence of this. Puritan millennialism was essentially spiritualist: a Joachite Third Age, a Fifth Monarchist thousand-year reign of Christ and his saints were, however literally intended, modes of envisaging a day in which all the elect should be immediately and permanently possessed by the Holy Spirit. But the paradox was that this primacy of the spirit operated against the tendency of apocalyptic to draw salvation back into time and tended rather to restore the eternal now of an earlier Christian tradition. It placed the individual saint where the Church had once been, in an immediate relation to the eternal, and gave him authority originating outside time for his actions within it. There is a relationship between Hobbes's insistence that covenants must be kept [60] and the debates at Putney as to whether men might find authority in their spiritual experience for regarding engagements as superseded; [61] and William Prynne's discovery that Quakers were Franciscans in disguise is only a somewhat idiosyncratic expression of a widespread Erastian realization that the struggle against sectaries was a second front of the war against papists.[62]

[60] *Ibid.*, i, 15 (Oakeshott, pp. 93–94).
[61] A. S. P. Woodhouse, *Puritanism and Liberty* (London, 1948), pp. 9–13, 25–36, 45–52, 86–95.
[62] William M. Lamont, *Marginal Prynne* (London, 1963), explains the curious but contemporary relation between apocalyptic and Erastianism in Prynne's thinking. See also his *Godly Rule: Politics and Religion, 1603–60* (London, 1969).

181

Hobbes, then, set out to destroy "enthusiasm," [63] which he considered a form of madness,[64] the sin of Korah, Dathan and Abiram, a doctrine that must place the authority of prophetic utterance at the disposal of any man who might claim it on grounds that could not be evaluated by his fellows. In attacking Bishop Butler's "very horrid thing" he stood at the outset of a century and a half's Anglican orthodoxy, but the manner of his attack does much to explain why that orthodoxy devoted much of its energy to attacking him. He denies the reality of "enthusiasm" or "inspiration"—defined as the infusion of God's spirit into that of a man—by ruthlessly denying both the reality of "spirit" in the ordinarily accepted sense of the term and the possibility of the individual's directly experiencing God except on the rarest of historic occasions. This denial was conducted by means, and we may be tempted to explain it as the consequence, of Hobbes's philosophical materialism. In a universe consisting of matter and motion "spirit" may be the name of an extremely subtle corporeal substance, or a metaphor helping to express the state of a man's thoughts and feelings, notably—but conventionally—on such occasions as he has heard God's word directly or indirectly; [65] there can be no justification for using it as a nonsense-word to express the ubiquity of a non-substance. Nor can we intelligibly use it to describe any medium of communication between God and man. When God communicates with men he does not enter their bodies himself—the only man in whom "the Godhead dwelt bodily" was Jesus [66] —or blow an extremely subtle wind into their nostrils; [67] nor,

[63] The word is used in *Leviathan*, i, 8 (Oakeshott, p. 49) and iii, 33 (Oakeshott, p. 246). The terms "inspiration" and "infusion" are, however, far more common: i, 3 (Oakeshott, p. 13); i, 8 (Oakeshott, pp. 47–50); iii, 32 (Oakeshott, p. 244); iii, 34 (Oakeshott, pp. 259, 264–65); iii, 36 (Oakeshott, pp. 280–82); iv, 45 (Oakeshott, p. 429); iv, 46 (Oakeshott, p. 445).

[64] *Ibid.*, i, 8 (Oakeshott, pp. 47–50).

[65] *Ibid.*, iii, 34 (Oakeshott, pp. 255–60).

[66] *Ibid.*, iii, 36 (Oakeshott, p. 280); iv, 45 (Oakeshott, p. 429).

[67] *Ibid.*, iii, 34 (Oakeshott, p. 264). When Christ breathed on his disciples, this was a sign (p. 429).

certainly, does he communicate with them through a shared non-substantial being. He speaks to them either mediately, through words, which are systems of motions transmitted through space and time to the senses—in a phrase of St Paul's which Hobbes quotes, "faith comes by hearing" [68]—or by super-natural revelations, of which we do not know very much, but may ask whether they are made by affecting the senses of men or, as in the case of Moses, by means altogether beyond our understanding. The men who receive these revelations—of which there have been none since the deaths of the first apostles —cannot communicate to other men the experiences by which they receive them, and it is only by opinion, faith and public authority—all of which involve the transmission of words—that others believe they were made. It is to such verbal, material, social and historical processes that a man who claims a direct "spiritual" revelation must appeal if he wishes others to accept his claim; he cannot invoke the word "spirit" in order to give himself authority and would do better to avoid its use altogether.

The argument has implications far beyond what can be discussed by elucidating the workings of a system of philosophical materialism. If God cannot be known to us through the operation of his spirit upon ours, he can be known to us, and can work upon us, only through his words, and knowledge of these words is historical knowledge; they were given to us in past time, and both their content and the faith we repose in them have been transmitted through complex social processes taking place in time and involving awareness of their earlier stages. It can be said, furthermore, that the God of revelation and faith acts upon men only through history and is present to them only in history. The God of nature and reason is known to all men through processes which involve no history; but if there have been no revelations and no miracles since the lifetimes of the

---

[68] *Ibid.*, iii, 29 (Oakeshott, p. 212); iii, 43 (Oakeshott, p. 387).

Christians who knew Jesus as a man,[69] then the God who acts positively to rule and redeem his peculiar people is not immediately present to us now. We have nothing of him except his word, and these prophetic and revealed utterances were given in past time and are acting upon us only through the modes of their transmission through subsequent time. Hobbes's God—of whom Bramhall asserted, and Hobbes did not deny, that he existed wholly in time[70]—begins to resemble the *deus absconditus* of modern radical theologians and, as has been the case with some of them, his operations are entirely eschatological. He was in direct relationship with us only when he spoke to us directly; that relationship will be restored only when he speaks to us directly again, which will be—the elect know through their faith in his given word—in his second kingdom which is to come.

Hobbes's nominalism, as well as his materialism, is at work here. By nominalism may be understood—if only for elucidation of the present context—a philosophy which asserts that our knowledge is of words, denoting things that are not to be understood in themselves, so that words are at once all-important to knowledge and imperfect in the knowledge they supply. Hobbes added, of course, that philosophy was a knowledge of the relation between ideas, arrived at by reflection on the content of words and logically certain in itself; but his system of prophecy is not a mere extension of his system of philosophy, and can be discussed without committing us to deciding how far the latter is consistent with the nominalist language which he undeniably uses. Now, a consequence of nominalism in this sense is that God is not to be known through understanding of

[69] *Ibid.*, iii, 37, contains Hobbes's doctrine concerning miracles, which are extraordinary works of God designed to procure credit to an extraordinary minister speaking directly from him. Cf. *Leviathan*, iii, 32 (Oakeshott, p. 246), marginal note: "Miracles ceasing, prophets cease, and the Scripture supplies their place."
[70] Bramhall, *Works*, IV (Oxford, 1844), 523–24; Hobbes, *English Works*, IV (n. 49, above).

his nature, but rather as will or power and through the revelations or prophecies—themselves words—which he wills to make known to us; and a further consequence is that these words may not be fully intelligible, and that what matters is rather the faith by which we acknowledge them to be God's words than the reason by which we apprehend their meaning.

Hobbes's God is one of whom we can know by reason only that he must exist and must be all-powerful. His nature is incomprehensible, and anything we may say about it is no more than language designed to honour his power.[71] When therefore such a God speaks to us, what is required is that we believe and acknowledge the words to be his rather than that our understanding be enriched by their contents; they can communicate to us, and their function is to communicate, primarily a reminder of his power and an injunction to obey him; and Hobbes indicates that nearly all religious and prophetic teaching is reducible to this form, including the injunction to obey and expect the kingdom of God that was and shall be over his peculiar elect. Faith in God's word is little more than acknowledgment of his power; the Ten Commandments,[72] the Old and New Testaments[73] convey little more than reminders and injunctions of that power; and, conversely, it is by the faith we repose in his word that his civil power over us, the subjection of our wills to his, is constituted. His civil and prophetic kingdom rests on a voluntary submission by the elect; we may refuse him that kingdom, or reject him after acceptance as the Jews did, by refusing or withdrawing the measure of faith necessary to constitute it. His word to the elect, given on peculiar occasions, is that his power is; the elect constitute his civil kingdom by believing that he spoke this word on peculiar occasions, through the mouths of peculiar men, and addressed it peculiarly to them. Such a civil kingdom was, from Moses to Samuel,

---

[71] *Ibid.*, ii, 31, *passim;* iii, 34 (Oakeshott, p. 257).
[72] *Ibid.*, iii, 42 (Oakeshott, pp. 339–40); iv, 45 (Oakeshott, p. 424).
[73] *Ibid.*, iii, 33 (Oakeshott, p. 253).

but it ceased to be; Christ, in whom we repose faith as God himself, promised the elect a restoration of that kingdom, but since it visibly does not exist at present, our faith in Christ must be our acceptance that he was God in person, restoring God's kingdom by uttering his word, but that he spoke the word and restored the kingdom in a future tense, by promising that he would come and rule again. Our relation to God is one of civil obedience. God is not here now in such a way that he can be so obeyed, but we ensure ourselves a place in his future obedience by believing that Christ was sent to promise that his kingdom would come again. God's word is invariably command, and our faith in it invariably acknowledgment of a kingdom; but at present we are acknowledging and constituting a future kingdom by believing the author of words uttered in a future tense. By believing that God, who has the power to rule, will come and rule again, we ensure ourselves a place in his kingdom. The whole structure of faith and salvation has been reduced to a system of statements in and about time. This is the inner meaning of Hobbes's premise that the one article of faith necessary to salvation is "Jesus is the Christ." [74]

This radical temporalization of salvation is the consequence of the sharpness of the distinctions Hobbes draws between the traditional trinity of experience, reason and faith; for this alone is sufficient to indicate that statements concerning God's relation to his peculiar people, since they cannot be universals, must be made not a-historically, but at particular times; and if faith is defined both as that by which statements of this order are accepted, and as that by which salvation is effected, then salvation becomes a matter of acceptance of a historical scheme. The content of the statements is of significance mainly as providing the scheme with a future, expectation of which becomes the principal means of salvation; but we are to be saved less because we have faith that God will save us than because we

[74] *Ibid.*, iii, 43 (Oakeshott, pp. 388–93).

186

acknowledge—and thus actualize—his power to do so. In Hobbes's theology, God's power is known to us far more certainly than his mercy or goodness, and we do not so much receive his grace as help to reconstitute his civil kingdom. This is not merely to temporalize Christian salvation, but to politicize it. Faith in and knowledge of God are mere acknowledgments of power; but that power is committed by words it has used, and we are committed by our faith that those words were spoken, to a scheme of its action in time.

The tactical thrust of Hobbes's argument is now clear. It is directed against new presbyter as well as old priest, and against new saint as well as old scholastic—against anyone, that is, who may claim that the process of salvation authorizes his civil actions or power in the present. The tactic of combining apocalyptic with mortalism served, as it always had, to destroy the claim that the Church possessed the keys to an individual's salvation at the hour of his death; he could be saved or damned only by an action which God was to take in the future, and the Church was merely a community of faithful expectant of that future act. Hobbes furthermore directed his radical nominalism against the claim of the schoolmen that there existed a structure of essences through which the character of the eternal might be apprehended by men in time and its actions upon time rendered accessible to reason; we shall see that he regarded the erection of this philosophy as the chief event in the history of the false church or "kingdom of darkness." But he also turned his nominalism against the saints with a systematic demolition of the claims of the spirit, as opposed to the temporal word, to act as the vehicle of salvation in time. The Joachite Spirituals had in their day sought to historize salvation by declaring that the Age of the Son was being superseded by the Age of the Spirit, in which God would be manifest in all men—a belief not unknown among Hobbes's contemporaries,[75] and, despite its revo-

---

[75] Gerrard Winstanley, James Nayler.

lutionary possibilities, capable of vesting the hierarchies of human society with sacerdotal authority. There is one point at which Hobbes's doctrine seems to echo Joachism: he suggests that God's Trinity may be known from his having been personated on earth three times—by Moses and the prophets as the Father, by Jesus as the Son, by the apostles and their successors as the Spirit.[76] But not only does his drastic handling of the term "spirit" render it more than usually difficult for him to give a satisfactory account of the Third Person of the Trinity;[77] the apostolic mission is little more than to represent the Son in his absence, or rather—since we should avoid using the word "represent" in its properly Hobbesian sense—to transmit through time the word that the Son came, redeemed us[78] and promised to return. The Christian present—the time now elapsing between the apostles and the general resurrection—is less a Kingdom of the Spirit than an era in which God is known to his peculiar people through the Word.

It follows that the apostles and their successors are not strictly prophets in either sense of the term. From Moses to Samuel there were, intermittently but frequently, prophets in the sense of *prolocutores*—men to whom God spoke and who relayed his words to the people, and through whom as well as the high priests God exercised his civil kingdom. The prophets of the Exile were *predictores*, men who exercised no civil authority, but were inspired (a metaphor, of course) to foretell the birth of Christ, by whom the kingdom would be restored. When Christ came, he did not restore the kingdom in this world but left words constituting his promise to do so in a future world; and once these words had been spoken by God

---

[76] *Leviathan*, i, 16 (Oakeshott, p. 107); iii, 33 (Oakeshott, p. 253); iii, 41 (Oakeshott, p. 322); iii, 42 (Oakeshott, pp. 323–24). Bramhall, *Works*, IV, 526–27; Hobbes, *English Works*, IV, 306, 310–12, 315–17.

[77] E.g. *Leviathan*, iii, 34 (Oakeshott, p. 265).

[78] For Hobbes's account of the redemption see *Leviathan*, iii, 41 (Oakeshott, pp. 316–17). Christ's three functions, those of a redeemer, a pastor and a ruler, are to be exercised sequentially in time.

himself in human form, there was no need for special revelations to other men which could merely repeat their substance. The apostles themselves, as men who had walked with God, would seem to have possessed extraordinary powers, but these were not transmissible; [79] and God ceased to perform miracles as signs of the authenticity of his word. Now that he had spoken words concerning his return, faith became a simple matter of accepting those words as spoken by him, and this was not to be done on the authority of other men's having received a special commission to speak for him. The age of prophets ended with that of miracles. The word was no longer spoken through chosen men; it had been spoken once and for all—since its content was essentially a promise concerning a future time—and faith was now to be reposed in it as spoken, recorded and transmitted. The business of the faithful was to expect the return (and very little more). They expected that Christ would return through believing that he had said he would, and the church was that organization through which they transmitted his words, and belief in them, to one another. Faith came by hearing.

But Christ, unlike Moses, had left no Tables of the Law, civilly promulgated to the people on a public occasion; since his kingdom was not of this world, i.e. was not then or now, but to come, he could not have done so. Hobbes emphasized, what the scholarship of his age could see well enough, that the New Testament was the result of a process, through which its various books had been written, assembled and recognized as canonical, taking place over time.[80] This brought us back to the problem, with which he had dealt early in *Leviathan*, of the mechanisms of belief and faith. It was not possible altogether to separate belief in the thing spoken from belief in the person speaking— the God of Jews and Christians was therefore especially *logos*,

[79] *Ibid.*, iii, 42 (Oakeshott, p. 351).
[80] *Ibid.*, iii, 33 (Oakeshott, pp. 252–53); iii, 42 (Oakeshott, pp. 338–39, 342, 345).

a God who had spoken [81]—and in the world of human continuity this raised the question of the human transmitter of words formerly spoken. Hobbes's famous remark that the cause of all religious change was "unpleasing priests" [82] was not a mere secularist's joke; he meant that loss of faith necessarily involved loss of credence in persons authorized to transmit belief-systems through social time. But this sort of credence, he had emphasized, meant our continued good opinion of the transmitters; the line of the ruling high priests had ended with the sons of Eli, that of the ruling prophets with the sons of Samuel, precisely because this opinion had been forfeited. It might seem, then, that faith, necessarily a historical and a social phenomenon, rested on no other foundation than the faithful's continued good opinion of the authorized speakers and transmitters of the word; and if the Christian communities had continued as voluntary congregations of believers, this would in fact have been the case. But a great historical transformation had prevented it. Instead, it had happened, either accidentally or providentially (but Hobbes does not state how), that entire civil societies had become Christian and that civil sovereigns had been converted to Christian belief, and this had brought the entire process of the transmission and determination of faith into the domain of public acts performed by civil authority as constituting public corporations. The task of deciding what words were to be believed, what writings regarded as canonical and what authors and doctors considered authentic and authoritative, now ceased to be performed by unincorporated opinion and fell instead to the civil sovereign; faith itself, always a decision,[83] became a public act, only to be performed by one whose authority rested on neither opinion nor faith.

[81] For Christ as the word made flesh see *Leviathan* iii, 36 (Oakeshott, pp. 274–75).

[82] *Ibid.*, i, 12 (Oakeshott, p. 80).

[83] *Ibid.*, i, 7 (Oakeshott, p. 40): "so the last opinion in search of the truth of past and future is called the JUDGMENT, or *resolute* and *final sentence* of him that *discourseth.*"

The sovereign's authority comes into being through the processes of natural civil reason, at least to the extent that reason makes us aware that natural laws exist, have to be obeyed and can be obeyed only in certain conditions, though Hobbes may never have made it plain how men became capable of the acts of fiction and personation by means of which the sovereign was created. At all events, he was not set up by, nor did his authority rest on, either opinion or faith, and we have already seen that there is no chapter of history which we need understand in order to understand this process. If we now ask by what kinds of intelligence the sovereign exercises his functions, that is, of course, a separate question from asking what authorizes him to perform them, and tends to divert our attention from the truth that his *raison d'être* is less to exert intelligence than to perform acts of will; but evidence can no doubt be found to indicate that Hobbes saw the sovereign's intelligence as consisting in civil philosophy rather than civil experience.[84] When we learn therefore that the sovereign, who owes his existence neither to faith nor to history, acquires an unlimited right to take the decisions of which faith consists, in the history which faith constitutes and acknowledges, it is tempting to conclude—something was said of this earlier—that the a-historical has somehow annexed and annulled the historical, and that the sovereign's decisions in matters of faith and observance will be taken with an eye to the needs of civil society and none to the imperatives of Christian belief. But this does not seem to be correct. Reason and nature command—reason indeed tells us that God commands —that we will the existence of civil society and will to give up to the sovereign our power of privately determining our social or public actions; and when the decisions of faith become public actions of public concern, reason commands that they be taken by the sovereign, since to do otherwise would be to erect other authorities, other than civil in their origins, but now

---

[84] This has been the usual interpretation of his *Dialogue of the Common Laws.*

capable of challenging him on his own grounds, which the nature of civil society commands must not be done. But it does not follow that the sovereign's decisions in matters of faith will be determined solely by considerations of the well-being of society. The situation which we are studying has arisen because civil societies and their sovereigns have become involved in the historical world of faith. Since they are so involved they have brought with them the considerations and the forms of intelligence which dictate their own self-perpetuation; but all that has happened is that the mechanisms of faith, the decisions to accept certain words as spoken by God and certain men as authoritatively transmitting them, have left the sphere of opinion and entered that of public obligation. The objects on which the mind is focused in belief—the words and acts said to be those of God, the writings and teachings of men—have not altered and cannot be the objects of rational knowledge. Hobbes may perhaps be shown to have cared too little about the possibility that the sovereign would take his decisions in the field of faith for reasons of civil prudence, but he cannot be shown to have substituted either prudence or philosophy for belief. The distinction he had formally drawn between these three modes of knowledge remained as sharp as ever.

We can now see that Hobbes's religious heterodoxy [85] is of a fideist-sceptical kind, very characteristic of its age, but not to be confused with the deist rationalism of the next century. He found himself faced by scholastics who invested both God and reality with timeless attributes or essences which could be rationally known, and by saints and enthusiasts who affirmed the existence of a world of spirit, operating within time, but giving the time-dwelling individual opportunity of direct contact with the eternal. Both positions seemed to him philosophically absurd because they intruded unreal entities upon the understanding, and politically dangerous because they intruded unreal

[85] Glover (in Brown, *Hobbes Studies*, n. 24, above) has argued the case for a good deal of orthodoxy in his thought as well.

forms of authority upon the government. In reply he asserted a radically nominalist theology, entailing a God of whom nothing could be known except his existence and his infinite power, and rehearsed the great rhythms of the Way of Negation [86] in order to dismiss the God of Greek and scholastic philosophy in favour of a purely Hebrew I AM. It may be that such a God, however much we may stress his simplicity and eternity, is condemned to exist within time, since if we can know nothing of his attributes we can apprehend him solely through his acts; when Bramhall reaffirmed the scholastic doctrine of the *nunc-stans* or eternal now, Hobbes replied that he could attach no meaning whatever to this concept. But in addition there was available, and was just then at the peak of its importance in English thought, an alternative rhetoric of God, in which affirmations concerning him were made not as philosophical attributions, but as historical statements, and he was shown not as exerting a timeless intelligibility, but as affirming his relation to a peculiar people, who could be located only in history, with the result that his acts concerning them must be located there too. Hobbes embraced the concept of the Judeo-Christian elect with the effect of confining the known and positive God within history and still more drastically separating the spheres of reason and faith; a consequence was that when the "mortal god" of political science entered the domain of faith and history, the power he exercised did not amount to a power to change or annul it.

If a God of history could be effectively employed in answer to the God of the schoolmen, he had become a paradigm for the saints and enthusiasts, who employed revelation and apocalypse as means of asserting their immediate spiritual links with him. Hobbes employed both materialist and nominalist weapons to destroy the concept of spirit altogether and leave our contact with God confined to knowledge of his words, and the content

[86] *Leviathan*, ii, 31 (Oakeshott, pp. 237–38).

of those words virtually confined to acts and affirmations of his power. Experience of God was conceivable only in the past and the future, the two times of the existence of his civil kingdom. To orthodox Christians this seemed, understandably and perhaps rightly, incompatible both with Christian faith as they had received it and with the existence of God as they considered they believed in him. But we cannot conclude that it was Hobbes's intention to affirm God's non-existence. He was simply denying that faith could affirm the existence of any but a God of history, and the more he repeated that denial the more he affirmed that God's reality; he was left with the irreducible concept of a God whose being was power, who was believed to have exerted power in the past and to have promised that he would return to exert power in the future, and with a conceptual system that included belief and historical authorities and from which he made no attempt to eliminate them. Having used apocalyptic against the scholastics, he could not eliminate it by further secularization; for if apocalyptic is a device for drawing God back into time, and if secularization is defined as the affirmation of the supremacy of time, then we need more than secularization to destroy apocalyptic. We need the replacement of belief by something else. Hobbes made no attempt to effect such a substitution. He treated belief with epistemological and brutal literalness, but the result was to leave intact the structure of historical authority towards which belief was directed. That structure included a future and an eschatology, and so Hobbes remained—inescapably but with no sign of a will to escape on his part—the author of two prophetic books.

The scheme of God's words and acts in time constitutes sacred history, but the stages by which the word and belief in it have been transmitted through time constitute what may be termed Christian history. This is a history of social communications and social structures, and the sensitivity to the variety of verbal and linguistic communication, characteristic both of late-Renaissance scholarship and of Hobbes's philosophy, makes him sharply aware of it. The history of belief includes both the processes by which the books of Scripture were written, disseminated, authorized and made canonical, and the processes by which Christian communities became coterminous with civil societies and the mechanisms of belief coterminous with the mechanisms of public law. There is another branch of history to which Hobbes's discoursing of religion commits him, and this is a history of error and perversion. He adopted what was long to remain the standard Protestant position that the greater part of the history of the Church consisted of Papal usurpation and its accompanying superstitions. Any polemicist who desires to reject as illegitimate the greater part of an existing and traditional order faces two simultaneous necessities, one for a necessarily somewhat anti-historical account of how things ought to be, the other for a necessarily non-normative account of how they came to be as they deplorably are; and this should warn us against being naïvely surprised when we find historical and unhistorical thinking together in such a man's works.[87] To Hobbes the Papal Church, and in no small measure the Anglican and Presbyterian Churches, all of which seemed to claim a civil authority apart from that of the civil sovereign, were prime examples of that which ought not to be but nevertheless was; and he set himself to explain the divagations from the norm which alone could account for their existence. As regards the Papal Church, there was available a well-established means of doing so. The apocalyptic history prevalent in most Protestant countries, and developed in England chiefly by John Foxe, confidently explained the rise and predicted the downfall of Roman authority by attributing it to the operations of Antichrist, a malign spiritual being operating through time and involved in the eschatology of the Book of Revelation and the subsequent commentaries thereon. This mode of explanation involved intensive reliance on allegory, typology, numerology and the rest of the

[87] I have tried to state this in greater theoretical completeness in essay 7 in this volume.

apparatus of prophetic interpretation. Hobbes had no liking for such intellectual pursuits; he preferred to take his metaphors singly; and, what was of far greater significance, he had carried his antipathy to talk of "spirit" and "spirits" to the point of denying the Devil and all his angels.[88] Apocalyptic for him was a verbal, not a spiritual mystery: not a matter of unveiling the esoteric history of the universe, but one of discovering what God had said he would do. It could therefore contain no account of what might have been done contrary to God's revealed will for mankind; and Hobbes's account of "the kingdom of darkness," the matter of the fourth book of *Leviathan,* rests formally on his express denial that the Pope is to be in any sense identified with Antichrist. This being is indeed mentioned in Scripture, but as one who shall come claiming falsely to be the returning Christ; and however many and various the false claims of the Pope, he has never asserted anything like that.[89] Exegesis is used to destroy mystical interpretation, and the illegitimate authority of Rome is reduced at one blow from the status of spiritual iniquity to that of intellectual error and deception. But the causes of error can be discovered where the mysteries of iniquity cannot, and the way is now open for Hobbes to study the Papal usurpation as a historical phenomenon. It is plain, however, that the explanations he provides originate in the need to provide alternatives for the mystical interpretations of traditional Protestant apocalyptic. The elaborate witticisms in which the Papacy is presented as a "kingdom of fairies" [90]—of unreal essences and authorities—do no more than erect substitutes for the rhetoric in which it appeared the kingdom of Satan and Antichrist, the Beast and the Whore;

---

[88] *Leviathan,* i, 8 (Oakeshott, pp. 50–51); iii, 34 (Oakeshott, p. 263); iii, 38 (Oakeshott, pp. 298–99); iv, 44 (Oakeshott, p. 397); iv, 45 (Oakeshott, pp. 421–22).

[89] *Ibid.,* iii, 42 (Oakeshott, pp. 364–65). Hobbes's point helps to explain the savagery of the punishments inflicted on James Nayler, who did apparently claim to be Christ.

[90] *Ibid.,* iv, 47 (Oakeshott, pp. 457–58).

and the description of the Church as the "ghost" of the Empire, "sitting crowned upon the grave thereof," is both a superb historical image and a piece of secularized apocalyptic—the new Babylon arisen in place of the old and sitting upon seven hills.

The history of error, which in Hobbes takes the place of Protestant apocalyptic history, records the temporary triumph [91] of priestcraft and Gentilism. The former rests on the false assertion that the Church, in some presently constituted form, is or represents the kingdom of God spoken in the Scriptures; on this are based the claims of presbyters, bishops, and above all the Pope, to exercise authority *jure divino* or *Dei gratia*—that is, to derive it from God without the intervention of the civil sovereign. While Hobbes consistently regards Papalism as the paradigmatic and most dangerous instance of this claim, and spends more time refuting it than any other,[92] he includes in his condemnation Laudian bishops,[93] Geneva presbyters [94] and, though only by implication, self-appointed prophets and visible saints; and out of all these he builds up a history of spiritual usurpation that cannot have been read with any pleasure by the dispossessed bishops of the Interregnum. First presbyters, then bishops and finally the Bishop of Rome asserted in the first Christian centuries claims to exercise authority direct from God; and in recent English history these "knots" upon Christian "liberty" [95] have been untied in the reverse order to that in

---

[91] *Ibid.*, iv, 46 (Oakeshott, p. 435): "old empty bottles of Gentilism, which the doctors of the Roman Church, either by negligence or ambition, have filled up again with the new wine of Christianity, that will not fail in time to break them."

[92] There is no Protestant counterpart to the two long refutations of Bellarmine: *Leviathan*, iii, 42 (Oakeshott, pp. 361–83); iv, 44 (Oakeshott, pp. 405–18).

[93] The references are not specific, but are to bishops claiming *jure divino* authority. E.g., *Leviathan*, iii, 42 (Oakeshott, p. 357). Hobbes's thinking here may be compared with that of Prynne; Lamont, *op. cit.*

[94] See the critique of Beza in *Leviathan*, iv, 44 (Oakeshott, pp. 406–7).

[95] Hobbes is speaking of "Christian liberty" in the severely orthodox Protestant sense.

which they were tied up—the Papal power having been destroyed by Queen Elizabeth, that of the bishops who still claimed authority *jure divino* by the presbyterians, and lastly that of the presbyterians by an agency Hobbes does not identify:

> . . . and so we are reduced to the independency of the primitive Christians, to follow Paul, or Cephas, or Apollos, every man as he liketh best; which, if it be without contention, and without measuring the doctrine of Christ by our affection to the person of his minister (the fault which the apostle reprehended in the Corinthians), is perhaps the best . . . there ought to be no power over the consciences of men but of the Word itself, working faith in every one, not always according to the purpose of them that plant and water, but of God himself that giveth the increase.[96]

Hobbes at this moment would have been content—as one suspects the majority of Englishmen would in 1651—with a system of independent congregations under civil rule, no less than with bishops who claimed only a *jure humano* authority, and there is a relationship between this ecclesiological position and the heightening of interest in apocalyptic observable in *Leviathan*. He would not feel that this progressive undoing of the chains of spiritual usurpation presaged the imminent return of Christ, because he did not hold that even faith enabled one to predict one event from another; prophecy enjoined us to expect, but did not empower us to presage. But he had written at length about apocalyptic because this was a necessary means of destroying the spiritual usurpations that England seemed to be overcoming at the end of the Civil Wars; and he was now in a position to argue that the fallacy of spiritual jurisdiction rested on a confusion of the timeless with time. He could not accuse the ecclesiastics (even the saints) of contending that Christ in

[96] *Leviathan*, iv, 47 (Oakeshott, pp. 455–56).

his kingdom had come again; the Papacy was not Antichrist; but he could accuse them of confounding, in his terms, the "kingdom of grace" with the "kingdom of glory," [97] of supposing that because a kingdom was promised for the future they could exercise in the present an authority which could only exist when the kingdom was restored. To make such a claim was to contend that the kingdom existed outside time and that they were its lieutenants within time—to repeat in another form the error of the *nunc-stans*. There was a considerable affinity between this and the error of believing in the doctrine of separated essences, which provides the second theme of the history of the Kingdom of Darkness.

This theme is the history of the importation into the revelation of the true God of the errors of the "Gentiles"—a term to all intents and purposes interchangeable with "Greeks and Romans." [98] The Gentiles, being ignorant of the physical processes of vision, took things which they imagined they saw for gods and disembodied spirits; [99] and later, being equally ignorant of the mental processes of the formation of ideas, took the words which they coined in excessive profusion for the names of real entities. [100] In this way was built up the kingdom of darkness, an empire of "insignificant speech" in which men were ruled by imaginary entities, bodiless and independent of space and time, manipulated by ecclesiastics to provide themselves with spiritual authority: a kingdom of spirits, then, maintained by superstition and scholasticism; a kingdom of ghosts which could only be compared to the kingdom of fairies supposed by folk-imagination to exist as an invisible double of our world, coterminous with it. All this was the result of the importation of Greek thought and mental habit into the revelation made by

[97] *Ibid.*, iii, 35 (Oakeshott, p. 270); iii, 42 (Oakeshott, p. 329); iv, 44 (Oakeshott, p. 399); iv, 47 (Oakeshott, p. 451).

[98] See the account of "Gentile" religion in *Leviathan*, i, 12 (Oakeshott, pp. 73–76).

[99] *Ibid.*, i, 12 (Oakeshott, p. 71); iv, 45 (Oakeshott, pp. 418–19).

[100] *Ibid.*, iv, 46 (Oakeshott, pp. 435–37).

God to the Jews and Christians. Hobbes's hatred of the contemporary universities is very largely a hatred of the Greek heritage which he saw them as carrying on, and which he saw as the foundation of the ecclesiastical conspiracy against civil authority and society.

Set in a different context, of course, this feature of Hobbes's thought appears as the "new philosophy" in revolt against the old, a Galilean and Cartesian rejection of Aristotelianism. But in the context in which it occurs, it depicts Hellenic superstition in opposition to, and as encroaching upon, the prophetic religion of Moses and Christ. One would like to know more about Hobbes's ideas of the historic relation between false philosophy, prophecy and true philosophy. Did the fact that God had revealed himself to the Jews and first Christians as acting and speaking words in time help save them from conceiving the erroneous belief in separated essences, which was only communicated to them by "contagion" from the Hellenized Jews of the Diaspora, the Hellenic and Hellenistic converts of the post-Pauline era? [101] Or was the true revelation helpless to resist false philosophy until the true philosophy had been independently arrived at? Hobbes's need to construct a historical dimension to his thought does not carry him to the construction of answers to these questions. It is plain, however, that he most rigorously separated the Hellenic from the Hebraic components of his cultural tradition and went further than any major philosopher since Augustine in rejecting the former and relying upon the latter. In this he must be most sharply separated from the English and French political deists of the next century, the lineage of Toland and Voltaire—classicists to a man, who sought to reduce the God of prophecy to a theorem in

----

[101] *Ibid.* (Oakeshott, pp. 419–20, 423, 430–35). Cf. Frances A. Yates, *Giordano Bruno and the Hermetic Tradition* (London, Chicago and Toronto, 1964), p. 437: "Thus it may be suggested, the true unifying principle of Mersenne's work [*Quaestiones in Genesim*, 1623] is Moses, an orthodox Moses, who, turning his face against magic, ushers in the new science." Hobbes had known Mersenne and his circle in Paris.

philosophy and, as Hobbes would certainly have predicted, put forward predominantly republican theories of politics in so doing. Hobbes was not of the opinion that Christianity was "reasonable" or "not mysterious," though he defined "mystery" with a razor as sharp as Ockham's and a good deal more recklessly wielded. The Christian mystery to him was the belief that God had spoken in history and had said that he would return in time. The God of prophecy and history was the only God of whom Hobbes would speak; the God of faith was the only God compatible with his political system.

[6]

Burke and the Ancient Constitution:
A Problem in the History of Ideas

THE INTENTION of this paper is to inquire into Burke's doctrine of traditionalism—as it may be termed—from a point of view not quite identical with that usually adopted. The aspect of Burke's thought thus isolated may or may not be the most important or the most characteristic, but it is the most familiar and that with which the student first becomes acquainted. Burke held—to summarize what may be found in a hundred text-books on the history of conservatism—that a nation's institutions were the fruit of its experience, that they had taken shape slowly as the result, and were in themselves the record, of a thousand adjustments to the needs of circumstance, each one of which, if it had been found by trial and error to answer recurrent needs, had been preserved in the usages and established rules of the nation concerned. He also held that political knowledge was the fruit of experience and that reason in this field had nothing to operate on except experience; from which it followed that, since the knowledge of an individual or a generation of individuals was limited by the amount of experience on which it was based, there was always a case for the view that the reason of the living, though it might clearly enough discern the disadvantages, might not fully perceive the advantages of existing and ancient institutions, for these might contain the fruits of more experience than was available to living individuals as the sum of their personal or reported experience of the world. It also followed that since the wisdom embodied in institutions was based on experience and nothing but experience, it could not be completely rationalized: that is, reduced to first principles which might be clearly enunciated, shown to be the cause of the institutions' first being set up, or employed to criticize their subsequent workings. There was, in short, always more in laws and institutions than met the eye of critical reason, always a case for them undiminished by anything that could be said against them.

All this is, of course, no more than elementary Burke, the first lesson learnt by every student of his thought. This essay is concerned with the way in which its presence in his thought should be historically explained. The account of political society here given is in a fairly obvious sense anti-rationalist: it endows the community with an inner life of growth and adaptation, and it denies to individual reason the power to see this process as a whole or to establish by its own efforts the principles on which the process is based. Burke's thought can, therefore, properly be set in opposition to any rationalist system of politics which presents political society as based on the assent of individual minds to universal principles rationally discerned. Such systems, of course, abounded in the eighteenth century, and Burke opposed these where he met with them. But this does not of itself justify us in supposing that the historical origins of Burke's thought are necessarily to be found in a reaction against political rationalism, as if the latter had conditioned all political thinking before his time and some special explanation needed to be found of his breaking with it. Yet many studies of his thought have been and perhaps still are based upon some such presumption. Meinecke and Sabine, for example, both supposed that the thought of Burke must be regarded as an effect and consequence of Hume's critique of rationalism,[1] and when Meinecke was constrained to admit that there was not enough evidence of Burke's having read Hume at the critical time, he fell back on the untestable hypothesis that Hume's teachings were "in the air"[2] and had infected Burke as a species of *influenza*. He was assuming that only some basic change of philosophical viewpoint could account for Burke's not conforming to a political rationalism which had hitherto dominated thought; and the assumption rests on a complex of misunderstandings which are still all too common among historians of ideas. We tend in the first place to assume that the ideas of a major thinker must be explained by co-ordinating them in a unified philosophy and discovering the common metaphysical or epistemological foundation on which they all rest; and we tend in the second place to simplify our field by the method of dialectical projection, by assuming that the thought of a particular period may be characterized as founded on certain common philosophical foundations and that the thought of the succeeding periods must be shown to have come into being as a result of some shift in these foundations. These methods are justified in some circumstances, but it is a misunderstanding to suppose that they must be adopted in all; and where we do not suppose this, some other means must be found of offering historical explanations of a man's ideas. We now know, for example, that Locke's political thought is not a simple extension of his philosophy, but an explanation of contemporary political experience offered to his contemporaries in one, and not the only one, of the modes of discourse they were accustomed to adopt.[3] The history of ideas may legitimately, though

[1] F. Meinecke, *Die Entstehung des Historismus* (2nd ed., Munich, 1946), part I, ch. VI; G. H. Sabine, *A History of Political Theory* (New York, 1945), ch. XXIX, pp. 605–7, 612, 614, 618.

[2] Meinecke, *op. cit.*, p. 278.

[3] P. Laslett, ed., *John Locke: Two Treatises of Government* (Cambridge, 1960), introduction; John Dunn, *The Political Thought of John Locke* (Cambridge, 1969).

not exclusively, be viewed as the history of the modes of explaining the world and its behaviour which have from time to time existed. Burke said clearly of his doctrine of traditionalism that it was a way of thinking which existed in the England of his time and had existed for so long that it was itself traditional. In this paper an attempt will be made to see if he was right in this assertion, and if so what the consequences may be for the historical understanding of his thought.

We may conveniently begin with a passage from the *Reflections on the Revolution in France* which, like most of the quotations from Burke to be made in this paper, is familiar to all students and is cited here in an attempt to establish the proper context in which it may be understood.

The third head of right, asserted by the pulpit of the Old Jewry, namely, the "right to form a government by ourselves," has, at least, as little countenance from any thing done at the Revolution, either in precedent or in principle, as the two first of their claims. The Revolution was made to preserve our *antient* indisputable laws and liberties, and that *antient* constitution of government which is our only security for law and liberty. If you are desirous of knowing the spirit of our constitution, and the policy which predominated in that great period which has secured it to this hour, pray look for both in our histories, in our records, in our acts of parliament, and journals of parliament, and not in the sermons of the Old Jewry, and the after-dinner toasts of the Revolution Society. In the former you will find other ideas and another language. Such a claim is as ill-suited to our temper and wishes as it is unsupported by any appearance of authority. The very idea of the fabrication of a new government is enough to fill us with disgust and horror. We wished at the period of the Revolution, and do now wish, to derive all we possess as *an inheritance from our forefathers*. Upon that body and stock of inheritance we have taken care not to inoculate any cyon alien to the nature of the original plant. All the reformations we have hitherto made, have proceeded upon the principle of reference to antiquity; and I hope, nay I am persuaded, that all those which possibly may be made hereafter, will be carefully formed upon analogical precedent, authority and example.

Our oldest reformation is that of Magna Charta. You will see that Sir Edward Coke, the great oracle of our law, and indeed all the great men who follow him, to Blackstone, are industrious to prove the pedigree of our liberties. They endeavour to prove, that the antient charter, the Magna Charta of King John, was connected with another positive charter from Henry I, and that both the one and the other were nothing more than a re-affirmance of the still more antient standing law of the kingdom. In the matter of fact, for the greater part, these authors appear to be in the right; perhaps not always; but if the lawyers mistake in some particulars, it proves my position still the more strongly; because it demonstrates the powerful prepossession towards antiquity, with which the minds of all our lawyers and legislators, and of all the people whom they wish to influence, have been always filled; and the stationary policy of this kingdom in considering their most sacred rights and franchises as an inheritance.[4]

Now, before assuming that this passage must be explained by attributing to Burke possession of any general theory of man and society, we can take one by one the statements of which it consists, and see both what is being said in them and to what order of statement they belong. Burke is simultaneously advocating and making an appeal to history—to "records, and acts of parliament, and journals of parliament"—and making a series

[4] Burke, *Reflections on the Revolution in France*, in *Works* (Bohn's Libraries ed., 1901), II, 304–5.

of statements about history; for he is saying that the practice of establishing the rules of political behaviour by an appeal to history conducted in this manner has been followed so regularly in the course of English history that it now constitutes a tradition of behaviour, a "stationary policy" which he hopes and believes will be maintained in future. The Revolution of 1688, he says, was conducted on the principle that there existed a body of ancient laws and liberties, and an ancient constitution guaranteeing them, and that all that was necessary in the conditions of that critical year was to reaffirm their existence; it was not conducted on the principle that under certain circumstances power "reverts to the society" and the people have a right to "erect a new form . . . as they think good." [5] Rights are not justified by abstract reason, but as an inheritance under positive laws; but for this assertion to have validity, it is necessary that the positive laws be as old as, or older than, the rights which they substantiate and—almost—the society which contains them. From Coke to Blackstone, Burke observes, the great English lawyers have steadily maintained that this is in fact the case with English law: that the laws and liberties of England are rooted in Magna Carta, and the Charter of 1215 in a body of law very much more ancient than itself. Burke inspects this historical statement; he thinks it very largely accurate, but adds that the fact that it has so constantly been made is of greater significance than the accuracy of its contents, because it demonstrates that Englishmen have always been concerned to establish their rights by appeal to their own past and not to abstract principles. This habit of mind he considers the most important fact in the history of English political behaviour.

Burke is talking history; he is discussing both a traditional interpretation of English history and the part which that interpretation has itself played in shaping English history; and the his-

---

[5] The words in quotation marks are, of course, from the closing sentence of Locke's *Second Treatise*. Burke did not mention that work in this part of the *Reflections*.

torical facts to which he alludes are such as we may ourselves discern and describe in terms not unlike his own. There really did exist a habit of conducting political discussion in England "upon the principle of reference to antiquity," upon the assumption that there existed an ancient constitution which was the justification of all rights and was itself justified primarily by its antiquity. The public and authorized theory of what had occurred in 1688–89—that on which the houses of the convention parliament had been able to agree and which was contained in the public documents of the time—really did base its interpretation on the doctrine of the ancient constitution, more than on the doctrines of contract, natural right and reason propounded by Sidney or Locke. The interpretation of history which that doctrine necessitated—involving the assertion that Magna Carta confirmed a charter of Henry I, which confirmed a charter of William I, which confirmed the laws of Edward the Confessor, which were themselves no more than a codification of law already ancient—had, as Burke remarks, been constantly put forward by lawyers from Coke to Blackstone. It was consequently still a living issue in Burke's own time; he feels called upon to comment on its truth or falsity, and though he has enough historical detachment to feel interested primarily in its significance as a long-held belief, its truth as history seems to him to be well established. What he is saying, then, is not a piece of antiquarian's lore, but an account of contemporary practice. This is how we conduct our politics, he is saying; how we have always conducted them. He is not calling upon his contemporaries to return to a seventeenth-century habit of mind, but assuming that it is still alive and meaningful among them. It will be of some significance to our understanding of Burke's thought if we decide that he was right in this assumption.

The plot thickens and becomes more suggestive when we observe that the habit of mind denoted by the term "ancient constitution" had already—during the seventeenth century—produced and given expression to ideas very like those of Burke's traditionalism, and (though this is of less importance) that Burke had some opportunity of knowing this. It is the evidence for such an assertion that we must next review, though it involves some repetition of what has been said elsewhere.[6]

The doctrine of the ancient constitution received its classical formulation, though probably not its original conception, about the year 1600. It was the work of common lawyers, and seems to have been shaped throughout by assumptions concerning the common law of England, deeply implanted in the mind of everyone trained in that study. These assumptions were first, that all the law in England might properly be termed common law; second, that common law was common custom, originating in the usages of the people and declared, interpreted and applied in the courts; third, that all custom was by definition immemorial, that which had been usage and law since time out of mind, so that any declaration of law, whether judgement or (with not quite the same certainty) statute, was a declaration that its content had been usage since time immemorial. These assumptions were now made the framework of an interpretation of history, one based on record, axiom and judgement rather than the statements of chroniclers and, therefore, containing at every turn the presumption that law was immemorial. It therefore became possible to believe that the whole framework of English law and (when that term came into use) the "constitution"—meaning the distribution by law of powers of declaring and applying the law—had existed from the obscure beginnings of English history, from a time earlier than the earliest historical evidences. Legal history, read upon the assumptions which were native and instinctive to a common lawyer, became a series of declarations that the law was immemorial. In this way grew up an elaborate body of myths, maintained with great tenacity by Englishmen of the seventeenth century and after, which taken

[6] What follows is to some extent a development and reformulation of some points made in Pocock, *The Ancient Constitution and the Feudal Law* (Cambridge, 1957), chs. II, VII and IX.

together form the cult of the "ancient constitution." It has elsewhere been argued that the idea of immemorial law was one of the cardinal political ideas of Stuart England; and since it has been found to have appeared, based consistently on the same assumptions, in every major controversy and in the mind of every important political thinker from Coke to Locke, the hypothesis has received some verification. This, then, is the doctrine and the habit of mind which Burke describes as "the stationary policy of this kingdom." [7]

It may be further characterized as the habit of interpreting English politics and society not with the aid of any political theory designed for the explanation of society in general, but in the light of those assumptions about English society which were already contained in its most distinctive and characteristic body of rules. That body of rules was the common law and when English political thought committed the supreme insularity of assuming that English politics and history already contained all that was necessary to their understanding, and did not require to be studied in the light of any foreign law or universal principle, it was to the unique character of the common law that English thinkers were referring. Of this Burke seems to have realized something; in a passage [8] closely following on the one already quoted, he speaks again of the age-old English practice of claiming their liberties

> as an *entailed inheritance* derived to us from our forefathers, and to be transmitted by us to our posterity; as an estate especially belonging to the people of this kingdom without any reference whatever to any other more general or prior right.

He goes on to say that this practice is "the happy result of following nature, which is wisdom without reflection and above it."

[7] For the foregoing see *Ancient Constitution*, ch. ii and generally.
[8] Burke, *op. cit.*, p. 306.

Whatever advantages are obtained by a state proceeding on these maxims, are locked fast as in a sort of family settlement; grasped as in a kind of mortmain for ever. By a constitutional policy, working after the pattern of nature, we receive, we hold, we transmit our government and our privileges, in the same manner in which we enjoy and transmit our property and our lives.[9]

Now the way of thinking and behaving which Burke is here recommending was founded upon an identification of the rules and spirit of English society with the rules and spirit of the common law; and the common law had taken shape as a law of real property. It cannot be quite coincidental that in these passages Burke is talking of the advantages which accrue when a people lay claim to their liberties on exactly the same principles as those on which they inherit their estates. From the words which have just been quoted he goes on without interruption to embark upon the famous passage which runs:

The institutions of policy, the goods of fortune, the gifts of Providence, are handed down, to us and from us, in the same course and order. Our political system is placed in a just correspondence and symmetry with the order of the world, and with the mode of existence decreed to a permanent body composed of transitory parts; wherein, by the disposition of a stupendous wisdom, moulding together the great mysterious incorporation of the human race, the whole, at one time, is never old, or middle-aged, or young, but in a condition of unchangeable constancy, moves on through the varied tenour of perpetual decay, fall, renovation, and progression.

This has many times been cited as evidence of Burke's vision of society as an organic community, not composed atomistically of self-regarding individuals; and so indeed it is. But if we seek

[9] Burke, *op. cit.*, p. 307.

for the historical genesis of these thoughts, may it not lie in the chain of association formed by the words "entail," "family settlement," "mortmain," "incorporation," which occur in that order in the passages that have been quoted? "In this choice of inheritance," Burke says, "we have given to our frame of polity the image of a relation in blood." [10] That is, we have made the state a family; but have we not done so by constituting it a family in the sense in which a family is a relation in law? By entailing our inheritance of liberties we have established a family settlement, based upon a mortmain; and it is when this is done, not in virtue of the tie of blood solely, that the family becomes an immortal corporation. We have made the state not only a family, but a trust; not so much a biological unity, or the image of one, as an undying *persona ficta,* which secures our liberties by vesting the possession of them in an immortal continuity. And all this has been done by the simple device—the most superb of all legal fictions—of identifying the principles of political liberty with the principles of our law of landed property. Burke sees this as an act of conformity with the order of nature, and it is not the intention of this essay to deny the importance which his conception of nature had in the formation of his political philosophy. But the above passages may at the same time be cited as evidence that he had achieved a genuine historical insight into the character of English political thinking. He says, quite explicitly, that it is the greatest accomplishment of our thought to have based our claim to liberty on an idea drawn from the law of real property; and historical inquiry seems to confirm that it was the influence of that law on political thought which had given rise to the very English way of thinking and behaving which Burke accurately describes, and with which he identifies himself.

It has now to be shown that a doctrine of traditionalism, very much akin to Burke's own, grew out of the concept of the an-

[10] Burke, *ibid.*

cient constitution. To do this we need to remind ourselves that this concept was founded on the identification of English law with custom, and that the term custom had more than one connotation for common lawyers. Primarily, it implied that all that was custom was immemorial; but this need not—though it often did—imply a static and unchanging content. A second implication, of no less importance than the first, was that custom was constantly being subjected to the test of experience, so that if immemorial it was, equally, always up to date, and that it was ultimately rooted in nothing other than experience. We may put the point in the words of Sir John Davies, James I's Attorney-General for Ireland, who had written: "the *Common Law of England* is nothing else but the *Common Custome* of the Realm." [11] The essence of this law was in immemorial usage; it consisted of a series of "reasonable acts once done," which, having been found "good and beneficial to the people," had been repeated "without interruption time out of mind" and so had become a law recognized, declared and recorded as such in the courts of common law. The act itself was nothing but a response to experience, and the test by which it had been found good and beneficial nothing but further experience. From about 1600, probably from much earlier, this concept lay at the heart of English thinking about law and exerted a potent influence on thinking about politics and society. It will be observed that though Davies refers to the act in usage as "reasonable," he nowhere suggests that its rationality was the proof that it was good and beneficial, still less that reason gave it the force of law. No doubt he regarded usage and experience as in some sense or other rational behaviour, but he does not equate law with reason; and both in his writings and in Coke's, signs may be found that common lawyers were already disposed to draw a distinction between the wisdom of the law, founded in experience, and the reflective reason of individuals, which they re-

[11] Davies, *Irish Reports* (1614—London ed. of 1674), Preface.

garded as a different instrument designed to produce different and perhaps lesser results.

Two famous quotations from Coke may make the point for us. The first is from his notorious and variously reported interview with James I.

> Then the king said, that he thought the law was founded upon reason, and that he and others had reason as well as the judges: to which it was answered by me, that true it was, that God had endowed his Majesty with excellent science, and great endowments of nature; but his Majesty was not learned in the laws of his realm of England, and causes which concern the life, or inheritance, or goods, or fortunes of his subjects are not to be decided by natural reason, but by the artificial reason and judgment of law, which law is an act which requires long study and experience before that a man can attain to the knowledge of it.[12]

The other is from *Calvin's Case:*

> our days upon the earth are but as a shadow in respect of the old ancient days and times past, wherein the laws have been by the wisdom of the most excellent men, in many successions of ages, by long and continuall experience, (the trial of light and truth) fined and refined, which no one man, (being of so short a time) albeit he had in his head the wisdom of all the men in the world, in any one age could ever have effected or attained unto.[13]

In both these passages Coke's contention appears to be the same. Philosophic reason could not by its own efforts reconstruct the law, because the law's origin is not in any philosophical assumption but in a multitude of particular decisions. The only way to know the law, therefore, is to know the law, by becoming acquainted with the innumerable decisions and digests of decisions which it contains. Selden believed that a deeper un-

[12] Coke, *Twelfth Reports*, Prohibitions del Roy (12 Co. Rep. 65).
[13] Coke, *Seventh Reports*, Calvin's Case (7 Co. Rep. 3b).

derstanding of the law could be attained by historical knowledge of the circumstances in which the various decisions had been taken, but Coke gives no sign of believing even that; for him, there was little to be known about the history of the law except that it was immemorial. No one man, by taking thought, could reproduce the infinitely complex train of experiences and decisions which had led the law to be what it was; and Coke seems also to be denying that there exist any means whereby the intellect can, by laying down axioms, assumptions or universal propositions, reproduce the law as a process of reasoning. The law, in short, cannot be reduced to general principles, or scientific laws, and their consequences; and in this very lawyer-like proposition we seem to have one origin of the long tradition of sceptical and conservative empiricism in English social thought. If so, the long outmoded concept of immemorial law has done much to make our thought what it is today; for it was the principle that the law was immemorial that made common lawyers realize that its origin was not in men's assent to universally acceptable propositions, but in "one emergency following upon another as wave follows wave; only one great fact with respect to which, since it is unique, there can be no generalizations." [14]

It seems, then, that an empirical and traditionalist way of thought, sceptical of systematic reason, formed part of the intellectual equipment of common lawyers and was grounded on the same assumptions as belief in the ancient constitution. With the next step in the story, we arrive at the first direct clash in the history of English political theory between this outlook and the rationalism which we learn from Burke to regard as its antithesis. A few years after the Restoration Thomas Hobbes completed his *Dialogue of the Common Laws*, and in this work set out to deny that the law of England was either immemorial custom or Coke's "artificial reason." [15] To Hobbes, consistent in this dialogue with the ideas of his major political

[14] H. A. L. Fisher's preface to his *History of Europe* (London, 1946), v.
[15] Hobbes, *English Works* (ed. Molesworth, 1839–45), VI, 5–7, 14–15, 62–63.

works, society was composed of and by individuals employing their "natural reason," which dictated to the individual that certain things must be done for his own preservation and, later, that certain things must be done by all for the preservation of all. To enforce the doing of these things a sovereign was set up, and doing them became a law for all when established as such by his command. But he did not possess more "natural reason," let alone reason of another sort, than that possessed by other men, and it was by the natural reason that he shared with his subjects that the laws he enjoined were seen to be necessary. All that was artificial about the sovereign was his power to command. Any doctrine of an artificial reason, known only to professionals as their craft mystery and ultimately inscrutable to reflective reason, appeared to Hobbes dangerous alike to the human mind and to the stability of the state, as tending to monopolise power in the hands of Bentham's Judge and Co. He therefore found it necessary to maintain that law was the product of natural reason and should be such as any intelligent individual might frame for himself; and in so far as the reason he spoke of was scientific, arguing logically from universal truths, Hobbes maintained the possibility of a social science. This was the ground on which he was met by Chief Justice Sir Matthew Hale—though Hale's reply remained unfinished and unpublished [16]—and both here and in his *History of the Common Law*, Hale set out in opposition to individualistic rationalism an empirical and traditionalist view of the law which can be shown to be founded on the common-law concept of custom.

Hale was a philosopher as well as a judge—though his philosophy was as case-made as his law—and he began his reply to

[16] It is printed as an appendix (pp. 499–513) to Vol. V of W. S. Holdsworth's *History of English Law* (London, 1924). A hint at the date of its composition may be found in John Aubrey's letter of 3 February 1673, in which he seeks to further the publication of a work on law by Hobbes, saying that Hale "has read it and much mislikes it" (*Brief Lives*, ed. Clark, 1898, I, 394). It is very improbable that Aubrey is referring to the *Elements of Law*, as some scholars have concluded.

Hobbes with epistemological considerations. Reason, he said, was the faculty of discerning the necessary connexions between things, and a man became expert at law, medicine or some other form of learning as he applied this faculty to different classes of things; so that, though the same faculty of reason might be at work in all cases, a man expert in one field might be hopelessly inept in another—it was the things of which a man had experience that determined the character of his knowledge, and the notion of a naturally reasonable individual who became, simply by applying his reason, good at making and applying laws must therefore be dismissed.[17] Law was a matter of applied morals, and this field was a specially complicated one; for the fact that a man was expert at moral philosophy, that is at discerning the connexions between moral ideas, was no guarantee of his success in applying these ideas to practical decisions. This was a class of problem in which Hale thought a power of discerning necessary connexions likely to be of very little use, for he was above all impressed with the complexity and instability of the human context in which such decisions had to be taken, and was disposed to regard each decision not as the recurrence of a regular phenomenon but as something unique. Two quotations may help to make his thought clear.

> . . . it is a thing of greatest difficulty, So to Contrive and Order any Lawe that while it remedyes or provides against one Inconvenience, it introduceth not a worse or an equall . . . the texture of Humane affairs is not unlike the Texture of a diseased bodey labouring under Maladies, it may be of so various natures that such Phisique as may be proper for the Cure of one of the maladies may be destructive in relation to the other, and the Cure of one disease may be the death of the patient.[18]

This instability of context affected not only the practical but the moral problem:

[17] Holdsworth, op. cit., V, 501–2.   [18] *Ibid.*, p. 503.

> . . . every Morall Action is or may be diversified from an-
> other by Circumstances which are of soe greate an Influ-
> ence into the true nature and determination of Morall
> Actions that they very frequently specifically difference
> Actions that are materially the Same, and give such Allayes
> and abatements or advances and improvements to them
> that Scarce two Morall Actions in the world are every way
> commensurate. And these Circumstances are Soe various
> and their Influx into Morall Actions so different and Soe
> difficult to be discerned, or adequately estimated, that the
> makeinge of Laws touching them is very difficult.[19]

Here, plainly, we have the social philosophy of a judge, a man
accustomed to viewing each moral problem on its merits as it
comes before him, and to viewing it as entangled in the endlessly complex web of practical social reality. This alone might
explain Hale's disposition to view each problem as a unique
complexity and to doubt whether there exist universally valid
patterns of thought with which natural reason may legislate for
society—to doubt, in short, the efficacy of a social science. But
we cannot leave out of account the further fact that Hale was
accustomed to dealing with such problems with the aid of a law
which already insisted that there were no universally valid rules,
only accumulated experience, and that the only outcome of experience was a precedent which never achieved finality as a universal rule. It is law of this kind which Hale goes on to recommend as an artificial reason more effective and reliable than
Hobbes's natural reason. Directly after the words last quoted,
we find him advocating reliance on ancient law in preference
to the dictates of individual reason, and his argument for doing
so comes in a double form. In the first place, he argues that experience does what reason cannot do—it finds out the "con-
veniences and inconveniences" that attend the operation of a
particular law, which the complexity and instability of the social
context render it impossible "for the wisest Council of Men

[19] *Ibid.*, p. 504.

att first to foresee." Secondly, and in consequence of this, he argues that ancient laws very often defy our criticisms, for the reason that while we have the law itself we no longer know the circumstances in which, or the reasons for which, it was originally made. Therefore we cannot criticize those reasons; but the mere fact that the law survives furnishes a presumption, not only that the law was originally good, but that it has adequately answered the needs of all the situations in which it has subsequently been invoked. There is a further presumption that it will adequately solve our problem, even though to our intellects, evaluating the problem and the law, it may not appear likely to do so.

From all this it seems to follow that the law is inscrutable; it is reasonable, Hale says, but our reason cannot tell why. Historical reconstruction cannot tell us, since the law itself may be the only evidence we have concerning its history; philosophical consideration cannot tell us, because the law is nothing but a record of particular decisions and is not founded on any universal rational propositions. It can only be known as a collection of particulars.

> Now if any the most refined Braine under heaven would goe about to Enquire by Speculation, or by reading of Plato or Aristotle, or by Considering the Laws of the Jewes, or other Nations, to find out how Landes descend in England, or how Estates are there transferred, or transmitted among us, he wou'd lose his Labour, and spend his Notions in vaine, till he acquainted himselfe with the Lawes of England, and the reason is because they are Institutions introduced by the will and Consent of others . . . the Positions and Conclusions in the Mathematicks have more Evidence in them, and are more Naturally Seated in the minde than Institutions of Laws, which in a greate measure depend upon the Consent and appointment of the first Institutors.[20]

[20] Holdsworth, *op. cit.*, V, 505.

The law does not consist of first principles and their logical consequences, the necessary connexions between which can be known by reason. It consists of a series of particular decisions, each of which was framed in circumstances no longer known and has been tested by experience in circumstances which may similarly have been forgotten. All that need—very often all that can—be known of it is that it survived an indefinite number of such tests, and this is enough to create a presumption that it is more efficacious than our intellects can comprehend. Such is Hale's reply to the rationalism of Thomas Hobbes, a reply which visibly gives expression to the social philosophy of the common law and is essentially a development of common-law assumptions concerning the law and its workings. Only an immemorial customary law could satisfy Hale's requirements or give birth to his ideas, for if law were founded on the decisions of known men in recorded circumstances it could be evaluated and criticized both on rational and on historical grounds and would lose the ultimate inscrutability with which Hale, a sceptical traditionalist, is seeking to invest it. There is little about custom in the reply to Hobbes, but in his *History of the Common Law*[21] Hale worked out, at length and with subtlety, a view of law as immemorial custom in perpetual adaptation.

On his interpretation of immemorial law, it was not necessary that it should have retained its present content since time beyond memory, for law consisted solely in a series of responses to particular exigencies and what rendered it immemorial was not the stability of its content but the continuity (since time beyond memory) of the process of adapting old precedents to new situations. As this process continued the old precedent became, by degrees and generally insensibly, both refined and enlarged, until it took on a meaning beyond anything those who

[21] This too was published posthumously in 1714. Since Hobbes's *Dialogue* was unpublished until 1682, the whole story of the contact between these two minds, of some importance to the understanding of the recurrent themes in English political thought, was overlooked until Holdsworth and Pollock brought it to light.

first established it could have intended. Therefore, one would not seek to know the meaning of a law by going back to the circumstances of its first institution, and indeed in most cases neither these nor the subsequent stages of its development could be accurately known. Hale united a subtle sense of historical growth with a high degree of scepticism as to the possibility of historical knowledge, and in this as in all else he was a true common lawyer in his thought. He regarded the records of the law as very nearly all the evidence existing concerning the history of the law, and these records, as he knew, did not often rehearse the circumstances in which they had been made and were in essence little more than a series of declarations of what the immemorial law was, through which nevertheless ran a thread of almost imperceptible change. Hale, therefore, despaired of knowing when any particular point in the law had originated, or of recovering its original meaning from its successive reformulations, or of establishing what the state of the law as a whole had been at any moment in time past; nor did he think that this mattered.[22] To him the law was in flux, constantly being restated by people, parliament and judges in response to their immediate practical needs, and what was of importance was that they had chosen to do this rather by restating old decisions than by creating new out of their rational estimate of each situation as it arose. Because they operated in this manner the law was perpetually in change and you could neither analyse what it was nor reconstruct its history; but they were constantly drawing on and applying the accumulated experience of their ancestors, even though they could not explain what it was nor demonstrate its rationality. Hale repeatedly uses the image of law as a river, and what matters to him is not the analysis of the water it contains but the unchecked continuity of its flow. Society constantly produces law; doing this by refin-

[22] The key passage for the above interpretation of Hale's thought is in ch. IV of his *History of the Common Law* (2nd ed., 1716, pp. 57–65). See also *Ancient Constitution*, pp. 174–78.

ing on old precedents, it accumulates a wisdom which is rooted in experience and never rationally demonstrable or capable of analysis into its elements. It is the fact that it is the record of society's experience that makes law immemorial.

Such is Sir Matthew Hale's philosophy of the common law; its kinship with the traditionalism we ascribe to Burke should be evident. The question now to be settled is that of the connexions between Burke and the common-law thought of the seventeenth century, and here we may begin by reminding ourselves that Burke alluded to the belief in an immemorial constitution as a thing well known to himself and his readers, of peculiar importance to the understanding of seventeenth-century constitutional history, and as a way of thinking still alive in his own time. Burke was then aware of common-law thought both as a phenomenon of the seventeenth century, and as a phenomenon of the eighteenth; and it may be worth commencing under the former head and investigating his knowledge of Hale as the common-law theorist whose ideas most resembled his own. There is no evidence to demonstrate that he knew the manuscript reply to Hobbes, though there were copies in the Harleian MSS. and in the collection of Francis Hargrave; [23] but the *History of the Common Law* was one of the standard books of the eighteenth century, and in an early work from Burke's hand we have his opinion of it. That opinion is unfavourable, but illuminating. There is a fragment, which may date from about Burke's thirtieth year, known under the title of *Essay Towards a History of the Laws of England*; after remarking that few attempts have been made to provide such a history, he continues:

> Lord Chief Justice Hale's History of the Common Law is, I think, the only one, good or bad, which we have. But with all the deference justly due to so great a name, we may venture to assert that this performance, though not with-

[23] Holdsworth, *op. cit.*, V, 499.

out merit, is wholly unworthy of the high reputation of its author: the sources of our English law are not well, nor indeed fairly, laid open; the ancient judicial proceedings are touched in a very slight and transient manner; and the great changes and remarkable revolutions in the law, together with their causes, down to his time, are scarcely mentioned.

Of this defect I think there were two principal causes; the first, a persuasion hardly to be eradicated from the minds of our lawyers, that the English law has continued very much in the same state from an antiquity to which they will allow hardly any sort of bounds. The second is, that it was formed and grew up among ourselves; that it is in every respect peculiar to this island; and that if the Roman or any foreign laws attempted to intrude into its composition, it has always had the vigour to shake them off, and return to the purity of its primitive constitution.

These opinions are flattering to national vanity and professional narrowness. . . . we have been, and in a great measure still are, extremely tenacious of them. If these principles are admitted, the history of the law must in a great measure be deemed superfluous. For to what purpose is a history of a law, of which it is impossible to trace the beginning, and which, during its continuance, has admitted no essential change? Or why should we search foreign laws, or histories, for explanation or ornament of that which is wholly our own; and by which we are effectually distinguished from all other countries? Thus the law has been confined, and drawn up into a narrow and inglorious study . . . which deduced the spirit of the law, not from original justice or legal conformity, but from causes foreign to it, and altogether whimsical. . . . the truth is, the present system of our laws, like our language and our learning, is a very mixed and heterogenous mass; in some respects our own; in more borrowed from the policy of foreign nations and compounded, altered and variously modified, according to the various necessities, which the manners, the religion and the commerce of the people have at different times imposed.[24]

Here the young Burke, perhaps not long out of the Middle Temple, shows the same vigorous awareness of the tradition of common-law thought and its belief in the ancient constitution as he was to display in the *Reflections*, thirty years later, when he wrote: "In the matter of fact, for the greater part, these authors appear to be in the right; perhaps not always." But here his attitude is hostile, and his criticism is founded on the quite accurate perception that if the law is absolutely unique and absolutely immemorial, there is nothing about its history that can usefully be said. In one sense, he was being unfair to Hale, who had many times denied that an immemorial law meant a law whose content never changed and had asserted, in words foreshadowing Burke's own, that the law had been transformed utterly in the course of its history. But the difference between Hale and Burke lies deeper: Burke here is asserting, what Hale had virtually denied, that the course of change in the law can be historically explained by relating it to the operation of factors outside the law and independently known. To Hale a legal decision was a response to some momentary situation, of which as a rule no record was preserved other than the decision to which it had given rise, so that there was little prospect of historical reconstruction. Burke is visibly of the opinion that there is more evidence about the history of the law than the law by itself supplies, and the crucial point of his difference with the common-law school lies here. In making this point, we should note that he speaks with two distinguishable voices. His insistence that the law is derived in large part from foreign na-

[24] Burke, *Works* (Bohn's Libraries ed., London, George Bell and Sons, 1877), VI, 413–16. This fragmentary study is usually exempted from the controversy concerning the authenticity of the *Essay Towards the Abridgment of the English History*, with which it has been printed.

tions may have been drawn from Spelman—whom he discusses [25]—or the other seventeenth-century scholars who had investigated the Germanic, feudal or Norman origins of much English law. But a certain emphasis should be given to Burke's use of the words "the spirit of our laws" and his reference to "the various necessities, which the manners, the religion and the commerce of the people have at different times imposed." Here is thoroughly eighteenth-century language: the idea that peoples or their institutions possess a "spirit," or historical character, which may be understood by relating it to just such things as "the manners, the religion and the commerce of the people," might come direct from Montesquieu or any of the Scottish historical sociologists with whom Burke was later to be acquainted.[26] The words prefigure the *Speech on Conciliation with America* and the orator who was to depict the "spirit" of the American colonists in as impressive a passage as eighteenth-century historiography contains. At this point in his thought, then, Burke is thoroughly of his age in believing that laws can be understood by reference to the operation of general social factors, and he rejects the empiricist mystique of the immemorial partly on these grounds. He implies clearly that the history of the law can be made intelligible.

But he knew, when writing this early essay, that if the law were truly immemorial and as Hale had described it, the reverse was true and its condition in the past could not be reconstructed. He therefore understood on what his position was based, and what its contrary was, and this helps us to understand the fact that in 1782 we find him reversing it and returning to a doctrine very like Hale's. In May of that year he composed but did not deliver the speech [27] *On a Motion Made in the House of Commons . . . for a Committee to Enquire into*

---

[25] Burke, *loc. cit.*, p. 414.

[26] C. P. Courtney, *Montesquieu and Burke* (Oxford, 1963).

[27] The speech does not occur in *Hansard*. In the editions of Burke's collected works it appears in an incomplete form.

the State of the Representation of the Commons in Parliament.
He divided the arguments he meant to oppose into two kinds.
First there was the claim that representation was the natural
right of the individual, and it was in answering this that Burke
used the following words:

> Our constitution is a prescriptive constitution; it is a con-
> stitution whose sole authority is that it has existed time
> out of mind. . . . Your king, your lords, your judges, your
> juries, grand and little, all are prescriptive; and what proves
> it is the disputes not yet concluded, and never near becom-
> ing so, when any of them first originated. Prescription is
> the most solid of all titles, not only to property, but, which
> is to secure that property, to government. . . . It is accom-
> panied with another ground of authority in the constitu-
> tion of the human mind—presumption. It is a presumption
> in favour of any settled scheme of government against any
> untried project, that a nation has long existed and flour-
> ished under it. It is a better presumption even of the choice
> of a nation, far better than any sudden and temporary ar-
> rangement by actual election. Because a nation is not an
> idea only of local extent, and individual momentary aggre-
> gation; but it is an idea of continuity, which extends in time
> as well as in numbers and in space. And this is a choice,
> not of one day, or one set of people, not a tumultuary and
> giddy choice; it is a deliberate election of ages and genera-
> tions; it is a constitution made by what is ten thousand
> times better than choice, it is made by the peculiar circum-
> stances, occasions, tempers, dispositions, and moral, civil
> and social habitudes of the people, which disclose them-
> selves only in a long space of time. It is a vestment which
> accommodates itself to the body. Nor is prescription of
> government formed upon blind, unmeaning prejudices—
> for man is a most unwise and a most wise being. The indi-
> vidual is foolish; the multitude, for the moment, is foolish,
> when they act without deliberation; but the species is wise,

and, when time is given to it, as a species it always acts right.[28]

Now these sentences (though never spoken by their author) are treasured in the anthologies of English conservatism and repeated in nearly every textbook on the history of political thought; but the meaning which they had for Burke and his intended auditors can be appreciated only when we regard them as a restatement of the classic and familiar doctrine of the ancient constitution, in which its two fundamental assumptions are brought out and elaborated. Burke's prescriptive constitution has two characteristics: it is immemorial—and this is what makes it prescriptive and gives it authority as a constitution— and it is customary, rooted in something "better than choice . . . the peculiar circumstances . . . and . . . habitudes of the people." This is Burke's argument against a reform of the representation founded upon the principle of natural right. Every word he uses may be paralleled from the traditional doctrines of the common lawyers, the doctrines he had once rejected in his criticism of Hale but was to espouse once again in the *Reflections*; and common-law thought, as Burke could have found it in Hale and was (wherever he learned it) expounding it here, contained an explicitly formulated theory of conservative traditionalism.

Was Burke an antiquarian, expounding seventeenth-century ways of thinking to a generation of uncomprehending Lockeans? This conclusion easily follows from some of the unstated assumptions upon which the history of ideas is commonly conducted,[29] but it can be disproved by the simple exercise of ob-

[28] Burke, *loc. cit.*, pp. 146–47.
[29] It is easy, for reasons glanced at earlier in this paper, to think of Locke as if he transformed the whole character of English political thinking and inaugurated a period in which it was conducted exclusively in rationalist terms. The present writer was once led (*Ancient Constitution*, p. 243) to speak of the customary concept of English law as "running underground" between Hale and Burke, and an American reviewer developed the idea of a "rationalist hiatus" in English thought. To such oversimplifications the history of ideas seems prone.

serving how Burke's draft of May 1782 develops. There is, he says, a second argument in favour of reform, which he now proceeds to answer in the same way as the argument based on natural right; and it consists in the assertion that the constitution has fallen away from its original principles—here supposed to include the principle of representation on the basis of numbers—and must now be restored to them. This argument Burke answers with an assertion of startling simplicity and yet venerable antiquity—one implicit in the debate between Hale and Hobbes; that an immemorial constitution is not based upon any original principles and that consequently none can be alleged as a means of evaluating its workings.

> To ask whether a thing which has always been the same stands to its usual principle, seems to me to be perfectly absurd; for how do you know the principles but from the construction? and if that remains the same, the principles remain the same. It is true, that to say your constitution is what it has been is no sufficient defence for those who say it is a bad constitution. It is an answer to those who say it is a degenerate constitution. . . .
>
> On what grounds do we go to restore our constitution to what it has been at one definite period, or to reform and reconstruct it upon principles more conformable to a sound theory of government? A prescriptive government, such as ours, never was the work of any legislator, never was made upon any foregone theory. It seems to me a preposterous way of reasoning, and a perfect confusion of ideas, to take the theories which learned and speculative men have made from that government, and then, supposing it made on those theories, which were made from it, to accuse the government as not corresponding with them.[30]

The sentiments of the second paragraph can be rediscovered in Professor Oakeshott's *Political Education*,[31] but the passage

[30] Burke, *loc. cit.*, p. 148.

[31] Michael Oakeshott, *Rationalism in Politics* (London, 1962), pp. 111–33.

as a whole might have been written by Hale. The requirements which the constitution has existed to satisfy can only be inferred from its structure, and if the structure is immemorial nothing can be inferred about its functioning at any particular time. Consequently, we can never know the principles on which it has functioned, either at its origin or at any subsequent period; and only by partial and speculative abstraction can we discover any principles which we may call common to its entire history. Its true basis, moreover, will not lie in these principles but in the mere fact of prescription. Burke, in fact, has reverted to the position he formerly rebuked Hale for adopting—that little or nothing can be known of the history of an immemorial constitution save that there is a great weight of presumption in its favour; and like Hale, he roots his argument in the idea that the law is immemorial and customary.

He developed this argument as a reply to the contention that the constitution had degenerated from its original principles. This doctrine was indeed employed by Pitt and other speakers for the motion of May 1782, and is a staple argument in the literature of the county movement. It was a crucial point in the thought of the neo-Harringtonian "country ideology" described in two previous essays, which, transmitted by Bolingbroke, James Burgh and the Society for Constitutional Information, may be seen living on through Major Cartwright into the literature of the next half-century of frustrated reformers.[32] Its importance for our purposes is that it was so clearly a partial rationalization of the traditional common-law doctrine. There exists an ancient constitution, it said, whose claim upon us lies largely in its antiquity; but this constitution was founded upon principles which can be known, and we are therefore able to know when it has degenerated from them and to restore it to them. This Burke denied. He was, therefore, faced not only with a rationalist doctrine based on a Lockean theory of natural right, but

[32] H. Butterfield, *George III, Lord North and the People* (1949), pp. 341–52; Christopher Hill, *Puritanism and Revolution* (1958), ch. III, "The Norman Yoke," pp. 94–122.

also with a modified form of the seventeenth-century "ancient constitution." It emerges that a political language was still in regular use in 1782, based on assumptions which had been established in English thought as far back as the age of Coke by the theory and practice of the common law and had not—as it is too easy to suppose they had—been submerged in a tide of rationalism.

In the conflicting ideologies of the first period of parliamentary reform it is possible to discern reaffirmations of a number of typical seventeenth-century ideas. For example, Leveller anti-Normanism—the doctrine that existing laws and institutions are unjust, being founded in Norman conquest and usurpation —reappears in Paine and Cartwright; and it has been argued elsewhere[33] that there is no need to suppose direct contact or transmission between the ideas of 1648 and 1780. In both periods it was usual to declare that the essential soundness of the laws was proved by their having survived the Conquest, and it is not to be wondered at if the same affirmation called forth the same negation; Overton, Paine and their adversaries all spoke the same language. Burke, too, was in the part of his thought under inspection repeating the assumptions of the seventeenth century. Faced with an argument for reform that presupposed the existence of an ancient constitution, he responded by pointing out the foundation on which that belief was really based: the identification of law with immemorial custom, from which it was possible to deduce an entire philosophy of sceptical conservatism and empirical traditionalism. Hale had deduced that philosophy and Burke, who also deduced it, was acquainted with part of Hale's work and had criticized it for the very positions he was afterwards to take up. But the present essay is not designed to show that Hale "influenced" Burke or that Burke "derived" his ideas from Hale; such phraseology is universally agreed to be inadequate. If any

[33] *Ancient Constitution*, p. 127.

importance attaches to Burke's readings in the ancient-constitution thought of the previous century, it may be that they helped to create his intense historical awareness of the common-law tradition as "the stationary policy of this kingdom"—as a factor in shaping English political thought and behaviour. The point which it seems most important to establish is that Hale and Burke reached similar conclusions because they were arguing from similar assumptions, from a common acceptance of a belief in immemorial customary law which, as Burke found it necessary to explain and Hale did not, was one of the cardinal beliefs of the society and tradition in which both men lived. Burke's traditionalism is rooted in a way of thought already traditional; it may be possible to discern, from the way in which he restated it, that it was a tradition beginning to fade. And it was possible for Burke's contemporary Tucker, as it had been possible for Hervey and the advocates of Walpole fifty years before, to repudiate the return to original principles by an argument as defiantly modernist as Burke's was traditionalist, but equally conservative.[34]

It is important that this analysis should not seem to claim too much. It is confined to one aspect of Burke's thought—his doctrine of the superior wisdom of traditional institutions—and it treats even that in isolation. There are many things in his social and political philosophy besides his traditionalism, and it is not suggested that his membership of the common-law tradition explains all or any of them. To understand their meaning and their presence among his ideas, it may well be necessary to invoke the natural law, the philosophy of Hume, the sociology of Montesquieu or the rise of a romantic sensibility, and even more complex operations will obviously be needed if any one aspect of his thought is to be reduced to philosophical unity with any other. It is certainly not suggested that Burke's unified view of reality—if he had one—was derived

[34] See above, pp. 141–43, and below, pp. 265–68.

from the common law; on the other hand it is suggested that in order to explain his traditionalism, regarded simply as an isolated factor, there is no need to suppose more than his continued employment and highly developed understanding of certain concepts which came from the common law (as he recognized) and were generally in use as part of the political language he spoke with his contemporaries. In this respect, Burke's thought was formed by the contemplation of English society and history with the aid of concepts traditionally used for that purpose, and by the contemplation of those concepts themselves.[35]

[35] For responses to this comment on the historical explanation of Burke, see Paul Lucas, "On Edmund Burke's Doctrine of Prescription: or, an Appeal from the New to the Old Lawyers," *The Historical Journal*, XI, 1 (1968), and Burleigh Taylor Wilkins, *The Problem of Burke's Political Philosophy* (Oxford, 1967).

[7]

Time, Institutions and Action;
An Essay on Traditions and
Their Understanding

Societies exist in time, and conserve images of themselves as continuously so existing. It follows that the consciousness of time acquired by the individual as a social animal is in large measure consciousness of his society's continuity and of the image of its continuity which that society possesses; and the understanding of time, and of human life as experienced in time, disseminated in a society, is an important part of that society's understanding of itself—of its structure and what legitimates it, of the modes of action which are possible to it and in it. There is a point at which historical and political theory meet, and it can be said without distortion that every society possesses a philosophy of history—a set of ideas about what happens, what can be known and what done, in time considered as a dimension of society—which is intimately a part of its consciousness and its functioning. How these images and ideas of time arise, function and develop may be studied as part of the science of society.

An essential feature of society is tradition—the handing on

233

of formed ways of acting, a formed way of living, to those beginning or developing their social membership—and the transmitter of a message cannot do without some image of a message which he has received and of the way in which he received it. Both images will be, in some way or other, conceptualisations of the mode of activity to be handed on, and it will be thought of as having been received by the transmitter from transmitters before him: his predecessors in a craft, his ancestors in a society, or both. Societies therefore look backward in time to those from whom "we" received what we now tell "you"; even the so-called "timeless" societies described by anthropologists are not really exceptions to this rule. But the variety of the ways in which societies have conceived the transmission of their traditions is very great indeed. This is not surprising when we consider, first, that the image of an activity's continuance must vary both with the character of the activity and with the ways in which practice of it may be thought to be transmitted; second, that any society or social complex envisaging its own continuity must do so in terms of those elements of its structure of which it is sufficiently aware to consider them continuous. Social activities and structures vary widely, and it cannot be predicted with certainty what elements of them will become institutionalised to the point of having stable and continuous images. Even in very simple societies, extrapolation of the image of the social structure in time can produce accounts varying widely, from one society to another, of "the past," that is of the way in which transmission has been and is being conducted. In complex societies, the past itself is complex; society consists of a number of patterns of behaviour, each of which generates its own "past" and need not be thought of as continuous in the same way as its neighbour; there may be contradiction between these "pasts," and even conflict.

Oakeshott has emphasised the extent to which a "tradition of behaviour" is not conceptualised, whether because its transmission takes place unnoticed or because it would not be appropriate to conceptualise it overmuch, consisting as it does in "intimations" and "nuances." [1] None the less conceptualisation of tradition is constantly going on, as it must if tradition is to function among self-conscious and communicative creatures, and we are beginning to see that it may take place in a variety of ways and give rise to a variety of mental phenomena. The concepts which we form from, and feed back into, tradition have the capacity to modify the content and character of the tradition conceptualised and even the extent to which it is conceived and regarded as a tradition. There consequently arise a wide variety of attitudes and strategies which men may adopt towards society's continuity and the sources of its authority; these are political phenomena, forming part of the organisation and extension of society's consciousness of, and in, its political life. In addition, however, since so large a part of men's consciousness of environment and time is gained through consciousness of the frame of social relationships which they inhabit, the conceptualisation of tradition is an important source of their images of society, time and history. The importance of these visibly transcends the political; we are looking at one of the origins of a distinctively human awareness.

In *The Discovery of Time* [2] Stephen Toulmin and June Goodfield have performed the interesting experiment of taking as their starting-point the consciousness of time to be expected of an archaic villager, limited to awareness of the continuity of his immediate social structure, and examining how this consciousness was progressively transformed by the thought of physical scientists where this raised the question of the time-dimension of the cosmos, by geological, palaeontological and archaeological discoveries, and by changes in social theory occasioned by or occasioning changes in the time-scheme within which human society was conceived to exist. They convincingly

---

[1] Michael Oakeshott, *Rationalism in Politics* (London, 1962), pp. 111–33 and the explanatory note on pp. 133–36.
[2] Volume III of *The Ancestry of Science* series (London, 1965).

show that there was two-way traffic between ideas about the character and processes of human society and ideas about the structure and processes of the physical universe; but their thesis is limited by the fact that it does not and cannot deal with ideas about time arising from the self-awareness of particular societies. The "time" they deal with is geochronic and cosmochronic; thought about society can have contributed to its "discovery" only to the extent—a very considerable one—that society was considered as a universal phenomenon, a central incident in the history of life, earth and cosmos. But what we call historical consciousness is social and subjective in its origins; it is a developed form of man's awareness of himself as existing and acting in a continuous context of social relationships, and must therefore begin with his awareness of a particular social continuity to which he himself belongs. But we have already seen that this awareness can take forms as many and varied as the social institutions with which it originates. We are following a line of enquiry distinct from that of Toulmin and Goodfield, concerned with an awareness of time that must have been multiple in its origins and its modes; we are forced to recognise that the history of historical awareness is necessarily distinct from that of the discovery of cosmic time, and that no unified "history of historiography" is likely ever to be written. Since each society has its own mode of conceiving its past, the history of its historical consciousness must in principle be peculiar to itself— even when it becomes conscious of its role within a greater history, even when historical consciousness is imported or imposed from without. We cannot, then, treat the history of historical thought as a unity, a progressive accumulation of insights starting from Hecataeus or Herodotus as the history of science can be said to start from Thales. It is part of the history of social self-awareness, and is as multiple as the social forms and social experiences in which that awareness develops.

We are, then, concerned with the conceptualisation of tradition, with the modes of social self-awareness and the attitudes towards tradition to which conceptualisation may give rise, and with the complex awareness of continuity which we call historical consciousness as one possible outcome of changes in this kind of thought. To understand what happened to the time-consciousness of the archaic villager, we must consider the consciousness of social continuity which the village, the city, the empire, the church or the nation—to go no further—required of their members, and we must enquire after the origins and occasions of changes in that consciousness. When we put it in this way, it is clear that the problem could be studied in the context of social development; the individual's time-consciousness could be looked on as changing in relation to changes in the organisation of society. But an alternative approach, which will be adopted here, is to elaborate and extend the model of a tradition which we have begun to build up, and attempt in doing so to discern the directions which conceptualisation of a tradition may be expected to take, and something of the alternatives, choices and strategies which may confront minds engaged in such conceptualisation.

A tradition, in its simplest form, may be thought of as an indefinite series of repetitions of an action, which on each occasion is performed on the assumption that it has been performed before; its performance is authorised—though the nature of the authorisation may vary widely—by the knowledge, or the assumption, of previous performance. In the pure state, as it were, such a tradition is without a conceivable beginning; each performance presupposes a previous performance, in infinite regress. Furthermore, it may well be that it is the assumption, rather than the factual information, of previous performance that is operative; each action provides the grounds for assuming that it had a predecessor. Traditions of this kind, then, are immemorial, and they are prescriptive and presumptive; and this was pointed out by Burke, who was an acute analyst, as well as an eloquent expositor, of the traditional society and its mind. This is perhaps the simplest set of assumptions which we can ascribe to the traditionalist mind, when it is sufficiently self-conscious to have ideas and assumptions about what it is doing and the society it is acting in; but the full exposition of these assumptions requires a sophisticated mind and highly subtle language, as the writings of Hale and Burke bear witness. It can happen, in favourable circumstances, that a society may conceive all the activities of which it is aware, the whole pattern of its structure as it visualises itself, in traditional terms. Such a society will conceive its past as an immemorial continuity, its structure as inherited from an infinitely receding chain of transmitters; timeless societies are those in which the links in the chain are no longer distinguished from one another, each transmitting ancestor being perhaps thought of as the reincarnation of his predecessor, and the process of transmission being compressed into a single timeless act instead of being drawn out into an endless chain. At a more sophisticated level of consciousness, the traditional society may insist that not only are its practices and usages inherited, but its conviction that they are so is itself inherited from an assumed chain of transmitters, so that its knowledge of its past is and can be no more than presumptive. It cannot even know—it can only presume—that it has always based itself on presumption, though with this self-validating chain of presumptions many societies have been enviably content.

The traditional conception of society is in several ways of enduring value to social theorists. Any social act does in fact presuppose an antecedent degree of socialisation, and it is conceptually impossible to imagine a social complex coming into existence at any single moment. Both in the seventeenth century and in the twentieth, it has been salutary to be reminded that society is indeed immemorial, and further that our knowledge of the social usages that have preceded us is inherited from those usages themselves, from the assumptions they encourage us to make and the intimations they permit us to pursue. But in the present essay we are concerned less with tradition as an objective fact, a necessary mode of social life, than with the conceptualisation of tradition, with what happens when a society forms an image of itself as a constant transmission of ways of living and behaving; and while it is possible for this self-awareness to take a strictly traditional form, for a society to envisage itself as immemorial, prescriptive, an inherited style of behaviour and thought, this is by no means the only form which conceptualisation of a tradition may take, nor will it necessarily retain the form it has once taken. Now when a change in a society's self-awareness has become at all widely disseminated, that society's styles of thinking and acting have been irreversibly altered. There may still be much in its traditions of behaviour which has not emerged into consciousness and perhaps never will; what has changed, however, is its mode of being and becoming conscious of itself and its existence in time, and once this has happened a society is no longer what it was. We are studying its political and cultural individuality, therefore, when we study the form which its self-awareness has for the present assumed.

Moreover, when we say that a society's image of its own continuous life may take forms other than the traditional, we mean that it may not conceive inheritance as its sole mode of reception, transmission as its sole mode of action, or presumption as its sole mode of knowledge. There are other ways in which behaviour and knowledge may be envisaged, and a society's departures from a purely traditional self-awareness may be enlargements of its political and social, indeed of its human, vocabulary. Nor need human existence in time be envisaged solely as existence in a stream of transmission. Once men are thought of as thinking and acting in ways other than those appropriate to the traditional framework, it becomes possible to envisage their behaviour in social time as a complex series of interactions between different modes of behaviour, of which the traditional is only one. At this point the social framework begins to appear the result or product of human action, instead

239

of merely its matrix; a historical mode of understanding begins to replace a traditional one, and what may be the most far-reaching of changes in a society's style has begun to appear.

A society thinks of itself in purely traditional terms in proportion as it is aware of itself simply as a cluster of institutionalised modes of transmitting behaviour. We may, somewhat in the manner of Victorian anthropologists, envisage a simple kinship society, in which everything is learned from the fathers before the shrines of the ancestors; in such a society, it is evident, everything will be thought of as transmitted, continuous, immemorial and—since each father must speak on the authority of his father—presumptive. It is needless to point out that no society is as simply linear as that; the kind of self-image which the model conveys can be found even in complex literate societies, where the kind and degree of institutionalisation have been favourable to its existence. In pre-industrial England, for example, all social and national institutions could be conceived as bound up with the common law, that law was conceived as custom, and the activity of law-making was conceived as the conversion into written precedents of unwritten usages whose sole authority was that of immemorial antiquity. Consequently, to the end of the eighteenth century it could be argued that the constitution was immemorial, its authority prescriptive and our knowledge of it presumptive. The character of English institutions, in short, was such as to favour the assumption that the only form of action was transmission and the only form of knowledge the inheritance of learning. But in sixteenth-century France we have the case of a complex institutional society where continuity in the past could not be conceived in terms of any single institution, but different institutions suggested the images of different modes of action. The *coutumes*, in force in some regions, suggested the authority of continuous usage; the Roman law, in force in others, suggested that of rational action; the royal jurisdiction and its *cours souveraines*, overarching and co-ordinating all, suggested an authority distinct from the other two but interacting with them; and by the end of the Religious

Wars French scholars were saying that their institutions could be understood only in terms of a history of the royal power's expansion at the expense of customary, seigneurial and provincial jurisdictions.[3] *Les rois ont fait la France.* A society's institutions, it is clear, may be either consolidated or discrete, homogeneous or various; it may inherit dialogue, dialectic or conflict between its traditions, and the impulse to replace tradition, first with another image of normative action and secondly with history as the vision of interplay between modes of action, may arise from within the inheritance. There are seams, after all, in the seamless web; or it may appear so to those who receive and wear the garment.

Institutionalisation, the necessary cause of traditionalism, may then be the cause of a society's tradition being conceived in terms other than purely traditional. But conceptualisation has a logic of its own, and images and concepts of a non-traditionalist kind may arise from causes lying within the process of giving a tradition conceptual form. So far we have imagined tradition as the concept of an activity's indefinite continuity, arrived at by extrapolating the concept of its continuity in the present and—when this is done rigorously—imagined as immemorial or without a beginning. But the foundation myths of Greek cities, in exploring which Hellenic historiography was obliged to begin, provide us with examples of traditions of a different sort. These do not arise from the extrapolation of institutional continuities, but consist in ascribing a sacred or epic origin to the society conceived as a whole. In the late and sophisticated form which the Greeks gave it, this activity became what is known as historisation; it was the historian's business to discover origins, preferably human inventors, for societies, institutions and arts.[4] But in its more purely mythopoeic form, this kind of "tradition" has the value of re-

[3] The most intensive study of this, written from a historicist point of view, is that of V. De Caprariis, *Propaganda e Pensiero Politico in Francia Durante le Guerre di Religione,* 1559–1572 (Naples, 1959).
[4] See M. I. Finley, *The Greek Historians* (London, 1959) and "Myth, Memory and History," *History and Theory,* IV, 3 (1965), pp. 281–302.

minding us that a society—whether tribe, city, culture-complex or civilisation—is not necessarily imagined as a whole only in consequence of being imagined as a cluster of institutionalised continuities. There may be an awareness of tradition less precise but equally vivid, and when this occurs society's continuity may not be explicable in institutional language at all. It may have to be expressed in terms of whatever vision of the world human perception and fantasy have been able to conceive by means other than the conceptualisation of institutional or even social traditions, and this vision may entail a very different image of time or none at all; in the great phrase attributed to Australian aboriginals, it may be "in the dreaming." But if institutional time and sacred time or non-time are juxtaposed, then society's time-consciousness is already a complex matter.

To describe a timeless existence, a sacred origin or an immemorial continuity, are all ways of conceptualising the continuous existence of society. The more precisely we imagine society as a series of concrete human actions in time, and time in terms of the sequence of such actions, the more we seem to move away from imagining society in terms of the sacred, as our use of the words "temporal" and "secular" indicates. Nevertheless, complex interrelations between different ways of envisaging time, society and action are constantly found in the thought of societies. In ancient China, for example, there seems to have been equal emphasis on the idea that the *li*, or governing rituals, originated in the creative acts of sacred heroes called the Former Kings, and on the idea that the truth concerning the acts of the Former Kings could only be inferred by presuming their continuity with the traditional character of the *li* as inherited by the present. It is possible at one and the same time to extrapolate the present form of an institution back into a remote antiquity, and to realise (the mythopoeic mind need not even realise) that the beginnings of such an institution are exceedingly hard to imagine, if only because they cannot be conceived in terms of the institution's functioning. A system conceived in none but traditional terms must be conceived as immemorial, since antecedent tradition is necessary in order to account for its existence at any moment; but few societies have been bold enough to assert that they have existed *ab aeterno*, or sophisticated enough to assert that a prescriptive or immemorial tradition is merely one whose beginnings are not to be found in any single moment or moments. Most societies have their culture-heroes or founding fathers; but to imagine traditions of behaviour originating in specific actions is to imagine actions whose creative power is not explained by any antecedent tradition. Hence the charismatic figures who stand at the mythical beginnings of so many traditions—the gods, heroes, prophets and legislators, who abound in the legends even of highly institutionalised societies and provide the inheritors of tradition with occasion to imagine politics and other activities as consisting of charismatic (which here includes rationalist [5]) instead of traditional action, and time as a sequence of such actions instead of as institutional continuity. What stands outside tradition is charismatic; where time itself is envisaged as the continuity of tradition, the charismatic may stand outside time and become the sacred. But if an activity is seen as a succession of charismatic or sacred actions, then a new vision of time may be constructed in terms of moments of creation rather than moments of transmission. This no doubt was what Oakeshott had in mind when he described the ethics of the self-made man as idolatry; [6] such a man must visualise his actions as unendingly creative and charismatic. It may nevertheless happen that the idea of a series of charismatic actions, even the vision of time as composed of a sequence of sacred acts, becomes part of the mental furniture of a society, so worn and domesticated with constant varying use that it may be described as belonging to society's traditions.

[5] The purely rational founder of a society is always a heroic and miraculous figure.

[6] *Rationalism in Politics*, p. 35.

"A tradition of behaviour," Oakeshott has truly written,[7] "is a tricky thing to get to know"; so much so, we now observe, that parts of it must be conceptualised in non-traditional terms. "The pursuit of the intimations" of such a tradition will not be the simple unfolding of a consistently traditional "style" of either thinking or acting. It will involve our envisaging charismatic figures, actions and styles of behaviour; these will run counter to the theme of transmission and continuity, setting up alternative images of action and authority. Within tradition there will be dialogue between the non-traditionalist and traditionalist voices with which it speaks, and the pursuit of intimations will involve us in conflict and contradiction, in problems of historical, philosophical and methodological interpretation, even in existential dilemmas of self-determination and self-definition. A tradition may be a turbid stream to swim in, full of backwaters, cross-currents and snags. Nevertheless the dialogue we have begun to depict has its logic and its strategies, and the next stage in our enquiry must be to map some of these.

A tradition, then, may stress either the continuity of the process of transmission, or the creative and charismatic origin of what is transmitted. The two are conceptually distinct and entail different images of action and of time; but they are dialectically related, and are often—perhaps normally—found together within the same tradition. A distinction may be drawn between traditions which conserve highly specific and significant images of the creative actions with which they began and of which they are in some way the continuation, and traditions which depict themselves as sheer continuity of usage or transmission and conserve little or no account of their beginnings. These two types are situated far apart on a spectrum whose ultra-violet and infra-red are, respectively, the sacred, which lies outside time, and the immemorial, which refuses to admit a beginning in or outside it. Burke's "prescriptive government"

[7] *Op. cit.*, p. 128.

which "never was the work of any legislator," Oakeshott's "tradition of behaviour" and his "bottomless and boundless sea," are traditions of pure usage; but we have seen that traditions which admit to no beginning at all are rare and rest, where they exist, on the accident of a society's being very highly institutionalised in a peculiar way. The assumption that everything in English society could be treated as an inheritance from some earlier time was after all a myth—and Burke knew it—resting on the further myth that everything in English law was custom. But if most traditions of usage make some acknowledgement to the idea of a creative origin, it is equally true that most traditions claiming to originate in a creative act have to admit that the authority of the initiating charisma has become merged with that of the chain of transmission through which it has been mediated—the well-known problem of the "routinisation of the charisma." Traditions once conceptualised are complex mental structures, and in the dialogues that occur within them, what Oakeshott has called the "abridgment" of tradition into an ideology is only one among a number of intellectual operations that may be carried out.

Ancient Chinese thought (in its Western translations) presents an interesting example of political ideas organised around a tradition more highly and consciously institutionalised than was ever possible for Hellenic thought. The *li* had supposedly been established in mythic time by the Former Kings, and to that extent charismatic figures and creative action formed part of Chinese imagery. But when Confucius, in a time of disorder, set out to intensify the impact of the inherited *li* upon society by eliciting a consciousness of the virtues which they contained, he did not associate these conceptualised virtues with the figures of the Former Kings so much as stress the continuity of their transmission from an ancient time which was known less by contemplating what the Former Kings had done in it than by presuming its continuity with the inheritance of the *li* in more recent times. When he called himself "a transmitter, not

245

a creator," he was not simply being modest about his own role; he meant that what he was teaching possessed the character of a tradition, whose authority was derived from the continuity of its transmission. But if transmission, not creation, was to be the central social act, then the role of the Former Kings, the creators, was liable to lose its importance. There are several recorded sayings in which Confucius makes it plain that we know what form the *li* possessed under Hsia and Yin, the earlier of the three dynasties which he thought historical, only by inference from our better documented knowledge of the usages of Chou, the most recent dynasty; and if we know Hsia and Yin only by presumption, the same may be true of the Former Kings. His confidence in his ability to know the past by inference and presumption was very high: he held that he could reconstruct what institutions had been like in the past by simple extrapolation from their form in the present, and regretted only that independent evidence did not survive to corroborate him.[8] (In Jacobean England Sir Edward Coke advised antiquarians against venturing to reconstruct the history of institutions without taking the advice of lawyers, who worked on the presumption of continuity.) Confucius is also said to have declared that since we knew what Yin had added to Hsia ritual, and what Chou had added to Yin, we could predict what additions would be made by any future dynasty succeeding Chou—a doctrine which carries "the pursuit of intimations" to a point where it becomes "the poverty of historicism." [9]

It was Mo Tzu, the first post-Confucian thinker to envisage the possibility of governing society by means other than inherited ritual, who declared to his adversaries: "You are only following the Chou, not the Hsia dynasty. Your antiquity does not go back far enough." [10] A familiar if important contrast may

---

[8] Above, p. 47. "Former Kings" and "Sage-Kings" are identical.
[9] Above, *ibid.*, and see "The Origins of Study of the Past," *Comparative Studies in Society and History*, IV, 2 (1962).
[10] Fung, *History of Chinese Philosophy*, p. 78.

be erected between the two positions. Confucius was a conservative; he was anxious to invest the present system with authority, and did so by regarding it as an inheritance from the past. Adopting a traditionalist position in a highly traditionalist society, he invested the present system with authority inherited from a former set of practices which themselves acquired it by inheritance from a remoter past . . . and so *ad infinitum*. In such a scheme of thought it is not necessary to know much about the mythical origins and founders; it may even be inappropriate to stress them overmuch. Institutionalisation tends to reduce, if hardly ever to eliminate, the importance of myth; it replaces a mythic dream-time with a secular time of institutional continuity. It is important to have a well-established foundation in the recent past on which to presume continuity with the remoter past; but to attempt independent knowledge of the remoter past is in Burke's phrase "preposterous" and in the Confucian Hsun Tzu's "like giving up one's own prince and following another's." [11] Our knowledge of the past is based on the presumption of transmission, and the subtleties of historical awareness which may arise in this style of thinking consist largely in awareness of how much more there is in a continuous tradition of behaviour than we need or can know.

But Mo Tzu was in the strict sense a radical: that is, he was adopting the posture appropriate to a rebel in a traditional society, which is that of a reactionary. He did not believe it any longer possible to govern society by the inherited means of ritual, and had an alternative set of arrangements to suggest; but it was nevertheless so far from possible in that society to forgo deriving authority from antiquity that he must suggest an alternative version of antiquity which would authorise his alternative arrangements. The appropriate location for his image of antiquity was the remotest accessible past, since there the presumption of continuity with the traditional present would

[11] Above, p. 72.

be hardest to apply and, once he had occupied the headwaters of tradition, he would be in a position to maintain that the stream had been diverted from its proper course. Instances of this radical strategy, the advocacy of return to the roots or sources, abound in the history of argument within systems of authority. To take examples from English history, the Levellers opposed to the traditional constitution the image of an idealised pre-Conquest England after which all had been Norman usurpation; and Bolingbroke, followed by the early parliamentary reformers, adopted the Machiavellian tactic of ascribing to the existing constitution "original principles" on which it had been founded, from which it had degenerated and to which it must be restored. To the latter argument, it is significant, two modes of reply may be detected. In one—represented by Lord Hervey and Josiah Tucker [12]—the past was repudiated as barbarous and no longer relevant; here the conservative's basic concern with the present was pushed to the point of brutal rejection of the appeal to history, a rejection however founded on a developed power of historical criticism. In the other, far more subtly traditional, Burke pointed out that an immemorial constitution can have no original principles, since a system whose knowledge of its own past is based exclusively on the presumption of transmission can never arrive at knowledge of them.

The radical's rejection of the traditional present forces him to adopt new positions. Once he has denied that the present derives authority from a past of which it is the presumptive continuation, three questions confront him. Since his image of the past as he says it was cannot be arrived at by presuming its continuity with a present it is designed to repudiate, how is that image arrived at and maintained? Secondly, since the

[12] Hervey, *Ancient and Modern Liberty Stated and Compared* (1734); Tucker, *Treatise on Civil Government* (1781). The same view was constantly advanced in the *London Journal*, which supported Walpole against Bolingbroke and the *Craftsman* in 1729–34. Isaac F. Kramnick, *Bolingbroke and His Circle: The Politics of Nostalgia in the Age of Walpole* (Cambridge, Mass., 1968), pp. 127–37.

past as he conceives it does not authorise the present, it cannot possess or transmit traditional authority; what authority does it then possess, or, in other words, why are we obliged to return to it? Thirdly, if it possessed and still possesses such authority, how have matters so fallen out that it is no longer actualised in our institutions? As the radical was, initially at least, a normative writer seeking to give authority to his programme rather than a historical writer seeking to explain what had happened, it is likely to be the second question that concerns him most, but the means by which he endows his image of the past with authority must be intimately bound up with the means by which he constructs it; since the function of the image is to contain and convey authority, the authority must to a large degree define the image. Mo Tzu indeed seems to have been impelled to open the whole problem of the nature of authority and its place in political society, but he was clearly a man of unusual philosophical capacity. In a traditional society possessing only a highly institutionalised present and the presumption of its continuity in a past, it is likely that the radical desiring a past to return to will be obliged to erect a myth—an image of the past owing most to the creative imagination and heavily endowed with charismatic authority; for if we assume that action and authority conceived as outside the stream of tradition must be conceived as in some way creative, charismatic or sacred, the radical's solution must be dictated by this necessity.

Much obviously depends on whether the tradition already contains images of creative or sacred action [13]—on whether, for instance, it defines the nature of the sacred act with which it began—for then the radical has only to depict the tradition as a departure or degeneration from its own beginnings, and authority may be defined as a recrudescence of the original charisma in the present. It was a weakness in Mo Tzu's position

[13] On this point—as elsewhere in this essay—I am indebted to correspondence with the late Marshall G. S. Hodgson of the University of Chicago.

that so little could be said about the Former Kings and the Hsia other than the presumption of their continuity with Chou usages. But great religious traditions in highly literate societies, which begin with detailed written expressions of inexpressible sacred events, will be in a peculiarly interesting position in this respect. Protestant thought, for example, began by making an intensive scholarly and critical endeavour to reconstruct the practices of the primitive church, as possessing the authority of revealed truth over the present, but later generated an increasingly illuminist attempt to attain through inspiration direct experience of the operations of the Spirit not only in primitive times but in all times. In Islam, where the reinterpretation of primitive documents is less possible, the radical Shi'i sectaries claimed that the charisma of the Prophet had passed to the hero 'Ali, and that those who did not give their allegiance to 'Ali were no true Muslims. In such cases as these a sacred charisma, never to be fully contained within the normal mechanisms of transmission, is thought of as awaiting outside time the faithful who seek or expect it within time. Apocalyptics develop elaborate schemes of prophecy, predicting the times and occasions on which the charisma will return to the temporal world; mystics pursue "the intersections of the timeless with time," regarding their occupation as extra-historical. But whether or not the operations of the timeless are conceptualised into a historic scheme, authority has been located outside time, and the strategy of return may end by abolishing its own necessity; "if a man think to be saved by the report of Christ's dying at Jerusalem, he is deceived." If the structure of time is the transmission of authority, an authority which may be had by direct contact with the timeless seems to abolish time altogether.

The strategy of return does not depend on the tradition's conserving any image of its sacred or other origins; if 'Ali and the Former Kings do not exist, the radical is often capable of inventing them. English common-law traditionalism repeatedly denied that the origins of tradition could be found at any specific moment,[14] but this did not prevent the Levellers locating in pre-Conquest England "the birthright of Englishmen," or the Georgian democrats locating at the same period the realisation of "the original principles of the constitution" and erecting the figure of Alfred into that of the English legislator who had established them. The tradition contained no specified charisma which could be vested exclusively in the Anglo-Saxons, but if we ask what sort of authority English radicals supposed the vanished past to exercise over the degenerate present, we find answers in which the charismatic and the rational are blended. The Levellers identified the inner light of the spirit in every man with his natural reason and the freedom to exercise it; they could both assert with Lilburne that institutions embodying that freedom had once existed in England and assert with Overton that it did not matter if they had not, since the authority of spirit and reason was independent of worldly happenings. The Georgian radicals had abridged the constitutional tradition into a Polybian-Machiavellian "science" of mixed government, according to which every stable constitution must be founded on certain principles, from which it might degenerate and to which it must be restored. Burke, as we know, contended that theories like these were always distilled from the constitutional inheritance which was then represented as degenerate from them, and that this was "a preposterous way of thinking and a perfect confusion of ideas." It might indeed be argued that the element of authority in each case did not belong to the common law and was borrowed from another strand of thought, Puritan or humanist, in the English inheritance; but in each case the authority vested in the past and enjoining a return to it was no longer located in a stream of transmission,

---

[14] See Davies, preface to *Irish Reports* (1612): "Neither could any one man ever vaunt, that like *Minos, Solon,* or *Lycurgus,* he was the first *Lawgiver* to our Nation. . . . Long experience, and many trials of what was best for the common good, did make the *Common Law.*"

but consisted in something—whether charismatic or rational—not dependent on time for its validity.

Here we seem to have established some fairly simple cases of "the abridgement of tradition into an ideology." The strategist of return, supposed to be making his departure like Mo Tzu from a situation of pure traditionalism, cannot invest the past in which he believes with the authority of tradition. He therefore borrows elements of charismatic or rational authority either from the tradition which he is criticising or from some other strand in his society's inheritance—it is worth noticing that the stream of transmission must already be bearing along elements of charisma or rationality, or elements easily conceptualised as such—and concentrates them wholly in his "past," in such a way as to deprive subsequent tradition of what now becomes a predominant form of authority, capable of commanding return to the past in which it was once fully actualised. But since traditional thought conceives time in terms of social transmission, an authority which has not been transmitted is not in time and does not depend for its validity on its having been actualised in the past. The strategy of return tends therefore to be self-abolishing.

The phenomenon is familiar enough, being that "radical," "rationalist" or "ideological" thinking which has been criticised from Hsun Tzu to Michael Oakeshott by those aware of the reality and ubiquity of tradition; the outlines of their criticism are also familiar. But there is a foreshortening of perspective into which a vivid awareness of tradition should not be allowed to lead us. We should beware of supposing that the criticism of tradition by those in search of an alternative basis for authority necessarily leads them into ideological postures, so that every dialogue between the conservers and the critics of a tradition is like that between Burke and Paine. This is simply not so; traditionalism has its own naïvety, which consists in exaggerating its own subtlety and the naïvety of its opponents. It can be empirically shown that the range of strategies open to both the conservative and the radical is greater than we have so far allowed, and that in confrontations between them the awareness of history is by no means all on one side. If the abridgement of tradition is ideology, the criticism of tradition may be history—the ascription to the past of a relation to the present more complex than mere transmission. The ideologist and the historian may be closer partners than seemed likely at first sight.

A tradition in the pure sense consists of a set of present usages and the presumption of their indefinite continuity; the only modes of social action which it conceives or recognises are use and transmission, and the radical critic is therefore driven to invent or import some other mode of action lying outside the tradition. But we have already seen that traditions of pure usage, containing no other concepts of action or authority, are on the whole rare. The majority contain some image of charismatic or other action, which the radical may employ to construct his strategy of return and develop into the foundations of his ideology. It further happens that few radicals find themselves confronted with a traditionalism so pure that it makes no other assertion about the past than that it is the indefinite antiquity of present usages. Factual statements are commonly made about actions taken or assertions of authority made in the past, and the basis on which these are made is seldom exclusively that of presumption. The character of these statements is all-important to the development of historiography. If they consist merely of allusions to sacred and timeless events, with no secular or institutional continuity with society's present, we are in a situation like that of the Greeks, unable to make any statement about the past which is not either myth or the rationalisation of myth; if they consist merely in presumptions of the continuity of present usages, we are in the situation already described, limited to either the presumption of antiquity or the invention of a timeless myth of charismatic action. But if they are made in such a way as to facilitate discussion of what happened and what authority it exerts over the present, then critical discussion of past, continuity and tradition becomes possible. It is when two men—who may be the conservative and the radical—begin making contradictory but discussable statements about the past and its relation to the present that historical thought can begin. We should observe, however, that it may well be the radical who wishes to initiate such a discussion, the conservative who denies that it can or should be held. It was the conservative and traditionalist Hsun Tzu who wrote: "Abandoned incorrigible people say ancient and present times were different in nature . . . The Sage cannot be so deceived." [15]

At this point literacy emerges as the force modifying the character of tradition. Should there have existed for a sufficient period the practice of conserving official records or literary expressions of what is taken to be the tradition's content, the conservative need not rely exclusively on the presumption of continuity, nor need the radical be confined to the construction of a charismatic myth. It will be open to the latter to recombine and reinterpret the evidences of the past so that they present an image other than that of the tradition, just as it will be open to the former to construct an image of society in the classical and canonical perfection it supposedly enjoyed in some ideal past. The traditionalist, however, will always distrust the classicist, seeing in him the well-meaning author of a potentially radical doctrine. Words—the Chinese philosophers used to point out, referring of course to ideograms—are rigid in their form and yet endlessly debatable in their meaning; the tradition is that of the actual practice of the *li* and words should be kept in a subsidiary role; if they become predominant, there must be a ruler with authority to interpret them, and since the basis of his authority must be above words and outside tradition, it must be arbitrary and unintelligible. The fact is that a literate

[15] Above, p. 73.

254

tradition is never a pure tradition, since the authority of written words is not dependent on usage and presumption only.[16] As durable material objects they cut across the processes of transmission and create new patterns of social time; they speak direct to remote generations, whose interpretation of them may differ from that of intervening transmitters of the tradition they express. If the position can be firmly maintained that documents are no more than occasional expressions of an essentially unwritten tradition, the doctrine that equates authority with simple transmission may survive; the concept of English politics we find in Burke is directly connected with the fact that common-law records were assumed to be declarations of an immemorial *jus non scriptum*. But every reader is a potential radical; non-traditional interpretations arise, and with them the question of the authority to be employed in reading and interpreting documents; this authority may be thought of as traditional, rational, charismatic or simply mysterious. Books breed sybils to read them, and the sybil's authority, recorded on the various occasions on which it is exercised, now enters the tradition, which increasingly becomes a record of the different interpretations which have been made of items in the social inheritance and the different modes of authority which have been asserted in making them. All these recorded facts are next made available to remote generations in ways that are more than merely traditional, and society's conceptualisation of its modes of transmission—which is to say its image of itself as existing continuously in time—becomes various, subjective and controversial. Documents tend to secularise traditions; they reduce them to a sequence of acts—whether the acts recorded, the acts of those recording them or the acts of those interpreting the records—taking place at distinguishable moments, in distinguishable circumstances, exercising and imposing distinguishable kinds and

[16] See Jack Goody and Ian Watt, "The Consequences of Literacy," in Goody (ed.), *Literacy in Traditional Societies* (Cambridge University Press, 1968).

degrees of authority. They reduce time from a simple conceptualisation of social continuity to that of an indefinite multiplicity of continuities, which—since in the last analysis they
represent different ideas of action, authority and transmission—
cannot be altogether consistent with one another.

The radical desiring to alter the traditional image of the past
has now many strategies open to him besides that of constructing a myth and investing it with a charisma. The past consists
of many recorded actions and images of authority, of which
the greater part must be acceptable to the conservative as well
as to himself; these may be selected and re-arranged so as to
provide a new image of the past and the sort of authority it
exercises upon the present; counter-interpretations may be put
forward and their rival claims may be discussed. Since the discussion of alternative versions of the past and their relation to
the present is what we mean by historiography, we may risk
the hypothesis that the beginnings of historiography are to be
found when, in a literate tradition, an attempt is made to alter
not so much the received facts of the past as the kind of authority which they exercise over the present; for this will bring
about the discussion of alternative versions of society's continuity as a means of transmitting authority. The concepts employed in constructing and discussing these versions will be
various, and will not all seem to us such as historians have any
business to be using. Depending upon what modes of authority
are supposed to be inherent in the tradition under discussion,
there will be timeless concepts of sacred or rational authority;
there will be concepts of action and transmission peculiar to
the tradition's institutional character, and taken for granted
without critical investigation; there will even be uncritical or
anti-critical employments of the concept of tradition. But the
possibility now exists of agreeing, first, that certain acts were
performed irrespective of the authority which they exercise, second, that certain forms of authority were asserted and recognised irrespective of whether they are or should be now ac-

knowledged. There now exists the possibility of two further stages in the growth of historical thought. The first is that of a "pure" or "objective" historiography, meaning the reconstruction of a past irrespective of the authority which it exercises over the present. This stage, it should be observed, has sometimes been reached by accident; classicists and radicals have discovered, with a sense of shock, that they have reconstructed the past in such terms that it can authorise only itself.[17] The second is the realisation of the complexity of tradition, the discovery that society's past contains and has transmitted all these modes of authority and of action, of which purely traditional authority and the activity of pure transmission form only one conceptualisation, so that the tradition has become a dialogue between its more and its less traditional—a dialectic between its traditional and its anti-traditional—modes of envisaging itself. If the former of these stages is more likely to be reached by radicals and classicists, the latter is more likely to be reached by conservatives and sometime traditionalists.

"The criticism of tradition is history"—a sentence the necessary counterpart of Henry Ford's "History is more or less bunk. It's tradition"—is now seen to mean that historiography emerges from the context of a discussion of various ways in which the past can authorise the present. In this discussion many concepts by no means appropriate to pure historiography will be constantly in use, and though the tendency to eliminate them and convert the discussion from the level of politics to that of history will be very strong, there is no reason to suppose that it will ever reach absolute completeness. In these circumstances we have to avoid the temptation—which has flawed several brilliant Italian works of the post-Crocean school—to single out those aspects of thought which we consider "historical" and

---

[17] A *locus classicus* of this sense of shock is Francois Hotman's *Anti-Tribonian* (1566). See Pocock, *The Ancient Constitution and the Feudal Law* (Cambridge, 1957), pp. 11–15, and Julian H. Franklin, *Jean Bodin and the Sixteenth-century Revolution in the Methodology of Law and History* (New York, 1963), pp. 46–58.

in their light to condemn others as "unhistorical" and writings containing concepts of the latter kind as less than "history." It is clearly wiser to consider pure historiography as one extreme of a wide spectrum of types of discussion, which will be intensified in proportion as modes of authorisation come to be looked on "objectively," i.e. in the same light as others. Since what we are concerned with is history, the light in question must be that of a common temporal context, and it should therefore seem—at least *prima facie*—that it will be hard to construct a historiography where the dominant mode of authority is and remains sacred. It is true that one of the main origins of modern historiography is found in the endeavours of sixteenth-century religious reformers to recover the exact text of Scripture and the exact institutional character of the primitive church. This led not only to counter-endeavours in the field of erudition on the part of their opponents, but to discussion of the modes of transmission of authority and the structure of the Christian community. The reformers' posture was radical; they meant to use their recoveries to prove that the historical church had failed to transmit authority and had consequently lost it; and like other exponents of the strategy of return, they faced the question of how to define the authority which had once existed and the authority by which they themselves claimed to know it. Since what was in dispute was an action of the sacred upon the world of time, the reformers claimed the authority of the sacred acting on and through themselves, their acts being conceived as opposed to tradition; they claimed both to interpret the past and to reform the present by personal authority and charisma, and the strategy of return duly proved, in a number of cases, self-abolishing. Their opponents pointed out that charisma was tending to replace transmission altogether, and advocated a return to the accepted modes of interpretation of the sacred origins, which were scholastic reason, institutionalised authority and prescriptive usage. The next step should ideally have been the construction of a vision of Christian history in which all these modes of authority and transmission were seen as acting together; but—apart from the political struggles which discouraged any such eirenic—so long as the Christian world is seen as an interrelation of the sacred and the temporal, the possibility of a Christian historiography depends on the extent to which that interrelation can be defined in terms which permit the temporal to be seen as the product of an inner dynamic.

In the emphasis which Hooker laid on the church as a traditional community, transmitting its interpretations of original revelation in ways which invested them chiefly with prescriptive and presumptive value, we recognise not merely an appeal to tradition as a mode of authority sometimes preferable to charisma, but an intensified awareness of the traditional community, which is often considered the ideal conservative response to the strategy of return. To the Shi'i fundamentalism which became a recourse to the charismatic figure of 'Ali, orthodox Sunni Muslims reply by declaring their loyalty to the Ummah, which is the historic Muslim community existing in time, somewhere containing all truth and, though it may contain imperfections and uncertainties as well, not to be broken up by those who are certain of their perfection. Here we have a heightened awareness of transmission as carried on in many modes and asserting many forms of authority; it makes possible—though this seems not to have been realised in Islam—that authentically historical awareness of the complexity of tradition as containing many modes of transmission which was mentioned earlier; and in its realisation that different assertions of authority must be weighed against one another and that a certain relativism attaches to them all, prescriptive awareness of authority and tradition may be renewed on a higher level. This has already been defined as the species of historical awareness which the conservative is especially likely to achieve, but it is important not to credit him with it too hastily and to realise the complexity of the dialogue with the radical that must precede it.

We have so far defined the anti-traditional thinker, not as

one who wishes to abolish the authority of the past or to impose a new conception of authority on society, but as one who, having denied that the past authorises the present by vesting it with continuity, is obliged to create a new past and invest it with an authority which easily abolishes the necessity of referring to a past at all. His thought is therefore Janus-faced, but we should pause before emphasising too ruthlessly the contradictions which it may contain. It tends to become unhistorical in the sense that it devises a mode of authority independent of social continuity; but it contains an equally visible tendency towards the historical reconstruction of the past in a shape which, together with the authority which it possesses for the present, it is the radical's peculiar contribution to leave uncertain and discussable. In a documented tradition his "past" will be a compost of assertions of fact and authority selected and rearranged from a common inheritance; he cannot help revealing, and leaving open to question, the methods by which he has done this. Furthermore, the more "factual" and the less "mythical"—these are not mutually exclusive categories—the past which he claims once existed, the more specific the authority which enjoins that it should exist again, the more he (or his readers, or his adversaries) may feel impelled to ask why it does not exist now: how has the unauthorised present come into being? He may reply, like Plato or Machiavelli, by averring that there exists a general tendency towards instability and degeneration in human affairs; but the more clearly he can differentiate the characteristics of his "past" from those of his "present," the more specific he may feel able to make his account of how the latter came to predominate. Boulainvilliers's account of the decline of the *noblesse* is more complex as a piece of historical explanation than his account of their original privileges; [18] the Georgian radicals, having erected the myth of a free medieval commonwealth of landowning warriors, ac-

[18] Comte de Boulainvilliers, *Essais sur la Noblesse de France, contenans une dissertation sur son origine et abaissement* (Amsterdam, 1732).

counted for its decline by tracing the rise of government finance, professional armies and parliamentary influence in ways
which passed through Hume to the Glasgow school. The radical
reconstructs the past in order to authorise the future; he
historises the present in order to deprive it of authority. Both
operations may give him a bias in favour of historical explanation, which may emerge almost against his wishes from the
very character of his enterprise; as with the radical legal humanists of the *mos gallicus,* who reconstructed Roman law in
order to imitate it instead of following the glossatorial tradition,
and then found they had reconstructed it in such detail that it
could not be imitated. The conservative may profit by such
mistakes, but could never have made them.

The repudiation of tradition, and the construction of a mode
of authority owing nothing to time or continuity, need not—
paradoxically enough—diminish a thinker's interest in the reconstruction of the past. Thomas Hobbes repudiated tradition
and constructed a mode of authority which has nothing prescriptive about it. Consequently, it is said, he regarded the study
of history as of limited illustrative or prudential value. He denied that the common law was Coke's "artificial reason," based
upon presumptive awareness of tradition, and said it was merely
the commands of natural reason rendered authoritative by the
sovereign. Yet it is precisely in his writings on English law [19]
that we find him among the advanced historical thinkers of his
day, conscious that the doctrine of immemorial custom could
be refuted by reconstructing the law as it had once been, the
feudal law of a feudal society. Nor did he adopt this line of
argument for merely polemical reasons. There is a visible relation between his denial that the past was a source of authority
for the present and his awareness that it could be explained
as existing in its own right; and his reconstruction of the past
was a piece of serious antiquarian thinking, not a mechanical

[19] *Behemoth* and *A Dialogue of the Common Laws;* in Molesworth,
ed., *English Works,* VI (London, 1839–45).

application of his abstract theories. Because his thought was unhistorical in one respect, it could be historical in another. A rationalist approach to authority and a historical approach to the past may be partners as well as opposites; this is only one of the complexities which follow from the radical's denial that authority is prescriptive.

In his now well-known reply to Hobbes on English law, Sir Matthew Hale raised the prescriptive theory of custom to a new level of sophistication. He wished to deny that law was a series of simple rational commands; he contended that law was custom, and that in a given custom nothing could be seen but the fruits of experience, shaped in a series of concrete situations to which no moment of commencement could be assigned, and thereafter tested in subsequent situations not identical with their predecessors but assimilated to them by practice. The details of these situations had not as a rule been recorded; the content of the law had been constantly refined on the presumption that it was being preserved; we could say of no item in the law when it had originated, nor could we trace the succession of contexts in which it had been shaped and modified. There was only the presumption that it had answered, and would continue to answer, in all the situations to which it was exposed; but this presumption was overwhelmingly strong.

Hsun Tzu had attacked the radical strategy of return by arguing that the past could not be known by means other than presumption. To know the ways of the Former Kings we must follow those of the Later Kings; to know those of the Later Kings we must follow the usages of Chou; to know those of Chou we must follow Confucius. Hale was attacking a rationalist theory of authority, which implied the possibility of independent knowledge of a past no longer prescriptive, by arguments essentially the same. It is important to observe how the traditionalist strategy shifts under attack. In a system of pure tradition, all knowledge is dependent upon transmission; the validity of transmitted knowledge can only be presumed, but since we have no means of knowledge other than transmission, this presumption must be made of all knowledge; the circle is closed. When therefore the radical, the rationalist or the antiquarian begin to assert that the past can be known by means that do not presume its continuity with the present, that the past does not authorise the present but enjoins another set of political arrangements, that authority can be found by means that do not locate it in the past, or that the past can be studied in ways that do not invest it with authority over the present, the conservative's strategy is—at this stage in the analysis—always the same. Against the rationalist, he avers that nothing can be known of a social institution or its authority which does not stress its continuity with the past to the point where that authority becomes inescapably prescriptive; against the radical, the antiquarian, even the historian, he avers that nothing is known of the past which is not based on transmission and does not compel the presumption of continuity between that past and the present (or between a remote past and a recent past of which the present is the continuation). But both Hsun Tzu and Hale reveal that his position has in fact altered. The radical avers, in one way or another, that the past can be known, and however insubstantial his grounds, he forces the conservative to reply that it cannot be known; it can only be presumed. The radical constructs his image of the past by re-arranging, modifying, and occasionally inverting or contradicting the concepts and documents in which some part of the contents of a tradition is conveyed in easily manageable shapes; and since the elements of his structure are abstracted from a context of which they form part and with the other elements of which they have unstated and presumptive relationships, the conservative is able to point out that the radical's past is a construct, an abstraction, of limited validity. There is of course a sense in which all knowledge in a tradition is of this kind; Confucius may have intended this when he said: "Shall I tell you what wisdom is? It is to know both what one knows and what one doesn't know." But in Hsun Tzu the stress on "what one doesn't know" is the stronger because assertions have been made about the possibility of knowing the past to have been other than the present, and in Hale the stress has become very strong and its expression very sophisticated. The past is a continuity, but a continuity of adaptation; the image of a body changing its cells, of a river changing its water, is more than once used; and we are being told that all we can ever know of the past is that it was unlike the present and yet continuous with it. Even this we cannot know so much as presume, for we cannot know what the past was like at any single moment. Such moments are inapprehensible. The tradition has become a flux, Hale's river that of Heraclitus and Cratylus.

No less than the radical, then, the conservative can think both historically and unhistorically. The radical asserts that the past can be known, but that some elements of it can be known out of their traditional context; the conservative asserts that all knowledge must be knowledge in a continuous social context, but denies to that knowledge any status more positive than that of presumption. It seems to be a sign of unconscious conservative bias in us, therefore, when we assert that Hale's thinking is "historical" and that of Hobbes "unhistorical," or make similar comparisons between Guicciardini and Machiavelli. Hale and Guicciardini certainly possessed a greater sense of the complexity and intractability of historical events, but at the same time they denied that events could be known or governed, if at all, by any but the most rigorously presumptive methods: traditional conservatism in Hale, merging into scepticism and stoicism in Guicciardini. Their opposites in each pair were trying, by the aid of concepts abstracted from their historical contexts, to make history more intelligible and governable. But the conservative's strategies do not end with this union of scepticism and traditionalism, typically conservative though it is. The increasing complexity of non-traditional thought faces him with other challenges, to which he makes other responses.

It may for instance happen that the radicals have captured the past. That is, they may have succeeded in re-arranging concepts about the past so as to form a pattern widely accepted as plausible and containing much that is acceptable and even dear to conservatives, but seeming to authorise in the present only a set of arrangements other than those actually existing. This seems to have happened in Georgian England, where the traditional image of "the ancient constitution" had been revised to form a quasi-classical image of an "ancient and balanced constitution," founded on principles from which, it was said, the present constitution was degenerate. In these circumstances there are several replies which conservatives may put forward. There is the traditionalist and prescriptive answer, advanced in this case by Burke, which denies that the principles of the constitution can be known, since they are nothing but continuities of immemorial usage. The more precise, however, the image of the past and its authority to which this answer is opposed, the harder it is to dissolve knowledge into presumption. There is the possibility of constructing a new version of the past, more persuasive than that of the radicals; but the more striking and original the intellectual means employed to do this, the less likely is it to furnish present arrangements with prescriptive authority. There is the further possibility of drastically denying that the past has authority over the present, and claiming for existing arrangements an authority derived from outside history. It should not surprise us to find this radical and pragmatic conservatism in close alliance with historical criticism; so at least it was in eighteenth-century England. For the century following the Exclusion controversy, it was a standard tactic of the defenders of the Court—especially when the Court was Hanoverian rather than Stuart—to employ the feudal interpretation to deny the antiquity of the constitution, whether immemorial or balanced, and argue that since the past was mainly darkness and despotism the principles of government, such as they were, must be extra-historical in their location and recent in their discovery. Until the advent of Burke altered the intellectual scene, a classicist appeal to the past was the weapon of English and American radicals, a critical rejection of history that of the Court. Nor is this a peculiarly eighteenth-century phenomenon. Against the "abandoned incorrigible people" who argued that past and present times were different in nature, Hsun Tzu demanded: "Why cannot the Sage be so deceived? I say it is because the Sage measures things by himself. Hence by himself he measures other men . . . by the Way he can completely comprehend things. Past and present are the same. Things that are the same in kind, though extended over long periods, continue to have the self-same principles."

If Hsun Tzu could pass from traditionalism to essentialism in a few brush-strokes, it might seem that all that has happened is merely a tactical reversion of roles; the conservative desires to defend things as they are, and it is simply an accident of the polemical situation which determines what argument he adopts. But to leave it at that would of course be superficial; there is in the conservative's mind a constancy of belief as well as of interest. His basic position is that the existing arrangements of society contain their own justification, that it is not justifiable to subject them wholly to be evaluated by some standard existing outside themselves; and since it is impossible to cease altogether from visualising the existing arrangements as inherited, the element of tradition never quite disappears from his thought. Hsun Tzu's Sage does not resolve his "Way" into "principles" which he proceeds to substitute for it; the Way continues to be the practice of the *li* and the pursuit of the intimations which they contain, and what he is really asserting is that he can find no time in the past in which the *li* were not active and their intimations valid—and intimations constantly present and valid may be termed principles. In eighteenth-century England the position was more complicated. Ancient and present times were allowed to be different in nature, and the conservative school employed both historical and rationalist

266

criticism to deny that the principles of government were to be found in the past; the same tactic was employed by Voltaire and other defenders of the *thèse royale* in France, against Montesquieu and the lesser advocates of the backward-looking *thèse nobiliaire*. Reversing the strategy of return, they argued that the true principles of government had been discovered only recently, about 1689, and that once they had been discovered their effect was to render the past irrelevant. If they were of recent discovery they were not contained in tradition, and we seem to be faced by a conservative argument abandoning the appeal to prescriptive sanction. But a pragmatic and a prescriptive conservatism are not as dissimilar in their intellectual style as may at first appear.

If the principles of government were of recent discovery, how had this discovery been made and what was the legitimacy of actions performed before—or indeed after—their discovery? It might be argued that the discovery was made as a result of the developing historical experience of the English people; this seems to be part of the very complex historical thought of David Hume.[20] But if actions performed before their discovery were not to be considered mere folly and barbarism, they must be explained and justified by something other than "the principles of government," in which case these "principles" could not be the sole source of authority for political actions. Unhistorical authority alleged by a conservative will be a different matter from unhistorical authority alleged by a radical. It will authorise an existing set of arrangements, whereas its radical counterpart authorises one that must be brought into existence, even if this is to be done by a return to the past; and a consequence is that the authority of the latter must stretch further and do more than that of the former. The conservative demands less of his "principles" and puts less into them; they will resemble less a comprehensive theory of government than a pragmatic justifica-

[20] Giarrizzo, *op. cit.*

tion of existing arrangements. Indeed, they may turn out on inspection to contain little more than the pragmatic statement that arrangements must be continued if they exist and must be made if they do not exist, and that somebody must attend to continuing or constructing them. There is certainly little more to the conservatism of that admirable eighteenth-century curmudgeon Josiah Tucker.

The conservative in his pragmatic vein is anxious that practical steps shall be taken and existing arrangements upheld, without being subjected to excessive scrutiny in the name of abstract principle. To ensure this he will even repudiate the continuity of past and present, which his prescriptive and traditionalist brother is so anxious to maintain. But prescriptive action is undertaken on nothing more than an assumption, which its defenders are memorably reluctant to see replaced by an abstraction; and that assumption is no more than the presumption of its continuity with earlier action, which must also be presumed—as a matter of practical necessity—of the majority of actions undertaken in a purely pragmatic spirit. A pragmatic action must have a context and make sense in that context. A prescriptive style, which appeals constantly to precedent, may have much in common with a pragmatic style, which appeals only to necessity; this is how it was that the conservatism of the eighteenth century could reflect the thought both of those who thought the Revolution justified by precedent and of those—the so-called *de facto* Tories—who thought it justified only by necessity. Burke was able to unite these lines of thought by demonstrating that neither entailed, and each rejected, the establishment of an abstract and recurrent "principle" of dethronement. Pragmatism is the establishment of a continuous style of behaviour which cannot any longer be presumed; this is the sense in which it is conservatism without traditions.

We may now see how it is that the conservative can unite the extremes of traditionalist veneration for a past and sceptical denial of the past's relevance for the present. He believes wholly in an established and continuous mode of behaviour, which contains within itself all the criteria by which it can be judged and so cannot be judged by any standard outside itself. The radical attempts to establish such a standard in the past, the rationalist outside it. The appeal to tradition can be used against the rationalist, to return all thinking to the context of a given social continuity. But the radical is in one way a more formidable opponent, because he has an alternative version of the prescribing past, and as soon as traditionalism becomes a means of denying that such a version can be reliably constructed, it becomes a mode of scepticism differing only in degree from outright denial that the past can be known or relevant. Historical scepticism becomes a conservative weapon when it becomes a means of denying that the present act or arrangement can be judged by some standard located as existing and emanating authority in the past. An act concerning which nothing can be said with certainty except that it must be presumed continuous with some antecedent act is not so very unlike an act of which not even that can be said, given only that it is our agreed purpose that a social continuity must be established and maintained. At this point it becomes a conservative interest to emphasise the discontinuity of history, its character as a series of discrete actions, where previously it was to his interest to emphasise the presumed continuity with which it transmitted authority and legitimation. If each act is unique it cannot be judged by comparison with any of its predecessors; but if its intent is to establish authority and continuity, it should be accepted as such and not condemned. A series of such acts will re-edify a presumptive tradition; and neo-conservative and neo-Burkean historians are seeking to reduce history once more to an esoteric and disenchanted narrative of the almost inscrutable acts of statesmen.

There is here an antinomian and anarchic strain in conservatism. Distrusting recurrence and regularity, it reduces history to a river into which one cannot step twice, with the consequence that it becomes difficult to step into it even once. It is interesting that the "abandoned incorrigible people," against whom Hsun Tzu declared the steadfastness of the Sage's self-discovered nature, were probably not radical heirs of Mo Tzu but Taoists; since an affinity between Oakeshott's thought and Taoism has been detected by some critics. The assertion that "past and present times are different in nature" is certainly to be detected in some Taoist writings, but it does not seem to mean that the past may be reconstructed by historical technique and seen to be different from the present. "Footprints," we are told, "are made by shoes, but they are far from being shoes"; an utterance which seems to indicate that history escapes our knowledge. The Taoist insistence on the undifferentiated unity of all reality led them, it appears, to repudiate all attempts to pin exact definitions on it. If then you tried to assert that the present was known and properly governed, the river would slip through your fingers as you tried to net it. But this argument goes from Cratylus to Heraclitus; if you cannot step into the river once, you cannot step into it twice either; and no more than Hale did the Taoists believe it possible to determine the state of the tradition at single moments, past or present. They therefore abandoned the use of all concepts in government, even the concept of government itself. This view shocked Hsun Tzu, who was inclined to regard the transmitted contents of tradition as a body of authoritative institutions and dogmas, but it is a natural if extreme development of an integral part of the traditionalist style; indeed, it seems likely that the Taoists reached their belief that no moment in the Way was the whole of the Way, and that consequently no moment was like another moment, partly through reflection on the nature of tradition. Because the intellect cannot grasp the full meaning of any act in the sequence of a tradition, it cannot grasp the whole meaning of the tradition; and consequently it is very easy to think of action as the carrying on of a style, the continuation of a mode of behaviour whose character can be apprehended but never analysed, and which in turn is realised in action rather than in conceptualisation. From this the Taoists went on to regard the whole of reality as a style—the Way —and to take that delight, which Oakeshott shares, in telling stories of craftsmen who could perform their tasks perfectly because they did not consider how to do them, who were perfect in their style because they did not conceive it as a style. But if politics is to be the practice of a pure style, the practical is in fact being absorbed by the contemplative, the pragmatic by the aesthetic; where the traditionalist legitimised his acts by presuming them continuous and the pragmatist acted to institute a continuity, the aesthetic statesman acts so that the continuous style of his actions may be contemplated and enjoyed. All three share a conservative style; they presume a tradition.

Disinterested historiography is possible only in stable societies, where the present is fortified by means other than the writing of histories. It is therefore part of the conservative style to emphasise that history is studied for its own sake, and in a well-known passage Oakeshott has compared the impure historian who expects the past to teach him something, with the pure historian for whom the past is dead, a beloved mistress whom he does not expect to talk sense. But if the past can be considered dead, this can only mean that society's relation with its past, which we have seen to be society's continuing structure and its own inner self, has been stabilised by means other than those of the historian. In less stable societies, Oakeshott's historian is an impossibility. For Machiavelli, who makes significant use of erotic imagery as regards the past, history is Fortune, a treacherous and savage virgin whom we can never fully possess, but who may well devour us if we do not master her; and the river may burst its banks in devastating flood.[21] Even in a

---

[21] *The Prince*, ch. 25.

stable society, there is a certain cosiness about the Oakeshottian *ménage*. The point about a mistress is that we are not obliged to live with her; Oakeshott's historian and his past maintain separate establishments. But once we define society's awareness of its structure as its awareness of its continuity, of the complexity of its relations with its past, the occasionally enjoyed mistress begins to assume more serious, more terrible and more moral possibilities. To the Florentines she was the maenad Fortune, an irrational and irresistible stream of happenings. To the Romantics she was (and is) the Goddess History, of their relationship with whom they expect a final consummation, only too likely to prove a *Liebestod*. The conservative style leaves her in the role of mistress, but it has been the aim of this essay to show that traditionalism and its refinements form only one voice in a dialogue with and within tradition, out of which arises a constant discussion and redefinition of the modes of continuity and authority which link past to present and give the present its structure. In that dialogue the past is to the present something more like a wife: an other self, perpetually explored.

[8]

On the Non-Revolutionary Character
of Paradigms: A Self-Criticism
and Afterpiece

T HE MEN whose thinking has come under study in these pages all inhabited pre-modern societies: that is to say, pre-technological and pre-revolutionary. They did not live in worlds where the transformation of the material and conceptual structures of existence was seen as a constant process and an experienced reality. It is noteworthy that this did not deprive them of concepts expressing the idea of a constant stream of mutability, one whose fluidity escaped the intellect's capacity to reduce it to apprehensible moments; the Chinese Tao, the Greek flux, the English tradition all possessed this character; but they lacked, as it is commonplace that pre-modern men generally did, any concept of an indefinite secular future, open-ended and continuously being created by human action, and they supposed that the future—the socially new—could come into being only as the result of sacred, divine or (in a severely limited number of cases) heroic creativity. Therefore they lacked what has been a historically dominant paradigm of human social action as creative of a future: the paradigm of revolutionary action. They lie outside an entire universe of revolutionary discourse, an idiom of dialectic, alienation and revolutionary struggle; their thought, even in its most disturbing forms, tends to be focused on the values of stability and continuity and its paradigms serve the function of controlling and interpreting experience rather than creating it. It does not seem to be coincidental that (the Chinese alone excepted) the historical period to which they all belong is that from the fifteenth to the eighteenth centuries, in which Western men were most fully engaged in reinterpreting, by one another's light, their social systems and the languages of thought transmitted to them by literary tradition, and in which historical awareness was, first, begotten by the sense of instability upon the sense of traditional continuity and, second, heightened by measuring the distance separating European society from its written and unwritten, classical and customary paradigms. The sense of time with which we have been engaged in interpreting these men's thought is essentially a sense of time as institutionalized, an awareness of the conventions and devices erected in society to maintain continuity and control contingency, rendered vivid and intense by an added awareness of what has in fact been happening to these institutions in time. Such is still the mode of consciousness with which professional historians everywhere operate, and yet it is very unlike the *sens de l'histoire* which presents history as the medium in which human existence itself is lived, at once the pre-condition of our being and the product of our phenomenological consciousness. Some profound and interesting divisions in modern life may be found along the line of this distinction. Historians need not be historicists; a non-revolutionary politics entails a different sort of historical awareness from a revolutionary one. In a time like the present, the practitioner of a given intellectual discipline does well to stop and consider what company it encourages him to keep.

Such generalizations, then, may be thought of as raising

certain questions concerning the limits and validity of the method, outlined in the first essay, which it has been the aim of this book to show in action. One may ask, to begin with, whether it has not been developed, and is not far better adapted, to deal with a classical rather than a romantic style in politics and political thought. Classical man's attitude towards his paradigms and traditions is critical; between the two extremes of erecting the paradigm into timeless unassailability and subjecting his intellect to the inapprehensibility of tradition, he explores both paradigm and tradition, using them, arguing over their use, inquiring into their diverse meanings and functions, and generally conducting that process of strategic conversation which is subsumed under the notion of paradigm change. But romantic man's attitude towards the same phenomena is better characterized as dialectical; being far more concerned with ego, self-expression and identity, he sees linguistic, cultural and political structures as the institutionalized means of self-expression and self-creation; but his characteristic posture is one of opposition and rebellion towards such structures. Being committed to the notion that he must not only assert, but create, himself, he is pre-committed to a future in which he will be other than he is now, so that any present identity which he may assert, or find asserted for him, will require to be re-created in the creation of a tomorrow; and so he characteristically places himself at that moment in time in which the existing institutions of self-creation are seen as no longer creating or even expressing the self (whose self? his or everybody's?) and therefore as malignantly hostile to the self's authenticity. Classical man tends to assume that he has an identity and to inquire what can be done with it; his political action is civic, an operation outwards from his presumed identity towards the presumed identities of other beings. Romantic man tends to assume that his identity requires to be asserted or discovered, and that hostile agencies are operating to thrust an identity not his own upon him; his political action is revolutionary, a transformation of the self, a reconstruction of the conditions under which selves are to be created, and an engagement in the presumed self-creations of others. It might seem, then, that the critical posture tends to conservatism, the dialectical to radicalism. The one is based on an act of provisional acceptance, the other on an act of necessary rejection; and the paradigm plays a positive and functional role in thought of the former kind, a negative and adversary role in thought of the latter.

Someone who studies the history of thought as based on paradigms and their transformations may then be asked whether his method does not predispose him to the study of relatively but irreducibly conservative modes of thinking and even—shifting the argument from the methodological to the ideological plane—whether it does not dispose him to conservatism or disguise a disposition already established. The crux of both questions would seem to be this: does not a concentration of attention upon the paradigm dispose us to ignore both what happens to the self when the paradigm is seen as hostile to it, and what happens when the paradigm is to be overthrown by revolutionary thought and action? It can be replied, in the first place, that the study of paradigms and their history does not debar us from including in our history the occurrence of paradigmatic revolutions. A great deal of the theory in the present volume is borrowed from a book entitled *The Structure of Scientific Revolutions,* in which the whole idea of an authoritative structure of paradigms is employed as a framework in which to present the further idea of a conceptual breakthrough, or moment of intellectual creation, that rapidly destroys some such edifice and transforms it into something else; and it is in terms such as Kuhn's that the history of intellectual revolutions has seemed to become possible to write for the first time. But in the field of politics, a defence along these lines would be hard to acquit of a certain formalism. A scientific revolution is not, at any rate primarily, a romantic act, designed

and intended to re-create the self of the scientist by transforming the world he lives in. It may have that effect; a great and
illumined discoverer may feel that he and his world have been
born anew; but the problem with which he has been wrestling
was not set up in those terms. In revolutionary politics, this
is precisely what happens. There has been the explicit assumption that self and society are engaged in such a way that the
transformation of society is the necessary pre-condition to the
growth of the self; and "revolution" is not merely the appropriate term in which to describe what has taken place, but was
the goal, and its realization the problem, proposed by the
thought-pattern which the revolutionary followed, and which
may even have involved the presupposition that revolutionary
transformation is the natural condition of man's being. To
equate the terms "revolutionary thought" and "conceptual
revolution," therefore, is at the least to deprive the former of
its character as praxis; and the question has still to be answered
whether the history of revolutionary thought can be dealt with
simply by setting up the idea of the paradigm and its diversity
of functions.

Formally again, this can be made to seem possible. We have
been thinking of the paradigm as a conceptual constellation
performing a diversity of authoritative functions in the political
speech of a society. We may now add to these functions that
of helping to provide the scaffolding for the assertion of the
individual ego's identity as a political being, and proceed to
trace the ways in which a conventional set of paradigms cease
to satisfy by their performance of this function, and a conceptual revolution occurs so that new paradigms assert new modes
of identity in new ways. If we proceed thus, the Kuhnian deline-
ation remains intact and may indeed guide the historian in
tracing the history of romantic revolutions in political thought.
So far, so good; but it may still be replied that something is
lacking, namely the role of the existential ego as an actor in the
stories that have been traced. To rebel against existing para-

digms is indeed to go in search of new ones; but it is also to assert what it is like to be without them, to experience the terror and freedom of existential creativity. Paradigms do not define this condition for us. We may think of them as serving to conceal it from us or as the output of the creativity it isolates— according as we think of the mask as that which we hide behind or that through which we speak—but it is not their function to express the nakedness of existential freedom or dereliction. They exist to provide an exit from this condition, whether that exit is a front door or a back; and the more highly articulated the structures of speech on which we focus our historical or political attention, the more our thought moves away from the romantic towards the classical situation.

The romantic characteristically adopts the posture of alienation, one from which established structures of all kinds are seen as "other" and "absurd." He is therefore well placed to know that this posture is not merely transient or recurrent, but integrally and existentially part of the human condition, and he has consequently evolved whole political philosophies which present alienation and revolution as human norms. To be political at all, he declares, is to be confronted with an "other," with an alien structure which denies one's identity, and to be under the necessity of affirming a new identity by transforming the political world. Romantic politics render permanent in the human situation that moment at which paradigms cease to define one's identity and rebellion against them becomes a necessity; and such politics are both inherently dialectical and "modernist" in the sense in which that word is used in speaking of art. More colloquially still, one may now speak of a "mod" or "pop" politics, and recent years have witnessed an increasing number of experiments in that line.

We may concede, then, that to define paradigms and their functions is to define one half only of the dialectical situation; once they are seen as "other," there is that which stands outside them. But the history of dialectical processes remains to be written, and here it should seem evident that the historian will employ paradigms of his own to give structure to the thought and language in which he describes the behavior of egos alienated and revolutionizing the "others" which have confronted them. He has no alternative to doing so, if he is to use language and be a historian at all; but in saying this we are of course defining him as Minerva's owl, one who imposes pattern on thrusts of creativity after they are over, critic to the historical actor's artist. To accept this circumscription of his (and our) role, however, leaves as yet unanswered one very important question. Will there be continuity between his paradigms and the actors' paradigms, his speech and the actors' speech? Since historians normally pay considerable attention to subjective interpretation, to presenting things as they presented themselves to those who did and suffered them, it is probable that there will; and this probability becomes greater when—as is frequently the case—we find there were rhetorics of revolution, of alienation, even of existential freedom and nihilism, available to and used by the actors. To the extent that these rhetorics were communicated and in common use, they will have operated paradigmatically to structure the thought, the behavior, and even the alienation of those who accepted them; and the moment of existential indefinability begins to recede towards such points of absurdity as the revolutionary's revolution against his revolution, the alienate's alienation from his own alienation. The historian on the other hand reacquires the freedom to use the romantic actor's paradigms for his own purposes and to trace histories of paradigmatic change in dialectical as in critical contexts. That it is possible to write a great history of political thought showing how it was aimed entirely at reaffirming a civilization's identity in terms of a totally transformed and transforming affirmation of time and history—a history written in intense and articulate awareness of all the existential problems involved—is known to all readers of Joseph Levenson's *Confucian China and Its Modern Fate*; and Levenson wrote rigorously in terms of the conceptual languages available to and transformed by his actors.

But there are still some fowl which have not come to our net. The tendency so far has been to think of utterance as in varying ways modifying paradigms in common use, altering the values of coinage in circulation; but it is possible to think of utterances which are intended to effect immediate and radical changes in the communications system itself in which they are uttered, and so in the political system. It has been seriously argued that Plato's dialogues were intended not merely to recommend, but actually to effect, increase in the authority of the written as compared with the spoken word; [1] and adepts of the rhetoric of the emergent nations have explained that one of its chief functions is to set up patterns of choric incantation shared by the speaker and his responding audience, which transform the relations between them, the roles and identities of both, and the matrices within which psychic mobilization and political action become possible.[2] When speech thus transforms the communications system, the utterance becomes a "happening" in its own right, and there are obviously respects in which the concept of "paradigm" no longer suffices to deal with what is taking place. A paradigm is less a happening than an institution: a reference point within the structure of consciousness, stable and durable enough to be used at more than one moment, and so by more than one actor in more than one way. It is this which makes theory possible, for we have defined theory as the explication of the diverse functions and meanings of

---

[1] Eric A. Havelock, *Preface to Plato* (Cambridge, Mass.: Harvard University Press, 1963).

[2] "Leaders . . . more like Adam naming the animals . . . who suddenly have a mass audience are in the transitional position of the man/animal who announces "Me Tarzan—you Jane," and a whole new range of possible activities opens up. . . . There is no symbolism involved; there is a chanted response between leader and mass, a cry of "uhuru" which may mean everything or nothing." N. Hillary, unpublished master's thesis, "Revolutionary Guerrilla War: Aspects of Violence and Political Change," University of Canterbury, 1967.

paradigms. If we could imagine a politics which consisted wholly of happenings and never of institutions, we should have that "mod" or "pop" politics mentioned a few paragraphs ago; and it would in theory engender no theory at all, since where everything is exploration there is nothing to explore. There is indeed theory of how to set up a politics of this kind, but it presupposes a structure of paradigms and other institutions which may be assailed and dialectically transformed. A purely "mod" politics would have passed beyond dialectic altogether, since there would never be a moment at which the antithesis or "other" could take shape. Perhaps a main reason for the comparative failure of revolution as a political style in our time—a reason why it has too often proved among the more monstrous and murderous frauds of a monstrous, murderous, and fraudulent century—is that, looking too hastily to the posthistoric phase of permanent total transformation, it has failed to recognize the speed at which its concepts become paradigms and its happenings institutions, and so has failed, on a number of notorious occasions, to control its own congelation into an authoritarian and bureaucratic structure, controlling men under the pretense of liberating them.

We have now to ask the question whether a totally revolutionary politics would not be anti-linguistic, in the sense that action would have replaced words as a transmitting medium, and whether the abolition of language would not prove depoliticizing and dehumanizing. It seems that language is of its nature paradigmatic: if I use words to communicate a message to you, it is that you may use the same words in sending a message of your own back to me, and your use of my words, from a point in the social texture which is not that occupied by me, must inevitably warp the implications with which I loaded them when I sent them out. We render these distortions harmless and valuable, so far as we can, by institutionalizing them; the words become paradigmatic, in the sense that they can be used by more than one speaker to convey more than one load or spin, and social communication becomes a sort of verbal tennis-match in which I am allowed to impose my spin on you, subject to the condition that you may impart your own spin in returning the ball to me. Critical discussion now becomes a consensual operation in which we discuss and compare the respective spins we have been imparting to the ball, and render the continuation of the game possible by discussing its rules and tactics—in short, its theory. We are presumed capable of altering and transforming the game by this sort of discussion; the game may be rendered open-ended by the presumption that its rules can never finally be written, and it may be very important to allow for discussion of whether it should be played at all; we bear in mind that there are so many players that there is room for some of them to conspire to impose a given interpretation of the rules upon the others, and danger that some existing state of the rules may become a juggernaut that crushes all the players. The problem of radical dissent is the problem of what to do when this is seen to have happened.

But a ball that can in no sense be returned has been fired out of the barrel of a gun. That is, to make a communication to me to which I am absolutely prevented from imparting my own sense in returning it is to make one which I am in fact forbidden to return, since I am forbidden to make any communication of my own in terms of the message I have just received. In the context of a political system, to send me a message in terms such that I cannot reply to it is an assertion of pure power over me. The bureaucrat does this by sending me a verbal message, or what appears to be such; but the weight of authority behind the words is so great that I am totally imprisoned by it. One can of course argue—and bureaucratic behavior often supports this—that in such a case the words will not be words at all, but gobbledygook; I shall be dealing with Kafka's Castle, or the Kosygin-Daley figure of Auden's *August 1968* ("the ogre cannot master Speech"). But to say this only reinforces the normative equation of language, paradigms, and politics. The romantic revolutionary—who sees paradigms as alien and imprisoning and may, as in the extreme case we are supposing, be intent on creating a world in which they never assume shape and authority at all—may achieve exactly the same result and become an ogre in his own right, by sending me a message composed of anti-words (and of these there are now plenty to be found). Such a message will typically be one of pure absurdity, as is now the case in certain forms of protest politics; and it offers me the choice of being imprisoned in an identity which the message seeks to define as absurd, or abandoning it to accept another identity which the message defines as non-absurd by not defining it at all. But is the conversation aesthetic or political? Am I talking to Chuang Tzu or Han Fei? If it is political, the fact that I cannot return any message renders his utterance an act of pure power over me, to which I cannot discern any limit. As Humpty Dumpty might have said: "What is the sound of one hand clapping? It depends whether it has a club in it." I avoid the mutual fallacies of Chicago and deal with my one-handed romantic as Alice dealt with Humpty Dumpty: keeping an eye open for any club that may appear in his hand and refraining from grasping one myself, I quietly direct a stream of paradigms at his vicinity. He calls this repressive tolerance, and it is true that we are playing a power game; but if his intentions are sociable, as he says they are, he may return my service and we may begin taking the shared risks of language again. If he does not, I may walk away from him, or clubs may be trumps. When Alice walked away, Humpty Dumpty fell down.

The tone of this essay is one of moderate unfriendliness towards the romantic revolutionary, though this should not (as it probably will) be overestimated. The writer has no particular sense of alienation—horror and scorn and fear and indignation are another matter—and distrusts the proximity of the romantic on the grounds that one reconstructing the world in order to transform his identity is rather too likely to devour my identity to serve his own metabolism. But this possibility is mentioned with deliberate mildness. To a very real extent, the relations between powers, races, and generations can be seen in terms of confrontations between those possessing identities and paradigms which it satisfies them to employ critically, and those whose identities can only be created by transforming the world seen as "other." We can explore the prospects of getting these worlds into dialogue, or we can align ourselves with one at the expense of denying the other's right to be as it is. This essay seeks to present the problem in terms of language, and has passed in the last few pages from viewing paradigms as heuristic devices for the historian to viewing their normative, communicative and political functions in society. In what remains it will be worth attempting to retrace this in fact circuitous journey: to present a political theory of language in which the historian of thought may be assigned an appropriate role.

Language is power, as both Greek and Chinese antiquity recognized. In the confrontation between classical and romantic, critical and dialectical politics, we have found two theories of how language functions in this capacity and recognized that the assertion of each theory is itself a mode of asserting power. To address ourselves, as we are now doing, to the possibility of getting the proponents of each into dialogue is to contemplate drawing them into a common language system. This will be a power system, and such systems being what they are, it will probably be loaded in various ways to the disadvantage of one or other party. It may seem, for instance, as if the revolutionary, in being commanded to enter into dialogue with the non-revolutionary, is being enjoined or compelled to abdicate, to enter into the system he is otherwise committed to transforming. What is happening is rather that, in the first place, limits are being set to his power to define persons as "other," as alien, as "system," "elite," "establishment," or whatever it may be; to inform them that they can say nothing to him, or he to them, which is not a unilateral exercise of power; and to set about transforming them unilaterally, that is, without listening to anything they may have to say for themselves. It follows, as a further consequence, that, if he is obliged to receive communications from his adversaries which modify the communications he is able to make in return, his mode of politics has indeed shifted some distance from the revolutionary towards the consensual. It would be pointless to deny that this is what we are trying to achieve. The non-revolutionary for his part—operating with an identity and an equipment of paradigms which he is prepared to criticize as need arises but from which he feels no radical alienation—is required to recognize that someone is trying to change him and his language for reasons which may be very hard to communicate to him. He is being offered the right to demand that messages be beamed towards him to which there is the possibility of his replying; but just as the revolutionary is denied the unilateral determination of the anti-language of change, the non-revolutionary is not allowed unilateral control of the paradigmatic structure of communication and reply. To the extent to which either party insists on playing Humpty Dumpty the process has broken down.

The problem just raised—that of the normative limits to be imposed on conservative or non-revolutionary behavior—provides an appropriate context in which to say something about the radical assault on empiricism and objectivism now going on in a number of academic professions. The tone of the campaign, and the behavior of some of its managers, carry disagreeable overtones of witch-hunting and even totalitarianism; but the theory of paradigms put forward in these pages leaves little doubt that there is something to be said for it. The charge leveled is that explanation implies acceptance, and that there is an irreducible taint of conservative ideology about the very notion of a fact. Now to accept certain phenomena as data is to commit oneself to the paradigmatic and linguistic structure which defines and circumscribes them. To view language as we have viewed it here is to view it as consisting of paradigms which simultaneously perform an indefinite number of linguistic and social functions, which enjoin and entail an indefinite number of authority structures, and which do all these things in so complex and simultaneous a context—namely, the total structure of social behavior itself—that to identify a single paradigmatic function as present can never isolate it from other possible functions which may be present at the same moment. There exist, it is true, a number of highly effective techniques, historical and positivist, for distinguishing between these functions; but these are effective only in proportion as the iceberg's tip may be made to emerge from implicitness into explicitness. It follows, not only that there is always more implicit in the language we use than we realize—we know what we say, but know not what we may be saying—but that in using a sociopolitical language at all, we commit ourselves to a tissue of political implications, to a variety of political functionings, and to the recommendation of a variety of authoritative structures, greater than we can critically distinguish at any one moment. The censors of the right and left, while disastrous, are not absolutely mistaken. To speak of a thing at all *is* to imply the possibility of its acceptance. We may not intend any such implication, but cannot eliminate such presences completely from our speech. The most rigorously-constructed utterance can be purified only of those implications which the author knows may be present and has sought to exclude; in the necessarily impure language of a common or social speech there must always be paradigmatic implications of which he is not conscious, or which he cannot exclude if he tries.

This after all is the law which guarantees us against the dictatorship of Humpty Dumpty or Big Brother. We can now see that the theory put forward to provide a matrix for the history of political ideas is at the same time a theory of the political language and the linguistic polity. Because men in speaking commit themselves to a load or fabric of meanings greater than they can control, it is possible for others in reply to employ the same words to convey the loads of meaning they desire to select. Communication is possible only because it is imperfect. Because we affect one another's most intimate behavior by the spins we impart to words as they pass to and fro between us, it is possible for the linguistic polity to synthesize conflict with the recognition of interdependency. Politics is a game of biases in the asymmetrical universe of society. What we have called paradigms are linguistic constructs recognized as carrying increasingly complex loads of biases, but at the same time carrying loads in excess of what can be predicted or controlled at a given moment; just as Clausewitz recognized that war would be impossible between two strategists each of whom could determine every consequence of his every act, so the polity of conversation would be impossible between two Humpty Dumpties. But as the complexity of function and the loads of implied and imputed authority carried by paradigms increase, so, it must be recognized, do persons engaging in paradigmatic communication commit themselves in increasing degree to patterns of implication beyond what they can control at a given moment; so that the danger that the implied authority structures will control them correspondingly increases with respect to each moment. This is what is meant when we think of negotiators imprisoned by their own agenda, though there the danger may arise from limitations consciously rather than unconsciously accepted. To speak at all is dangerous, and we need to pay attention both to what we may be saying and to the political context in which we may be saying it.

There is then a clear case against any participant in a politics of language who means by "objectivity" a rigorous determination to talk only in terms of a fixed set of paradigms, and the dissenter from a given practice does well to be wary of the terms on which he is drawn into discussing it. The proper meaning of "objectivity" in this context is something like "participation in a communications game possible to all players," and neither conservative nor radical satisfies this criterion if he insists on unilaterally determining the game's structure. The question we are considering is how the criterion can be met if one player's attitude towards the paradigm structure is that known as alienation. The practitioner of classical or critical politics concentrates on widening all parties' modes of awareness of the universe of implications within which they are communicating; but we have seen that critical exploration presupposes a provisional acceptance of the universe to be explored, and therefore a provisional willingness to live in a universe which eludes more than a measure of control. It is precisely this willingness that the romantic withholds, wholly or provisionally; not that he necessarily aspires to complete control of the linguistic or social universe (what makes him sometimes dangerous is that he sometimes does), but that, preoccupied with its function of defining and making intelligible his subjective identity, he sees it as having failed to do this to such a degree that its paradigms and language have become meaningless when spoken to or by him.

It is clear that—at the linguistic level—what he requires is not the critical exploration of paradigms alone; the gap may be too wide for that to be of immediate use; but rather the performance of those speech-acts, mentioned earlier, whose function is to transform the communications system and bring about the erection of a linguistic universe in which he can see himself to exist. It is logical, too, to suppose that these will tend to have the character of "propaganda by deed"—less, that is, of speech as action than of action as speech. But it is implicit in the romantic's own postulates that in transforming the communications system he is not merely re-creating his own identity but operating upon the identities of others; and the norms of politics require that this be a two-way process. The simplest statement of the case against nearly all forms of dialectical politics is that, purporting to be games for two or more players, they are games in which the name of the victor is predetermined and all the rules set in his favor when the game begins; and it could be argued that what is now needed is a theory of romantic politics which passes beyond revolution to polity and presents the process of mutual determination and transformation of identities as one in which any number of persons can take part, not merely as a sterile and sado-masochist entanglement between Ego and a dehumanized and dehumanizing Other. The revolutionary has his own brand of the universal sin of thinking no one human but himself.

Some highly interesting experiments in this direction have recently been made known by the writings of Henry S. Kariel [3] and in certain theories of intentionality and intersubjectivity of the phenomenological school.[4] In their popular form, however —"encounter groups" and the like—such explorations are said to suffer from the extreme poverty of their linguistic systems, though this is not a vice of which one would accuse Kariel. It is not enough to denounce language in its existing form if one neglects to provide any symbolic tokenage by which the players in the game may exchange messages, each with the spin imparted to it by its transmitter; and once we have readmitted the possibility of such a tokenage, we are on the way back to the construction of paradigms. We are also presupposing that the political game is to be played among persons whose alienation and anxiety for self-re-creation is rather sharply unequal; and both a role and recognition of its legitimacy must be found for the relatively sophisticated conservative we have imagined as the practitioner of classical and critical politics. If he will be more anxious than the alienate for the perpetuation of a system of paradigms, he will be correspondingly more critically alert to the processes by which the romantic's speech-acts crystallize into paradigms—we have seen that the latter's failure to recog-

[3] E.g., *Open Systems: Arenas for Political Action* (Itasca, Illinois: F. E. Peacock Publishers, 1969) and "Expanding the Political Present," *American Political Science Review*, XLIII, 3 (1969).

[4] Novices, like the author, in this field of theory may be assisted by Donald M. Lowe, "Intentionality and the Method of History," to be published in M. Natanson, ed., *Phenomenology and the Social Sciences* (Evanston, Ill.: Northwestern University Press). Kariel's footnotes also provide much bibliography.

nize that this is happening has frequently been his destruction —and the critic's role in the dialectic we are supposing may be that of converting speech-acts into paradigms while encouraging awareness of the conceptual diversity of what is happening. The romantic may have to be muzzled the while to prevent his incessantly proclaiming that the whole process is being robbed of authenticity; he is not permitted the exclusive determination of what that is.

Processes of this kind will still have histories that can be written in terms of the production, modification, and transformation of paradigms; but it remains possible to argue that they will be too mercurial to produce the superstructures of political theory. Our concept of theory requires that the paradigms remain stable long enough to be critically explored and to permit further paradigms for this sort of exploration to take shape. A polity of creative intersubjectivity, such as we have imagined, is clearly one in which the production and rejection of identities and languages will take place at a very high rate. We might restore the concept of "pop politics" by arguing that in such a polity the medium will be the message; that it will in fact be analogous to that presaged communications universe of electronic intersubjectivity in which concepts and images will not stay fixed long enough for the individual to determine his identity by self-location with regard to a conceptual and paradigmatic structure. This is to look beyond alienation to a postromantic politics—a polity of swinging ants, some would call it. But only if individuals disappear, is authority likely to disappear. So long as the individual is there at all, he will feel the need of points of fixity by which to define himself, even if he defines himself by rebelling against them; and in a communicative and political society, these points will become paradigms. At this stage it will be noticed that conservative and revolutionary have become identical, and there is reason to think that our third person, the historian, will join himself to them. In the wholly intersubjective society neither critical conservatism nor dialectical revolution may seem possible, just as in the electronic society words do not retain their written or printed meanings. But this reminds us that no alternative to the fixed visibility of the written or printed word has yet been found as a means of letting us question—letting us scrutinize or take a second look at—the meaning of what is being told us. Unless, in the aquarian society, power is going to be totally and evenly diffused—as seems unlikely—this will remain a matter of some importance; and one can imagine books and other forms of printed matter serving as deliberately introduced blockages,[5] compelling the merchants of images to slow down the production and transformation of their output so that we can inspect it. To the book corresponds the paradigm; and unless authority is completely unlocalized in a society of near-total fluidity, to compel it to stand still and declare its location and character will be as much a radical as a conservative activity. In such a continuum, besides, the historian could no longer be adequately described as Minerva's owl, coming along when all is over to impose a retrospective pattern upon it. To the extent to which he could oblige his society to organize its concepts in retrospection, he would be obliging it to organize them into paradigms—to admit that it had been doing something, that that something could be ordered in a certain way and that what it was doing now could be ordered with respect to that ordering. Orwell saw that we might be governed by bureaucrats who could switch the patterns of the past at will. If we are to imagine the different threat of government by high-speed manipulators who disorganize the whole structuring of time, it is a first challenge to their power to offer them such a structure and defy them to disorganize it. It is in fact this which historians have always been doing, and their relation to the paradigms of society has always been both conservative and radical.

[5] I have elsewhere described these as "spanners in the networks." See "Working on Ideas in Time," in L. P. Curtis, Jr., ed., *The Historian's Workshop* (New York: Alfred A. Knopf, 1970).

J. G. A. POCOCK

J. G. A. Pocock insists on describing himself as both political scientist and historian. Since graduating from Cambridge University, he has taught at St. John's College, Cambridge, the University of Canterbury, Christchurch, New Zealand, and, since 1966, Washington University, St. Louis, Missouri. He was a founder-member of the Conference for the Study of Political Thought, and has work in progress on Machiavelli, on the theory of Florentine republicanism and on James Harrington.